Monks in the World

Monks in the World

Seeking God in a Frantic Culture

WILLIAM THIELE

WIPF & STOCK · Eugene, Oregon

MONKS IN THE WORLD
Seeking God in a Frantic Culture

Copyright © 2014 William Thiele. All rights reserved. Except for brief quotations in critical publications or reviews, no part of this book may be reproduced in any manner without prior written permission from the publisher. Write: Permissions, Wipf and Stock Publishers, 199 W. 8th Ave., Suite 3, Eugene, OR 97401.

Wipf & Stock
An Imprint of Wipf and Stock Publishers
199 W. 8th Ave., Suite 3
Eugene, OR 97401

www.wipfandstock.com

ISBN 13: 978-1-62564-540-1

Manufactured in the U.S.A.

This book is dedicated to the people of the School for Contemplative Living and their willingness to practice the presence of God as they serve the world.

Contents

Acknowledgments | xi

Introduction | xii

1 An Uncertain Birthing | 1
    Break Those Vows!
    The Early Days
    Are We Real Yet?
    Naming

2 Foundations: Before There Was a School | 25
    Introducing the Inner Sanctuary
    Margaret's Story
    Jacob's Story
    Finding an Inner Sanctuary
    Encountering the Inner Sanctuary
    Silence
    Stillness
    Harry's Story
    Julia's Story
    Solitude
    Jesse's Story
    Christ in the Desert
    Searching for a Sanctuary Abroad
    Stepping through the Door
    Carol's Story
    Relaxing
    Mary's Story
    Sally's Story
    Commitment

Wisdom's Source
Myrna's Story
Simple Being
James's Story
The Way of Centering Prayer
Mike's Story

3   Stories of Practicing the Presence | 67

Catching Sight of a Monk
The Way of the Contemplative
On Contemplative Evangelism
On the Importance of Daily Practice
Bringing Presence into the World
Bowing School
Suffering with Community
Two Places We Belong
The Core Contemplative Attitudes
Being in the Presence: Listening in Stillness
Bringing Presence: Serving with Joy in the Wild World
Stories of Serving in Joy
Serving without Joy
More on Contemplative Service
Centering, Mudding, and Cancer
The Myth of "I Can't"
Belonging in Community
Centering and Texting
She Stayed Back
The Pleasure of Craft without Toil: Seven Parables of Contemplative Living
Birthing Your Own School
A Contemplative Pledge
Vows for a Contemplative Community
Out on This Vacant Lot Called Prayer . . . Wanting

4   The Dark Side of Contemplation | 138

Faux Monk
Imperfection
Snack Food
On Contemplative Discouragement
Loss of Our Calling
Facing Emptiness
Lostness: When Darkness Falls
Nowhere to Hide: Feeling Painful Feelings

5 Practicing the Presence | 163
  Ten Ways to Meditate
  Beginning Stillness: An Exercise
  Stepping through the Door: An Exercise
  Prelude to the Inner Sanctuary: A Relaxation Exercise
  Entering the Inner Sanctuary: Three Ways In
  Physical Experience
  A Breath Exercise
  A Visual Exercise
  A Hearing Exercise
  Retreats
  Sacred Circle: Shoulder Rubbing Practice
  Centering Prayer

6 Poems of Practicing the Presence | 188
  There Is a Stillness
  Regardez et Ecoutez
  Holding Near the Deep Presence
  Mountain in Rain
  Tasting Light: Breakfast of Tears and Mist
  When There Are No Words: Spirit!
  Today I Take My Seat
  If I Miss Seeing
  The Many Different Feet
  On the Eve of a New Year
  On the Eve of Thanksgiving
  On the Virtues of Being Blind and Deaf
  There Is This Other Knowing . . .
  Desperation: An Epilogue
  We Shelter Each Other

Desperation: An Epilogue

Resources | 215
Bibliography | 217

Acknowledgments

I AM SO VERY grateful to my wife Carol for her years of inspiration in the art of simple being and the practice of radiating loving-kindness within our family and into the world. She has been my greatest teacher. She also encouraged me to write not only theoretical material, but also stories. I am grateful to my family for always supporting me in being who I am, and to my brother Roger for his great marketing help. I have been blessed by my spiritual directors, Dolly Smith and Sister Jane McKinlay, and by a multitude of friends who participate in our School for Contemplative Living as learners and teachers.

Our steering committee members have served faithfully to help us chart a course through stormy seas. They have included Joan Bicocchi, Rev. Irvin Boudreaux, Mark Bugg, Dr. Francis Coolidge, Rev. Maggie Dawson, Sister Janet Franklin, Rev. Susan Gaumer, Jane Knight, Vivien Michals, Beth Morgan, Anna Maria Signorelli, Dolly Smith, Jennifer Standish, Susan Vanderkuy, and Rev. Callie Winn.

We have all been taught the contemplative path by cherished guest teachers Father Richard Rohr, Dr. Roberta Bondi, Brother Dr. Ephrem Arcement, the Reverend Dr. Tilden Edwards, and the Reverend Dr. Elaine Heath. We have also been blessed by numerous local teachers who have shared contemplative instruction through their workshops in art, centering prayer, dance, journaling, labyrinth walks, music, tai chi, and much more.

I am also appreciative of the support and help of my first copyeditor, Theresa Vigour, with an early draft of the manuscript, and for the practical help of Alex Fus, Christian Amondson, Matthew Wimer, and the editors and staff at Wipf and Stock in preparing this manuscript for publication.

Introduction

YOU HAVE IN YOUR hands a collection of stories about everyday contemplatives, people who live normal, stressful lives, except that our first priority is practicing the presence of God as monks living in the real world. We live in a monastery without walls, a monastery of the heart. We are seekers of God and seekers of a life centered in cultivating heartfulness, radiating loving-kindness, and bringing God's presence with us as we serve the world, each in our own unique ways.

I am sharing this spiritual memoir because our adventures in finding an inner sanctuary and creating contemplative communities for mutual support on our spiritual journeys show that you could have this life too. I know this because there is nothing special about us. We are regular people becoming messy contemplatives. We are ever beginners, and always will be. Yet something simple and wonderful is happening among us because the Spirit is moving.

I believe reading our stories will inspire those of you who long for a deepening spiritual life in a fast-paced culture. I write for those of you who have wrongly believed that others can live this kind of contemplative life because they are more spiritual than you. Our stories will surely show you otherwise. I write for those of you who believe monks are all pious bachelors living quiet lives in peaceful monasteries isolated from the world. You will be encouraged to know we are men and women busy living stressful lives and that our only peaceful moments are discovered in our inner monasteries one moment at a time. I write for those of you who feel a longing for something more. You need and deserve to have hope in finding that something more within yourself.

In this book, you will read about a group of male and female spiritual seekers who came together to birth a School for Contemplative Living.

But this school is not like your usual institution. Our school is not run by education experts or professors of intellectual information, but is instead being born by struggling people who find shelter in each other. We are truly teaching each other through experience, comparing practical notes on what works and what doesn't work in our spiritual lives. We are peers sharing a contemplative journey and learning this path from each other. We don't have a school building. Our school is located in the heart, and we find it among each other as we gather all over New Orleans.

In the first chapter, I will share some aspects of how a school for messy contemplatives is being born in and around New Orleans since the devastation of Hurricane Katrina. I hope you will read these pages wondering whether a contemplative community could be born for you too, wherever you live. In the second chapter, I share some of my own joy in discovering an inner sanctuary. I will tell you stories of the many people who helped me learn contemplative practices and attitudes even before the first vision came to us for forming contemplative communities in our area.

In the third chapter, I share many of our stories about learning to practice God's presence in our personal lives. I also offer details on how God's presence manifests through our lives in various forms of service. I hope you will find clear examples of our imperfections as we strike out on the journey of contemplative living as monks in the real world. You will find a list of core contemplative attitudes, our own contemplative pledge, a model for contemplative vows, and even some suggestions for birthing your own contemplative school.

In the fourth chapter, I cover some aspects of the dark side of contemplation. If you thought monks had it easy, think again. There's nothing easy about opening your heart and mind each day, or in encountering all that is within and around you. Facing each aspect of our shadow side, confronting every buried feeling, and letting them come bubbling up so they can be released is anything but escapism. In reading this chapter, you might find some of your favorite myths about contemplatives busted.

In the fifth chapter, I cover a variety of ways we practice the presence of God. Even so, I barely scratch the surface. There are literally a million ways "to kneel and kiss the ground," as the Sufi poet Rumi said.[1] So I share some of our favorite techniques within our particular communities. The section on "Ten Ways to Meditate" is an example of one of our classes.

---

1. Rumi, *Essential Rumi*, 36.

In the sixth chapter, I offer you some contemplative poetry, poetic expressions of a few aspects of contemplative living. I hope the poetic muse who moves through me at times will capture you as she has me. She has a way of dispensing with intellectual concepts and taking us straight into the heart.

The book concludes with an epilogue on how we create contemplative communities out of desperation, not from any kind of spiritual superiority. Our local model is really about learning to shelter each other on this journey. Then I list some additional resources for expanding your own contemplative life and a short bibliography of useful texts.

We are still in the process of our own birthing, but I can tell you it has been an amazing adventure. We have been tremendously helped in learning our contemplative path by the visits and teachings of Father Richard Rohr, Dr. Roberta Bondi, the Reverend Dr. Tilden Edwards, the Reverend Dr. Elaine Heath, Brother David Vryhof, and Brother Dr. Ephrem Arcement.

Yet our early years have been filled with lots of wandering in the dark, feeling lost, and finding our way as best we can. It seems that no amount of skilled teaching can make one a contemplative on its own. Great moments of inspiration do not substitute for the daily work of cultivating one's inner life. And doing the work cannot substitute for the reality that we are only opening our hands to receive the gift of God's presence. In the end, our stories are evidence of God manifesting herself in the world.

Our part is the intention and willingness to plod along in practicing God's presence day after day, year after year. And by God's grace, I can truly say there are now monks living in our corner of the real world whose monastery is in the heart, and who are actually birthing a school where we teach each other the sacred art of contemplative living. I have every hope that reading our stories will help you hear the divine call to join us in becoming monks in the world.

1

An Uncertain Birthing

Here in the international gumbo of cultures called New Orleans, I once saw a vision of spiritual pilgrims sitting together in stillness. Now, a School for Contemplative Living is being birthed out of the longing need among spiritual seekers in south Louisiana, and I have the privilege of being part of it. This birthing is happening in a land of bayous, rivers, and hurricanes that bring the Gulf of Mexico flooding into our laps. This might be an unlikely location to gather monks whose monastery is the world. But maybe this is exactly where we need such gatherings to support people seeking the solid ground of our beings. Perhaps this is where the spiritual search in the heart of every person can lead us home.

In a country biased in favor of people who climb the ladder of success higher and faster than anyone else, a call came into my heart to walk slowly, together with others, in equality around meditative labyrinths and nature paths. In a world obsessed with high-tech gadgetry and competition to purchase the very latest model of whatever-is-next before anyone else, a longing arose to share simple friendship with our poorest neighbors. Together we are being schooled in giving and receiving love in face-to-face encounters.

How odd that the Divine Trickster always seems to tug us spiritual seekers off in opposite directions from mainstream society and religious culture. As people in America are being driven to speed up, those in our monastery without walls are being led to slow down. We are tired of the frantic pace of American society and its pressure on us human hamsters to keep racing nowhere fast. As multi-tasking becomes a cultural expectation, our Inner Voice says, "Find the one main thing and live that."

As the god of capitalism pushes us to do anything necessary for the chance to make more money, a small group of imperfect followers is being called to a great giveaway of our money, our possessions, and our time. Yet this kind of going against the flow is all but impossible for most of us, except in little moments of grace when something bigger than ourselves pulls us along. Even then we all need a great deal of support from each other to take the time to think about anyone but ourselves. How did this new adventure start to become a quiet little revolution in our part of the world?

I am telling you the story of how this uncertain birthing began and how our school for contemplatives continues to arise. I am hoping that our story will resonate with your own need to find an inner sanctuary among fellow seekers in the wild world of postmodern American life.

Birth is always uncertain, since we never really know what will happen next. The birth of our school is no different, for no one can prepare us for how messy such a birth may be. Our map for this birth has been that first vision of spiritual pilgrims sitting together in stillness, along with a lot of guessing about what might need to happen next to achieve that vision. The uncertainty of it all reminds me of an earlier birth experience.

I saw my first birth as an eighteen-year-old medical volunteer working to vaccinate children in Guatemala. A midwife in the little Guatemalan village of Panzos was encountering complications with an impending birth and called on my volunteer partner and I to assist her with our tiny bit of medical training. She called us into a makeshift delivery area, and that's where things got really messy.

Let's just say that as teenaged boys, we had no business assisting in a birth. It wasn't pretty, and I had no idea birth could be that scary, painful, loud, squishy—amazing. After that tiny human being came forth from the Guatemalan woman's body, we sat silently in our rooms for the rest of the day. We literally couldn't speak. Silent stillness can often be like that: We are so overwhelmed by life that we just don't know what to say, and so we sit together in awe and silence. This feeling of genuine contemplation is a long way from any manufactured, super-spiritual state of mind in which we are in control and only trying to act holy.

The birthing of an organic community of human beings can also be scary, painful, uncertain, and amazing. Like childbirth, the process happens a moment at a time. We might all think we know how birth works, but reality has a way of showing us we are not in control and that we do not know ahead of time what's coming.

In birthing a community, you start forward and then fall backwards, much like labor's many starts and stops. There is rarely a predictable linear plan to follow. There is only a mental message after the fact saying, "Oh, so that's how this is going to work." It is a moment-by-moment revelation. And like all births, the birth of a community offers no guarantees. We might think we know how things will happen, but we never really do. The whole thing could die tomorrow.

The birthing of our spiritual community might sound more romantic if I could tell you we had a plan from the beginning. But in truth, we don't even have a very solid plan now—something is being birthed between us, and we are as surprised as anyone else to see what unfolds. We try to keep our eyes and ears open, watching for whatever appears to be coming next. But contemplative living is more like those two teens watching their first birth: We stand in awe, we are amazed and sometimes dismayed, we fall silent, and now in our contemplative communities, we do a lot of sitting in stillness together in hopes of practicing the presence of God in our midst. We do so not because we are super-spiritual, but out of desperation and deep need.

The stories that follow tell how this birth began and how our community is continuing to emerge. We are in the early years of forming contemplative communities around the New Orleans region, so we are still like children who do not know what they will be when they grow up. This is as it should be. A contemplative life is always going to require immense trust, like stepping into the dark. Thus, these stories are like charting a course in reverse, after the voyage has begun. All I can tell you is where we have been since the hurricane forced me and other spiritual pilgrims to reassess our lives and spiritual journeys. I cannot say what will happen next. This is how things unfolded as contemplative communities began to be born in the dangerous, soulful, sinister, sacred, and still recovering world called N'awlins following the 2005 destruction of Hurricane Katrina.

BREAK THOSE VOWS!

I was drawn to form a contemplative spiritual community after that monster storm ripped through our lives. A vision has been coming to me ever since, slowly creeping through my imagination to form a picture of people coming together as a community to practice being in God's presence. In the vision, we support each other in taking baby steps towards living simply, authentically, and fully in our oneness with the One. We come together to remind each other that we are not alone in this desire. And we carry our desire and diverse ways of practicing oneness into our daily lives in the world.

In this still-forming vision, a monastery without walls is being birthed. When I explain this to most people, I often get looks of blankness, confusion, even consternation. And I don't know what to say next, because all of my words about this kind of life can't seem to capture what is seeking to be born. I envision a community of contemplatives, beings who simply want to build their lives and service around experiencing their oneness with the Great Love.

When I say "monastery," most people picture medieval male monks wearing long, dark robes who cut themselves off from the world behind high stone walls to protect their isolated solitude. People imagine pious men walking around with their hands folded in prayer all day long, or pouring over ancient texts that have little to do with today's postmodern life.

But that's just it. The monastery in my vision has no walls. This is a monastery of the heart. The people of this monastery are men and women who dress in ordinary clothes and live in homes and families out in the world. We go to work in a multitude of different jobs. We aren't all on some unified mission to build a new hospital or any other tangible project. We spend much of our day like everyone else, carrying on with the business of everyday life.

And yet, we are all engaged in an invisible inward mission. We want to cultivate our awareness of the presence of God within us every day, and we want to carry that presence with us wherever we go, serving in and through that presence. And that is about as counter-cultural as anything I can think of.

I believe we Americans share one common religion: capitalism. From the time we get up until we fall asleep at night, and maybe even in our dreams, we Americans are supposed to dedicate our full attention to making more money. We are to seek better-paying jobs wherever that enterprise takes us, even if it means uprooting our lives and families. If we do stop to think of others, it tends to be in some self-serving way, like giving a little gift to some church or charity to ease our guilt for having so much.

At this time in my life, I cannot envision anything further from a spiritual life than capitalism. It's a god that wears us out and never ever says enough. It doesn't ease up. Even on vacation, we believe we should still keep our Blackberry on in case the office needs us, or watch the news to see what's happening with our stock portfolio, or leverage some chance meeting into a networking opportunity. Can't we see how crazy this is?

The people in my dream of community, who can't bow down to *that* god any longer, have felt for a long time an inner gnawing hunger for a deeper life. The hollowness of the American dream has not satisfied us. In fact, it has never even come close. And finally, after a long time of trying to be part of this culture, we are rising up one by one to say, "Enough!" Maybe the loss of so many of our homes and possessions in the hurricane helped us to cross that threshold of letting go.

We who are forming this monastery without walls are finding we no longer even have a choice. We see the vows required by the religion of capitalism, and even popular religion, and realize we have to break those vows. But let's be clear, the vows we must break might have tentacles that stretch deep into our own psyches. The currents of culture, popular religion, and even our own unconscious minds create a powerful pressure to quit swimming upstream and just go with the flow.

Some of us "monasterians," people creating a monastery of the heart, met in 2012 to begin a discussion of what it would mean to live by a common rule of life. We talked about the usual baby boomer resistance to rules or any institution that demands loyalty. Since I have been thinking for several years now about what kind of vows this community might adopt, and since people in monasteries and spiritual communities have often committed to live by a shared way of life, I have come to some tentative conclusions.

First, there is a storm coming our way. When people like us resist the vows dictated by the larger culture's rules, there is always a price to pay. Institutions, even religious ones, resist change, and they especially resist people who seek to bring about change. Even if we secretly, inwardly break the vows of what is acceptable to the majority of people around us, there will be a rub. Conflicts will arise and tensions will emerge. So we might as well begin preparing for that conflict.

My friend Dr. Jim O'Neill spoke this truth concerning spirituality and religion years ago. He said, "Spiritual leaders [and, we might add, followers] very often conflict with religious leaders." There it is, simple and clear, a warning for all those who follow a spiritual path. Religions are frequently distorted by the impulse to protect their own entrenched system, and so they have to stifle any spiritual renewal movement, which they see as a threat.

One example of this truth is seen in George Fox, the unintentional founder of the Religious Society of Friends in the seventeenth century, which later became known as Quakers. He felt he had to break the vows of common culture in his day. Fox could not in good conscience bow and tip his hat in homage to the wealthy upper classes as he passed them on the street. He could not hold his tongue when he felt led to speak to church authorities from his heart. He was led by the light of the Christ Spirit within to speak his truth. Fox was repeatedly beaten and imprisoned for these radical acts. But he had taken a vow to follow that light within, and felt he must be true to his personal vows whatever the cost, even at the expense of breaking the vows of accepted culture.

A century later, John Wesley, an Anglican clergyman, felt a similar call to stop playing by the rules of the religious status quo. He could not bow down to the religious authorities, and so churches refused to let him speak from their pulpits. Wesley turned instead to the people in the streets and the fields. He made a vow of holy living and called others to live out their beliefs, serving with the poor and preaching the love of Christ wherever they could.

Perhaps, in their own unique ways, George Fox and John Wesley were simply harkening back to the life Christ, who after all got himself into all kinds of trouble by clashing with religious authorities and breaking the vow to follow the rules of established religion. When he took the vow to make God's compassion his central calling, to welcome *all* into God's kingdom, to speak the words of God as they welled up inside him, Christ was living out a vow that eventually cost him his life. Things do not tend to go smoothly when people break the vows of the dominant culture, including religious culture.

So it is that even today, any of us who want to form a monastery without walls, to live a consecrated life, and to break the vows of popular culture by seeking to adopt a simple spiritual life should first pause to count the costs. We shouldn't fool ourselves, for even our own unconscious vows will trip us up time and again.

Maybe we don't even realize we have made vows of our own. Some voice within might be saying, "I need everyone's approval," or "I should never call attention to myself," or "I must fit in," or some other impossible internal vow. I have tried all those vows and many more: "Don't make so much money," and the opposite, "You should make a lot more money," or "You had better focus on retirement," and "Spiritual people never worry about money, they just trust God." I won't bore you with the multitude of other unconscious vows that come and go in my psyche, but I bet you have a few too.

After we break vows of culture like worshipping the god of capitalism, and vows of religion like putting loyalty to the system over God's truth, and once we break unconscious vows to inner gods of approval or social propriety, what's left to vow? To what purpose can we give our whole hearts and lives, or at least as much as we can muster at any one moment? What vow can a monasterian truly make?

I first saw my one simple, yet impossibly challenging vow painted on the wall of a house in New Orleans a few years ago. I had probably passed the house a hundred times as I took the exit ramp off the interstate to Saint Charles Avenue. I had never noticed the words scrawled on a deteriorating wall whose paint had almost faded completely. But one day, as always happens in spiritual life, an inner nudge turned my attention over my right shoulder as I waited for the stoplight to change.

On the fading forest green wall of that house, in bold pink print, were the words, "Let love rule." So there it is in all its embarrassing simplicity, my one real vow. I hope to be a monk who lives within a community of other followers who will help me take a stab at living this vow. I know I cannot follow this path alone. I always slip up by trying to seem loving, or to look loving. My ego gets in the way, checking over my shoulder to see if anyone is watching when I offer some little act of service. Or, if no one else is around, I might perform some small loving act and then think to myself, "Wow, William, you're quite a guy," which seems to cancel out any good I might have done.

I don't expect that Mother Teresa of Calcutta, Saint Francis of Assisi, or any other real lovers of the world wasted too much time thinking about themselves. But for people like me, ego keeps trying to regain its ascendency. It wants to clamber back onto the throne of my life and rule. It can't stand the thought that some other ruler, like love, might take its place.

So the dilemma of my vision of a monastery without walls is simple: How can I found a movement with others when I can barely even practice the very thing I'm called to do? I find there are two answers from which I must start. First, begin as you are right now, and second, ask for help.

Begin as you are right now means that just for today, I vow to practice opening myself to follow love's lead. Since I do not know the way ahead, I must become willing to "Let love rule." And I do that by sitting quietly every day that I can, breathing and opening my heart to the Great Love as best as I can. I set aside some time each morning to engage this practice, and I try to remember to open myself to that leading again and again throughout the day. I believe this simple vow summarizes what Jesus emphasized as the first and second commandments to love God, ourselves, and our neighbors (Matt 22:35–40).

When I forget, as the Quaker author Thomas Kelly teaches in *A Testament of Devotion*, I try not to waste time in self-recrimination. I just start over again. I do not try to be good. In fact, I do not *do* anything at all. I practice being—I try to just *be* in the presence of the One. That One is the very love I need and the love the world needs too.

But since I am constantly lapsing, or practicing oneness for a little bit and then feeling self-righteous about it, I also have to ask for help. I finally understand that I need community. I can't live any semblance of a spiritual life alone. I can't make love the essence of my spiritual path all by myself. If I am to "Let love rule," I have to find help to stay on that path.

And so let it be declared this day, with my hopes high that some good can come out of all of this, that I need a community of people to help me gradually learn to "Let love rule." If we're lucky, my helpers on this path will also be helped to live consecrated lives. Maybe a whole community of us can form a monastery without walls in which we monasterians may practice this one simple, impossibly demanding vow and help each other along this path.

Would you join me? Do you need help, as I do? Could we learn to help each other live a life of love in the twenty-first century, following God into the life that was planned for us all from the foundation of the world? Would you also vow, as best you can, to "Let love rule"? Please do. I, for one, could use the friends. If you want to come along with us, keep reading to see whether this calling to become a monasterian with others as part of a contemplative school might be your next vocation in life.

THE EARLY DAYS

I want to back up to explore the early days of how all this monastery business began. Sometimes knowing your beginnings, remembering how things got started, helps to ground the purpose and intention of what comes next. I trace the roots of this contemplative movement around New Orleans back to our responses to the descent of Hurricane Katrina in the late summer of 2005.

As with most disasters that sweep through any community, the people left behind are usually clueless about how to get through the endlessly traumatic aftermath. Most of us just hunker down and do the best we can to get through each day. We work on our own homes and we stop to help the next person. Such caring people often burn through energy we didn't know we had in trying to rebuild a life for ourselves and for others. We hope to reclaim a life that at least bears some resemblance to normal. What we reluctantly discover is that there will be a new normal, no matter how much we had hoped to reconstruct the life we used to know.

I went pretty crazy in the first year of recovery after the devastation of Katrina. That is one of the reasons I eventually had to begin a new way of life that includes creating contemplative communities. In my work as counselor and associate pastor of a church, I felt inundated with people's stories of their traumas. Everybody had a terrible story in those days. And most everybody needed to tell that story to anyone who would listen. We all did it. Telling the story was part of processing what had happened to us. But for a listener like me, taking in those stories of devastation every day and then coming home to face my own destroyed home through the slow process of reconstruction became overwhelming.

By the summer of 2006, I began to awaken to how overwhelmed I really felt. I was shocked to take a phone call from a new counseling client and see in my appointment book that I was about to take on my thirty-fifth client for that week. As I looked ahead to the next week, I saw that there were already thirty-five sessions scheduled for that week as well. For some reason that number made me wake up to how completely I had exceeded my boundaries.

My own absence of boundaries scared me. It was like I awakened from a dream to see I was living an unrecognizable alternate life. For on top of scheduling ten more weekly counseling clients than my normal counseling load of twenty-five, I was also working at least thirty hours a week to meet the needs of people from church. I felt dazed to find myself working essentially two full-time jobs.

The discovery shocked me so much that I immediately closed my counseling practice to new clients. But even that meager attempt to set a boundary didn't help much, because I still felt responsible for the many people I had already committed to help. In a desperate attempt to discern what the hell was going on with me, I begged my wife to leave with me for two weeks' vacation in Europe to sort things out. We had a little insurance money left over from the house repairs, and I convinced her to use it to take off.

For reasons I couldn't explain, I was drawn to go visit very old monasteries where monks had been living the contemplative life for many centuries. I felt a need to get away from the self-imposed stress of caring for so many people and look instead for places of stillness and centered prayerfulness. I didn't really know what I was longing for. Maybe it was mostly escape. And maybe I needed some kind of respite far from the world of disasters and recovery stories so I could lean toward my inner self and rediscover my own center.

For two weeks in September of 2006, we walked along Mediterranean beaches in France and Italy and visited monasteries from Nice to Piona Abbey on Lake Como. I remember being especially moved upon learning that Piona Abbey had been a place of contemplative prayer for a thousand years. The Italian word for silence, *silenzio*, was carved into the wood just outside this simple Benedictine chapel, and it resonated with something my soul longed for. Walking beside Italian monks in silence caused my soul to arise. I knew they were living the life of the contemplative community that I so needed. I didn't know what to do with this inner knowledge, but something visceral was emerging and calling me.

Being in those places was rejuvenating, but when I resumed my life near New Orleans, all of the same suffering people were still waiting for me. I didn't know how to sustain a centered life in the middle of all of those needs, and my small commitment of twenty to thirty minutes of centering prayer by myself each morning was not enough.

Throughout 2006, my spiritual director, Dolly, had been hearing my stories, longings, uncertainties, and vague dreams. She was intrigued by what seemed to be trying to be born in me, even though it was all about as clear as mud. She never tried to tell me what to do about it. She didn't ply me with advice. But Dolly did offer me steady support in trying to find some clarity. She could sense that God was in the longings that were wooing me, and her confidence in that helped me explore further.

Over time, Dolly helped me sense that a kind of ecumenical contemplative order might be part of the dream, and yet she tried to hold back and say as little as possible so as not to get ahead of what I was ready to hear or see. On the other hand, she would challenge me sometimes as an insight arose in her, as when she asked me to examine my own reluctance to be like a monk who, in effect, walks around with an empty begging bowl—needing other people to fill the bowl when I just can't do things alone.

Through those conversations with Dolly, I realized more than ever how much people engaged in sincere spiritual journeys need supportive guides who have the hope, faith, and trust we need when we feel like we are walking alone in the dark. Dolly knew things before I did. Yet she was careful not to get ahead of my own revelation—I guess she knew not to try to do God's work. Her steady presence of listening, of knowing spiritual things without saying them, of challenging me when it was needed, and supporting my own small steps was a big help in charting this course through unknown territory. Altogether, Dolly worked with me for about seven years. That particular year of discernment was an especially important part of this work as a new vision arose.

By the late fall of 2006, I felt I had to leave my counseling practice for another three weeks to keep asking what my life was trying to tell me. I took off for the Abbey of Gethsemani in Kentucky, where Thomas Merton had been a monk. He was the first contemplative I had ever read, a prolific author on the contemplative life, and something in me wanted to connect with him. I wanted to join him in the pursuit of a more contemplative life on the very grounds that he had walked.

My dad offered to ride with me from Nashville, Tenessee, and on a brisk autumn morning we set out in search of something I couldn't really explain. Maybe you too have felt an inner tug drawing you toward something without any clear understanding of what that longing is about. So it was that we arrived at Gethsemani Abbey with that vague sense of searching as my only guide.

We walked into the rugged stone chapel just as the monks were chanting the psalms. As we slipped out, I noticed the remarkable words, "God alone," etched into the stone arch leading to a small garden walkway. I remembered the full passage from Psalm 62:1, "My soul waits in silence for God only" (NASB). My own soul replied, "Yes, I too wait in silence for God alone." I felt a real kinship with those monks, and yet I never spoke to one of them.

I did not yet know enough about what I was experiencing to voice it to a stranger. But I did tell my dad I wanted to spend a little time alone on the monastery grounds. I walked off through that cold and blustery day to a spot on a hill, and tears welled up within me. I wanted to make my own vow right there, but I didn't have any model for what to say. I remembered what one of the Benedictine monks at Saint Joseph Abbey near our home had told us during our silent summer retreats: Monks are simply seeking God each day. In that moment, I made a simple commitment to live a contemplative life as best I could. I told God, "I am seeking you alone." Then I got too cold and headed back to meet my dad in the gift shop.

I looked around at the little symbols of monastic life for sale in the gift shop. I decided to buy two small clay signs as reminders of what was welling up inside me. One said, "Be still, and know that I am God," (Ps 46:10). The other was that summary of the phrase from Psalm 62:1, "God Alone." I keep one in my home as I write these words. The other is in my office. Wouldn't it be wonderful if all we needed to sustain a contemplative life was a couple of signs with lines of Scripture etched into them?

After my dad and I made it back to Nashville, I made an appointment with Rev. Jerry Haas, who was then guiding a nationwide program for spiritual formation supported by an organization known as The Upper Room. My spiritual friend and colleague, Rev. Carole Cotton Winn, had suggested I meet with Jerry to discuss my longings and to see what resources he might be aware of that might help me in my unfolding journey. He made several suggestions for connections around the country and mentioned several books that he hoped might help. But the main thing I took away from that visit was that Rev. Jerry took my vague longing seriously. He supported me in going forward to search for that unknown something that he felt God was obviously drawing me toward.

When I returned to my world, I started telling a few people I was going to be making some big changes in my life, even though I did not yet know what was unfolding. I was feeling an urge to drop everything and start off in some new direction. My friend Carole challenged me to be cautious about walking away from everything before I had an inkling of what I was walking toward. She wisely suggested I make a one-quarter turn in my life, which didn't require forsaking everything I had been working on up to that time. I listened carefully and wondered how such a thing might look.

I then invited the United Methodist district superintendent Rev. Ralph Ford, a kind of pastor of pastors in our region, to come over to our house so I could tell him about my longings. I spoke in sketchy language about seeking a place of ministry where I could devote less time to hearing everyone's crises all day, every day, and more time to cultivating spiritual growth in small groups. Ralph didn't know what I was talking about any more than I did, but like Jerry and Carole and another pastoral friend, Rev. Don Cottrill, he was supportive. He didn't say I was crazy, even though I myself felt pretty crazy.

Despite the level of stress I had been feeling through the disaster recovery process, I was also making more money in those years than I had ever imagined I could. I guess that's what working two jobs will do for you: more money and less inner life. So in some ways, the urge to leave all of that behind should have seemed crazy, especially when the only clarity I had about where I was heading was toward some yet-to-be-defined spiritual formation ministry.

But even my close friends with whom I was co-pastoring the church, John and Marie Williams, did not respond to my announcement with an appropriately reasonable sentiment such as "You are freakin' crazy!" Of all people, they might have had the most to lose when I said I felt the need to walk away from the church and the counseling ministry housed in our church. After all, they were still new on the scene of that church community and they depended on me to meet many of the church's pastoral care needs, especially while congregants continued their struggle to get their houses and lives back together. They admitted that my news was not what they wanted to hear, but they also were very gracious in saying they would support me in whatever direction I was heading.

By the spring of 2007, the United Methodist denomination found a possible place of service for me and offered me a job in the middle of the still-devastated city of New Orleans. I have to say part of me thought, "Why in the hell would I want to spend even more time in a disaster zone?" But another part was just ready for a change and still seeking a new space in which to birth something that I still could not define.

So after discussing the opportunity with my wife, I said yes to becoming the half-time pastor of a tiny church of sixteen people who had just decided to begin rebuilding, as well as the half-time associate pastor of a larger church undergoing a five million dollar renovation of their devastated building. Neither place had well-defined expectations of me. The call seemed to be to just go in and do some good.

That suited me fine, because it left some wiggle room for me to dream a dream of how to start creating small spiritual formation communities. Serving two churches in New Orleans when there were still no homeless shelters, few services for the poor, and hardly one hundred physicians to cover the whole city was not like walking silently alongside the monks at Piona Abbey surrounded by the Italian Alps. It wasn't rejuvenating. It wasn't peaceful. It surely wasn't reserving lots of extra time for God alone.

On the other hand, I was completely free to start experimenting. I had never been the only pastor of a spiritual community of any size, so from that very first Sunday in June of 2007, I could try new things, like asking people to speak out in worship and tell me some of their mystical experiences. I just asked, "When have you felt like you were part of something bigger than yourself or known that you were in God's presence?" Having no interest in trying to be in charge or in telling people how I thought they should do things, I was ready to co-create worship and community with them. I was a total novice and I knew it. I expect they did too.

While I was investigating this new calling, I also learned there was already an established contemplative community known as the New Orleans chapter of Contemplative Outreach. They had been meeting once a month for several years and had established a core group who were friends on a contemplative path. Their monthly meeting was in the very church I was asked to pastor.

One group meeting once a month was not nearly enough of what I was needing, so I asked two of the facilitators if they would be willing to provide a training workshop at our home in the suburbs. I hoped to create a contemplative community there as well. Our facilitators, Vivien Michals and Anna Maria Signorelli, were willing, and we found a date to schedule a new group on a Saturday in the late spring of 2007. In time, Vivien and Anna Maria were becoming some of my new best friends on this challenging contemplative path.

After a small group of us went through an introductory workshop on centering prayer held in our home on the Doubloon Bayou, we followed up with a suggested series of DVDs created by Father Thomas Keating, a co-founder of the international network called Contemplative Outreach.[1] We started with a group of about ten people. Many of us had pursued a spiritual life for many years. But most had never been trained in a specific form of prayer that could lead into contemplative prayer.

As we discussed the DVDs and practiced centering prayer together each week, a frequent theme emerged: "What am I supposed to be getting out of this?" I guess this is a common question for human beings to ask. We just tend to presume that every experience is a kind of product

---

1. Please see the "Resources" section for further details on Contemplative Outreach and related organizations.

that promises to deliver results, preferably in our first moments of trying it out. Some of the group began to fall away after those early weeks of practice. Others hung in there with us.

I am not sure I could say what anyone else was hoping for early on. But I knew I wanted to have a consistent practice group to help support my own desire to practice God's presence. And some of us did sustain a pretty regular practice of centering prayer. We gathered weekly for group practice and mutual support. That early formation lasted for about a year, though even with newcomers joining us occasionally, the group size began to dwindle.

As we ended up with only three of us from the original group of ten who returned week after week in that first year, I began to fear that this little experiment was about to come to an end. I didn't want it to end. But I didn't want the group to get so small that we were never sure whether anyone would be there either.

Then it happened. A simple moment of spiritual insight found me and became a vision of what would become my future. It was early evening when we began our centering time together in our home. The sun was setting over the cypress swamp outside the picture windows of our meeting room. The birds were still whistling. Several of our rabbits were munching on the grass. It was a peaceful pastoral scene on the bayou. After we had our initial check-in, we began to settle in for shared prayer in silence. I believe Beth Morgan and Jane Knight, two of our most faithful contemplative friends, were with us that evening.

It was during our prescribed twenty-minute period of centering prayer that I had a bit of a mystical experience. I was going down into that deep place in the soul where we are simply one with all that is. I found myself imagining that I was rising up towards the ceiling and looking down on the three of us, similar to some people's descriptions of near-death experiences. But I wasn't near death and I wasn't hallucinating. I was just seeing us practicing the presence of God together, experiencing oneness with the One together. I was a silent witness to an exquisite moment.

It hit me that this very moment of knowing oneness is a treasure, and that other people deserve to experience the spiritual richness we were discovering. I remembered what Jesus said about the kingdom of heaven being like someone who found a treasure in a field and who sold everything he had to buy that field (Matt 13:44). I knew clearly then and there that I had found a treasure, an inner experience of that which matters more than anything else: the home of the living God in the sanctuary of my soul.

I felt an old familiar ache, a longing dream of sharing this practice in the world. That moment was my clear call to become what I have later referred to as a contemplative missionary. Sometimes little moments change everything if only we are awake, open, and receptive to our own transformation.

That moment connected with an experience I had in 1992 while on a retreat for spiritual leaders. I had taken the week off from work and from writing of my dissertation. The staff of the Shalem Institute for Spiritual Formation was guiding us through five days of silent presence with God. All week I had been praying for direction about where to serve once I completed my PhD in counseling. I had been imagining all kinds of exciting possibilities and felt sure there would be a place where I could help change the world with my newfound gifts and training.

In the middle of this week of silence, I awakened from a nap. A phrase came immediately to my mind like a direct message from God: "Called to a life of prayer for the world." I started crying. I felt tremendously humbled, or maybe even humiliated. My ego was crushed. I thought, "What? After all these years of work to get a doctorate in counseling I am being called to a life of prayer for the world?" It seemed to me that I had just received a giant demotion. After fantasizing about some great new place of service, a real job with a real salary attached, and after sincerely believing God was going to reveal such a place, I was in no way prepared for this kind of calling. My ego took a tumble. But something in me felt the truth of the call.

So maybe what happened in that moment of evening prayer sitting in a room with two friends within and two rabbits outside was another calling to a life of prayer for the world. Perhaps I was finally coming back to my true home and original calling.

I experienced the early birthing of a monastery without walls through a simple vision of us sharing what we were already doing—practicing the presence of God in a little community. Suddenly it didn't matter that our community had dwindled to only three people. My vision was a sense that there might be other people out in the world who could truly benefit from the gift the group practice was offering. I felt I had discovered a treasure that I wanted to pass on. That was in the late spring of 2008. I had been serving in New Orleans for a year but was still living at our bayou home in the suburbs.

Shortly after that pivotal evening, we made the logical decision to let the weekly group at our home disband for the summer. But my friend Jane suggested that we email the larger group who started the journey with us to see if they would like to make a mutual commitment to practice together-apart for the summer. In other words, we asked the others to join us on Thursday mornings, or whenever they were able to, for a time of centering prayer practice in our own chosen places. It was like saying, "Hey, let's all do it wherever we are, and maybe it will help us sustain a sense of community to know we are all practicing on the same day."

It might sound like an insignificant decision, but it worked. Practicing daily prayer is hard enough to sustain in groups, much less alone, and so why not use the help of just knowing that others are practicing too? It was one of our earliest discoveries that the Spirit in and among us could use almost anything to help nudge us along on a contemplative path.

By that fall, Jane suggested that we commit to gather once a month and offered to host the group in her home. She also took the initiative of issuing a monthly personalized invitation with a quote, an experience, or thought to remind us that we were in this together. Her little email became the invitation we needed to gather month after month, as we were able, to be in each other's company as we longed for the company of God together.

I share these details about our early days of forming one small contemplative community both to show how simple this process can be and also how flexible we have to be in experimenting with different ways of being. It took a workshop, some DVDs, a weekly commitment, a disbanding, a promise to practice apart, a reconstituting on a monthly basis, and the willingness of one of us to offer her home and invite us back into presence together.

But something else drew us to one another and helped us stick together as a contemplative community. There was a real affection among us. Most of us in that first group had known each other for years. We trusted each other. We did not fear being judged, or at least not much. And I believe this freedom to let down our guard and just be ourselves together helped us stay with our commitment to gather on a regular basis.

I also believe that practicing the presence of God together over time creates a unique bond between people. The act of sitting together in the Presence, the Source of all compassion, was creating a reservoir of loving-kindness within and between us, though this was beneath our consciousness. I believe practicing the presence, as the fundamental act of contemplative communities, brings a sense of union that can't be explained by the fact that the first group had known each other already. It was more than that. There is some mystery at work in the depths of our souls when our union with God also unites us with each other.

That first group showed us that unitive consciousness is like an organic connective tissue that can hold us together even when we are apart. I feel this connection even now, though I have not personally been able to sit with that particular group for months. This mysterious connective tissue of the Spirit grew within and between us over months of sharing our practice together. I have seen it happen again and again in other groups over time, even within those groups who simply gather to practice and then go their own way with very little discussion of our lives.

Those were the nuts and bolts of our first group in the suburbs of New Orleans before we had birthed a network of contemplative groups all around the region. In time we formed another group, and then another. We experimented with a variety of styles for our groups and offered some new approaches such as sacred yoga or an occasional special program on some aspect of contemplative living.

We were like blind people feeling our way in the dark. But we overcame our fears about the whole thing failing by adopting the attitude that anything was worth a try. Our longing to be in the presence of the sacred overrode our concerns that it might fall apart over time. So we created groups each month to practice exercises like sacred reading (*lectio divina*), sacred viewing of art (*visio divina*), sacred writing (*scriptio divina*), sacred music (*audio divina*), sacred yoga and dance, sacred conversation (*conversatio divina*), and several forms of walking meditation in nature and through labyrinths.

After this process of experimental emergence had established itself and we had formed a number of weekly groups for centering prayer and various studies, I decided to propose that the people in my church join together in support of the birthing of this unfolding mission. There was not an abundance of enthusiasm. Some even said, "Monks, monasteries, and contemplation—we don't know what you're talking about."

So I stepped back and discussed all of this with one of my newest New Orleans friends. Francis had been seeking to establish his own contemplative practice for years. He understood the need for mutual support among all of us burned-out slobs who were doing our best to recover from the hurricane. He was serving as a philosophy professor in a local Catholic university as the school put itself back together following the devastating hurricane. Through it all, Francis was caring for his wife, son, and himself as best he could.

From the first time we met, I knew I was finding a soul mate in Francis. He got me, and I think I got him. We both knew what it was like to take on the needs of too many recovering people without finding enough support for our own needs. We both recognized the specific need to spend much more time connecting with others who sought to fill their inner tanks by practicing the presence of God. We both knew we wanted more support for our practice of the presence, but we didn't have any clear map for how to get there.

I asked Francis if he would come voice these concerns in our church, and he agreed. Somehow I thought if my congregants were having trouble understanding what I was saying, they might catch it better from a different voice. From his first sentences, it looked like this was true. He spoke of the importance of following a model set forth by Father Richard Rohr that unites contemplation and action. He described how overwhelmed people need time to let go and allow God to direct us and emphasized how much we need a union of prayer and action.

I was a bit shocked and honestly a little dismayed when a few of the biggest detractors in the church said things like, "Now we understand. He makes sense." I guess I took that response as a bit of a slap in the face, thinking, "Isn't that what I have been saying all along?" But all jealousy aside, some of the people did get it. And I think it was one of the first times some of them had gotten their minds around anything beyond the immediate survival of the church community after the big storm.

Over time, I realized that one small church community was not really the place to look for a home base for this unfolding vision. There was just not enough interest in the mission. There were only a few people in that early core group from the church who were drawn to anything contemplative. So I realized I needed to broaden my scope and began to seek companions from many spiritual communities around town.

This is partly how we began to be ecumenical in nature. My sense was that within any particular church community, there might be a small handful of people who were drawn to a more contemplative life. Maybe it was a false impression, but I had the regular experience that anywhere from 1 percent to at most 10 percent of a religious community would have any particular interest in the life of a contemplative.

I also learned early on that forming a spiritual community happens one person at a time. Even the people who were extremely drawn to the idea initially might show up for one gathering and then disappear for months. Other people would attend occasional meetings as they were able and eventually find other activities to occupy their time. I began to lower my expectations that we would become a consistent core group of contemplatives who would get to know each other in ever-deepening ways over time. I started to realize that we would become more of a rag-tag collection of whoever-happens-to-be-here-today-is-the-community.

ARE WE REAL YET?

One of the disturbing and persistent questions that kept arising in my mind through these several years of birthing was this: Are we real yet? Are we actually a contemplative community? Or are we more of a collection of small contemplative groups? Are we just a handful of people exploring the contemplative life occasionally? The uncertainty of who would even show up for any given class discussion or practice group helped to feed these questions.

I suppose my own image of a traditional monastery is of a committed group of men and women who have answered a call to live together in one place. I can easily define such people as a contemplative community. Learning about some of the new monastic communities who have been founded since around the year 2000 has taught me that they too tend to live together, or at least in close proximity.[2]

So are *we* real yet? Are we, who do not live together or even necessarily close to one another, in any way a monastery or a contemplative community? My answer is that I believe we qualify as a monastery of the heart, a contemplative community in spirit. For in our hearts, each and every person is looking for God when we show up, seeking both greater intimacy with God and with fellow seekers of God.

We are also a contemplative community by virtue of our intention. We share the intention of practicing the presence of God each day as best we can. We might use different practices at times. We might be more or less able to keep that intention at times. But each one of us who shows up has the intention of deepening our connection with the divine. From the newcomer who walks into a group on any given week to the earliest

---

2. For more about the ways several intentional Christian communities envision new monasticism, see Rutba House, *School(s) for Conversion*, and the writings of Shane Claiborne and Jonathan Wilson-Hartgrove.

participants in the centering prayer groups formed by Contemplative Outreach, we are all seekers of God who intend to learn to practice the presence of God together.

By January of 2009, some of us had met several times to discuss how to become a contemplative community. We had formed an initial steering committee to pursue that goal and had received our first non-profit donations toward the cause. Donations have been coming in ever since. They have been used to provide salary support for me to serve as a founding spiritual director for the School for Contemplative Living (the name we adopted after several stabs at putting words to what we were becoming). They have also been used to create and sustain a website, pay honorariums to local guest speakers, and eventually to pay the expenses to invite authors and retreat leaders to come educate all of us on various aspects of contemplative living.

So what makes us real? Is it the steering committee? If we were to turn the steering committee into a formal board of directors with a set of rules for governance, would that make us real? Is it the donations? If you receive money in support of a cause, does that make you real? Do people have to live together to be a real community?

Here is my belief. We could dissolve the steering committee tomorrow, stop receiving donations this week, and cancel my role as spiritual director by the end of the month. On paper we would cease to exist. And perhaps the School for Contemplative Living would become history too. But because we are a real contemplative community, we would continue nevertheless because we are seekers of God who are drawn together by a hunger to practice God's presence with each other. We have nothing else to stand on than this common longing, intention, and practice. So on this we stand.

Now, an unusual mixture of people from many neighborhoods around New Orleans are slowly being tugged, led, spoken to, and called to birth a monastery without walls. We are creating a School for Contemplative Living with no buildings, professors, or formal curriculum. And based on the flimsy stuff of inner nudges, intuitions, hints, dreams, and visions, we have begun our fledgling commitment to become like monks in the world. Our task is building a monastery without walls, something Sister Joan Chittister calls *The Monastery of the Heart*.[3]

---

3. See Chittister, *Monastery of the Heart*, for a beautiful and poetic description of the monastery without walls we seek to create.

How paradoxical to know you are being guided to birth something for which there is no clear model. What would it look like to have a room full of students who are also the faculty? How would it work if the class curriculum only appears as we start the class? How would you locate a school that moves around like a gypsy caravan, shifting the classroom from a home to a church, from a senior center to a university campus, from a homeless ministry to an apartment, and from a law school to a hospital? Who knows, we might one day host meetings in a prison. We might serve prostitutes seeking to leave that kind of life. We might get to share contemplative practices with local AIDS patients. Opportunities for contemplative service will keep appearing, and we will follow them where we find them.

Our School for Contemplative Living has been birthed in these ways: We extend invitations to fellow seekers or small groups make a request for guidance, we explore the readiness of individuals and groups to experience transformation, and we slowly locate a core group of potential contemplatives to begin training each other.

Sometimes the inner longings remain strong, spiritual roots deepen, and a group sticks together. Sometimes people get too busy and a group evaporates. Some groups gradually grow into a small monastery over time, with a sustained collection of seekers and an openness to newcomers. Some groups start the contemplative journey together, but the cares of this world replace the call of the Inner Voice, numbers dwindle, and the group falls by the wayside. The call is to offer each other the solace of fellow seekers on a contemplative path, not to control outcomes or guarantee results.

NAMING

There are no titles or hierarchies in this contemplative school. No one calls themselves a monk, or a contemplative missionary, or clergy, or laity. Students are also faculty. Perhaps the word "learners" best expresses the desire that brings us here. So when I adopt various terms to try to capture the spirit of what seems to be happening among us, I am reaching for words to get at something that is wordless. I am trying to describe something that does not need to be named in our communities.

No formal vows have been made, though our core groups have discussed this possibility many times. Imagine, if you can, a group of followers of the Way of Christ who are dissolving the categories that separate so they can just learn to *be* contemplatives. We will keep discussing the question of a shared rule of life, an expression that could help bind us together as a community. But we are determined to avoid exclusions if at all possible.

In the contemplative communities of the school, we could call each other contemplative missionaries when we have made an inner commitment to follow this path. In essence, we are saying, "I want to practice the presence of God in all I do." For some of us, practicing the presence becomes the heart of our lives. This commitment translates into private practice, group practice, and shared practice in the world.

Each of us comes to follow a call to daily contemplation in a form that best suits our own personality and lifestyle. We engage in various contemplative practices privately and in small groups. There is no pretention here to perfect the practice of God's presence. Clearly, in all our fumbling efforts to seek a living God within and all around us, there is no other option than to just keep practicing.

As contemplative missionaries, we are not content to spend just a few minutes in daily practice followed by a day full of forgetting the presence of God in the hustle and bustle of catching the speed train called life. As monks in the world, we are no longer content with the split between spiritual practice and our daily involvement in the world.

We want to find an inner rhythm for uniting contemplation and action, being present to God's presence and serving the world, which is what Saint Benedict called *ora et labora* (prayer and work).[4] We want to become contemplatives in action, as indicated in the Latin expression, *simul in actione contemplativus*, attributed to Jesuit Jerónimo Nadal (1507–1580) by our friend Dr. Ricardo Marquez. Ricardo says this union of contemplation and action expresses what the Jesuit spirituality calls forth in our experience.

As we are able to, we want to bring a quality of contemplative presence into the whole day so that contemplation and action become one. Father Richard Rohr emphasizes this goal as a path for Franciscans and all contemplatives. And yet we keep lapsing in our own practice repeatedly. This means we are ever beginners in practicing messy contemplation—devout in heart, but often forgetting, and then remembering to simply begin again.

---

4. Saint Benedict, *Rule of Benedict*, 2.

If you want to know more about my own background as a budding contemplative before we became this collection of constant beginners practicing messy contemplation, read the next chapter. It covers my own history with contemplative practice and the many people from whom I learned along the way. You might find it helpful to follow the contemplative journey of one regular person, one spiritual pilgrim, before the first vision of gathering contemplative communities arose. Current stories of our unfolding contemplative communities resume in chapter 3. Have some fun, take your time, compare your own experiences with prayer and service, and let your intuition lead you toward your own true home.

2

Foundations
Before There Was a School

BEFORE MOVING FURTHER INTO stories of what has been happening among us lately, I want to turn back in time to lay the groundwork for our emergence. Every school has a foundation, a platform on which it is built, a history of why it came into being. Although the stories of what happened around Hurricane Katrina and thereafter are important, I think we have to go further back to understand some foundational experiences of our messy mystery called contemplative living.

In each of our lives, there is a story that unfolds a moment at a time. In the first chapter, I described the beginnings of the School for Contemplative Living. In the third chapter, I will recount current history as it is unfolding among us now. What about the groundwork, the prelude, and the interwoven story beneath the current story? Would you step back for a moment with me and look with curiosity and wonder at how seemingly unrelated and random moments can become an interconnected story? That is how I would describe the treasure of discovering that there is an amazing inner sanctuary of the soul, a place within us all, which is the very home of God.

INTRODUCING THE INNER SANCTUARY

"Deep within us all there is an amazing inner sanctuary of the soul, a holy place, a Divine Center, a speaking Voice, to which we may continuously return."

—Thomas Kelly[1]

Learning to live in the "amazing inner sanctuary of the soul," and sharing that practice with others, has become my greatest aspiration. Notice that I say "sharing" that practice. I am not interested in just speaking or writing about the fact that there is an inner sanctuary. My true calling seems to be experiencing the inner sanctuary and seeking to share that experience with others. This is the way I want to practice my work of caring for souls. Actually, it is the only way I want to *live* now. And this is what I share with you in this chapter.

Thomas Kelly's phrase above has been speaking its truth to me for more than two decades. These words have become the foundation of my life and work. When I get up in the morning, they are there, calling me to practice. When I end my day, they are there, asking if I have lived from my inner sanctuary today. All through the day, as I meet with other seekers, the open heart of God within these words is close at hand, hoping I will invite the people I meet to visit their own inner sanctuaries.

This calling to live from an inner sanctuary and share it with others was an early development in my own life. After the experience of Hurricane Katrina, the calling evolved into forming a School for Contemplative Living so that groups of us could enter the inner sanctuary together as members of small contemplative communities.

When I go a day or two without the spiritual practice of resting in this inner sanctuary, I become too easily frazzled. I keep trying to do things on my own, and I tend to get overwhelmed sooner rather than later in the day. On these days, I long for the moment when I can ease up and let the serenity return. For in my heart, I now know that the inner sanctuary is the very source of serenity, wisdom, and the Great Love we call God.

Thomas Kelly was a Quaker author who wrote *A Testament of Devotion* in 1941. He captured my imagination in 1992, when I was researching my dissertation. His quote above literally turned my religious

---

1. Kelly, *Testament of Devotion*, 3. Kelly's Christian devotional classic is immensely inspiring for developing one's own experience of an inner sanctuary, and it was the reason I sought out my first Quaker community.

life around. Just that one phrase was enough to send a Southern Baptist Christian then completing his second degree from a Baptist seminary on a hunt to find a local Friends Meeting. What I found at that Quaker gathering eventually led me to seek membership in the Friends Meeting of New Orleans. This meeting became a home for my soul, as well as quite a change from the religious tradition that had trained me for thirty-five years up to that point. Why did I consider such a change?

Kelly's call to enter the inner sanctuary again and again through the day began to transform my life and work. I was excited to realize that the One I had searched for all my life was already there, just waiting to be noticed and loved in my own soul. And the peace of mind and heart I needed proved to be inside me, even if it was not always easy to locate. I needed a simple, spiritual practice and a daily commitment to keep showing up to help that experience of peace and God's presence to become real.

Kelly's phrase, "deep within us all," was particularly important to me. My experience of leading daily spirituality groups with psychiatric patients for ten years had proven that the ability to enter the inner sanctuary of the soul was not limited to the spiritually elite. In fact, I was always astounded with the degree of clarity and wisdom patients would sometimes share after a few minutes of listening for that inner voice. When George Fox, founder of the Religious Society of Friends, spoke of that of God in everyone, he was speaking of what I had witnessed for a decade. "Deep within us all" really means *all*.

Margaret's Story

Margaret's story[2] reflects an example of how "deep within us all" means everyone. In the early 1990s, she came to the psychiatric hospital where I led spirituality groups. She had become too depressed to care for herself. Margaret was deeply despondent. Getting out of bed, preparing her own meals, and even leaving the house had become impossible feats for this sixty-year-old with frosted hair and a tired face. Despite having asked her a multitude of questions in taking the typical patient history for her medical record, no one really knew the source of her depression. So no one knew where to begin to help her healing.

---

2. All the names in these stories have been changed except for those of our friends in the school.

I offered my counseling and ministry as the Clinical Director of Spirituality Programs for a psychiatric hospital in those days. That meant I led optional groups for inpatients and outpatients who were willing to integrate their spirituality or lack thereof with their healing process. Amazingly, 99 percent of the patients and even some of the staff members would attend the daily groups. The patients included people admitted for depression, anxiety, addictions, trauma, and mental illnesses. One day in the spirituality group I was leading, the source of the depression that was hammering Margaret, and the way to her healing, became clear.

That day, I asked the group to sit quietly, let their minds settle, listen to the peaceful music, close their eyes, allow their thoughts to drift along without trying to control their direction, and open their hearts to a wise Inner Voice that might bring whatever was needed. In the hospital I used such terms for God. Margaret had been unreachable up to that point. But for some reason, on that day, in that hour, she was ready to relax, settle in, and open herself.

As we concluded our period of silent inner listening, we turned the dimmed lights back up. Margaret's eyes were wet. I offered the practitioners a chance to share their experience with the group if they wished. After a brief pause, Margaret spoke up. She quietly cried as she told us of her vision of her deceased son. Despite their alienated relationship through the years of her son's drug addiction, despite the fact that he had treated her abusively right up to the point of his fatal overdose, and despite her years of conflicted guilt for never being able to reach him, a healing vision had come to restore her sense of wholeness. What Thomas Kelly called a "speaking Voice" had come to Margaret as she rested in her own inner sanctuary.

Without any effort to think of her son, an image had emerged that had the power to bring her back to wholeness. She saw her son walking away from her, hand in hand with God. Her son turned to look over his shoulder at her. As he looked her in the eyes, he simply said, "It's okay now, Mom. I love you." With that, he turned and walked away, still holding God's hand.

Margaret's face was now radiant, awash in tears. The freshness of a new experience of serenity had replaced the old exhaustion of guilt and grief. Margaret became whole again that day, even if her healing process would take a while. She learned that "all" included her too. She had experienced firsthand the speaking Voice that brings us the serenity we long for. She found an inner holy place, a Divine Center, the dwelling place of the

Most High. She learned that "deep within us all" really means *all*—it even meant her! Inviting others to find their inner sanctuary eventually became the heart of my calling in forming the School for Contemplative Living.

Jacob's Story

Judeo-Christian Scriptures tell an interesting story of another kind of holy place. The story is of Jacob and his dream of angels ascending and descending a ladder into heaven. The dream occurred along his journey. The experience was so profound that he built an altar at the place of the dream. He named the place *Bethel*, the Hebrew word for the house of God. How else can we mark the place in the psyche where we have entered an inner sanctuary?

Jacob's vision included being spoken to personally by God. There was even a promise that would continue for generations to come, for Jacob heard his Lord saying, "the land on which you lie, I will give it to you . . . and in you and your descendants shall all the families of the earth be blessed. And behold, I am with you, and will keep you wherever you go" (Gen 28:13–15 NASB).

These amazing messages from a speaking Voice filled Jacob with awe. He associated his wonder with the location. As he awoke from his sleep, he said, "Surely the Lord is in this place, and I did not know it," exclaiming, "How awesome is this place! This is none other than the house of God, and this is the gate of heaven" (Gen 28:16–17 NASB).

Jacob's story illustrates the amazement that comes when we have special, spiritual experiences in the inner sanctuary. We refer to the moment of the experience as a holy place, a place where we have encountered the Divine in the center of our beings. Sometimes, if the moment is especially blessed, we may inwardly hear a speaking Voice.

Perhaps you will want to stop reading for a bit, take a moment to examine your life, and remember times when you, too, had to stop and say, "Surely the Lord is in this place, and I did not know it." Even better, let your awareness in this present moment settle down into that holy place. Listen to the silence, and breathe. Let go of efforts to control the experience, and for a few moments become aware that here too, the Lord is in this place where you now sit.

Moments such as these can be holy if we allow them to be. And once experienced, we often feel a craving for more. We might decide we want to keep coming back. Thomas Kelly had a phrase for this too. He wrote that the inner sanctuary is a place "to which we may continuously return."[3] The practice of continuously returning had been missing from my daily life before reading Thomas Kelly. My religious tradition, like many others, had encouraged daily quiet time for reading Scripture and reflecting on its personal meaning. But this business of committing to rest in God's presence within the inner sanctuary for an extended period each day was somehow different. As we say among Friends, it spoke to my need.

Something palpable began to happen as I began to practice being in the inner sanctuary each day. Yet it took other teachers to help me understand the transformation beginning inside me, and still other teachers to help me apply this practice to my work. Through reading or personal contact, these teachers have included Mother Teresa, Thomas Merton, Jesus, Saint Augustine, the Psalmist, Dr. Herbert Benson, Dr. Jon Kabat-Zinn, Dr. Gerald May, and Father Thomas Keating. More recent teachers who visited our community have included Father Richard Rohr, Dr. Roberta Bondi, the Reverend Dr. Tilden Edwards, the Reverend Dr. Elaine Heath, and Brother Dr. Ephrem Arcement.

FINDING AN INNER SANCTUARY

The secret of finding an inner sanctuary has been sought for thousands of years. Perhaps people from other traditions don't refer to their experience as an inner sanctuary, but I am amazed by the similarities between my own daily practice and experiences such as a daily quiet time, Buddhist meditation, yoga, centering prayer, relaxation-response, healing touch, and other healing practices.

I like the fact that my practice is linked to the practices of other spiritual seekers from many traditions for millennia. This encourages me to continue daily practice even when I find it difficult to set aside the time again and again each day. It is as though I am part of a long tradition and worldwide community that spans divergent religious beliefs, all of us seekers of an inner sanctuary.

I treasure the experience of leaning gently into the sanctuary inside my being. Even if I were the only one, I would have to continue practicing. I have visited my true home. Now I want to live there and to share it with others. I did not have to go on a trek to Tibet or make a pilgrimage

---

3. Kelly, *Testament of Devotion*, 3.

some other holy land to find it. Neither do you. My travels have led me to many places, but what I was seeking was always on the inside. I believe what you are seeking is inside you too.

If you realized that there really *is* an amazing inner sanctuary in the depths of your own soul, would you take the risk and look within? Would you want to learn how to enter this deep inner realm? Would you let your yearning for a holy place help you find your way inside, where wholeness and holiness become one?

Even if you are sometimes afraid of encountering the Divine, will you let your longing encourage you to face the center of yourself, to meet your Maker there? Will you confront the doubting mind and listen for clear, wise, personal guidance from a speaking Voice? Once you locate that placeless place, will you return, even continuously? If you continue to read, this is the journey ahead. Each story, poem, quotation, and personal experience is meant to help you find your way in.

In this chapter, I will tell you stories about how I found the secret of this inner sanctuary, and who helped me find it. The stories included here are not meant to be exhaustive in covering everything others have taught me. Rather they are hints at the riches of inner learning we can find in spiritual guides from the past and present. These stories come from the days before we had a School for Contemplative Living.

For instance, although I am a follower of Christ, I only included a few short words from Jesus in this introductory section. This is not meant to belittle the importance of Jesus' teachings on how to live a spiritual life. The phrase I quoted is just one example of a clear, concise message from Jesus that has really spoken to me on the subject of an inner sanctuary.

Throughout the book you will find stories of how others have responded to finding their true home. The stories are just hints at what the discovery of this amazing place in the soul can mean. Such encounters do not come easy, for they require inner work, commitment to daily practice, and perseverance when the way is unclear.

Inner work challenges most of us at the core of our beings. You may even find yourself stirred in your depths from just reading about the inner sanctuary. This stirring might arise if you practice some of the suggested exercises. If so, be patient, full of care for the One who has been waiting for you all of your life, even your own soul. Take the time to get to know this truest essence of who you are. Find your way to the sanctuary inside you. Your true home is worth it. As you read, may you be led to find your own inner sanctuary. If you do find it, savor the moment.

ENCOUNTERING THE INNER SANCTUARY

There are many means of encountering the inner sanctuary of the soul. I will share a few of my own ways, as well as some of the guides who helped me. In learning from these guides, a few principles of the contemplative life became clear to me, as I hope they will for you.

A contemplative life is one that focuses on the direct experience of God. This does not mean we can control or call up these encounters. A contemplative is simply one who seeks out such encounters. Seeking the direct experience of God comes to shape the person's whole life. A contemplative no longer sets aside a time to be spiritual and then spends the rest of their day in real life. Rather, contemplative life itself comes to be about seeking God in all things, in all moments.

The word "contemplation" is often used to imply a pattern of thinking. Some say they are contemplating a subject when they think something over for any length of time. But the root words for "contemplation" are *con* (intensive prefix) and *templum* (temple). To be in contemplation is to be in the temple. In the Christian tradition, contemplation is a particular way of being within the temple. Contemplation is union or oneness with God, and is itself a gift from God. The gift cannot be earned or forced, but receptivity to the gift can be cultivated.

This chapter is about ways of cultivating our receptiveness to the gift of oneness with God. This oneness occurs in the inner sanctuary of the soul. Four ways we can prepare ourselves for the encounter with God in the inner sanctuary are by practicing silence, stillness, solitude, and simple being.

Silence

"I always begin my prayer in silence, for it is in the silence of the heart that God speaks. God is the friend of silence . . . Prayer feeds the soul."

—Mother Teresa[4]

When I was thirty, I had the opportunity to visit Bangladesh and India. A lifelong dream was realized when I got to meet Mother Teresa of Calcutta and observe the daily life and work of her nuns. They knew the secret of the inner sanctuary, obviously, or they could not have endured even an

---

4. Mother Teresa, *Simple Path*, 7.

hour of what they faced every day. The smells alone, much less the sight of the impoverished people living in the streets of Calcutta while traveling from the airport to my accommodations, were enough to freeze me on a cot for hours. I was wondering why I came and how soon I could get away from Calcutta.

But I'm so glad I stayed. Over those few days, I had the opportunity to meet Mother Teresa. I learned that the nuns of her order lived a moment-by-moment practice. To me, it was the secret to their survival in that seemingly God-forsaken world. But what was this secret of the global order known as the Missionaries of Charity?

Contemplative prayer was at least part of the nuns' secret. They did not pray because they were more holy or dedicated than most people (though they may have been). Prayer was their means of survival! It was their way of depending on a power greater than themselves. If there is such a thing as living in contemplation, living "with temple" throughout one's day, these nuns surely demonstrated both that the practice is possible and that the secret can be practiced even in the most stressful of places.

The nuns got up at 5:00 a.m. each morning to spend an hour in silent, private prayer. This is the prayer of contemplation. In saying, "I always begin my prayer in silence, for it is in the silence of the heart that God speaks," Mother Teresa explains that God is the friend of silence, and that we can hear God speak when we learn to silence our hearts each day. Such silence is hard to achieve anywhere, but perhaps nowhere is more difficult than where she lived her practice in Calcutta. The sounds of the city were endless. The nuns lived in a Mother House located in the center of town. There was no protection from the noise or the needs. Their life was anything but cloistered from the world.

Finding a silence from which God can speak each day does not mean escaping the world around us. It does, however, mean cultivating inner silence, and that is quite hard enough. Mother Teresa was fond of referring to inner and outer silence. Places of solitude can help us cultivate inner silence, and we will turn to that topic next. But what if we are living in the kind of noisy, needy, fast-paced world Mother Teresa lived in? Is inner silence just a fantasy for the religiously pious?

The nuns' practice of getting up for an hour of silent prayer every morning spoke volumes to me. These women were teaching by their own example how to prepare to encounter God in the inner sanctuary. Their willingness, commitment, and dedication to serve the needs of those who

Mother Teresa called "the poorest of the poor" continues to inspire the world. But not everyone seems to understand the importance of preparing themselves for their external encounter with the world by preparing themselves for an inward encounter with God.

I don't think we can over-emphasize what a difference it makes to set aside a period each day for cultivating these encounters in one's daily life. We can go out into the stress of daily life under our own feeble strength if we wish. We can try to act like we have the power in ourselves to be competent in the face of the daily uncertainty of what life may bring. But these women, these Missionaries of Charity, were practicing another way.

Their practice began each day in silence, the silence of the heart. In that silent place, they opened their hearts to the coming of the Creator. They opened themselves to receive the strength to face what they could not face alone. They opened to receive the love that could flow into and through them all day long while they faced the neediest people on the planet. They opened to the coming of a higher wisdom than their own, so that decisions could be founded in the Great Wisdom.

Such opening takes time. Silence of the heart is not an experience that can be popped into the microwave in seconds. It cannot be sped up. It is the antithesis of what our pop culture teaches—that everything that takes time should be discarded in favor of a quicker way.

Taking the time for the heart to grow silent requires a fierce commitment. It means resisting a hundred impulses that come along, calling us to race off for this or that. It means committing to stay still even when the urge to jump up seems overwhelming. Inner silence cannot be forced upon the soul. It is to be eased into, slowly, moment-by-moment. I believe this was why the nuns committed to such a long period of silent prayer at the start of each day.

Mother Teresa encouraged all her sisters to give themselves over to this practice. Then there were corporate prayers and mass from 6:00 to 7:00 a.m. This act of joining together as a community was also important. The gathering occurred in silence. There was a kind of beauty to this silent filing into the large room, one by one, and waiting for the collective silence to be broken by singing, prayers, and a homily. Silence of the heart may take a while to achieve, and it should not be exited abruptly. Even in a world of such intense and demanding needs as the streets of Calcutta, there was still time to slowly move into and out of the silent place in the soul that is a true inner sanctuary.

After breakfast and chores, the nuns went out into the streets to look for the dying and the orphans—for whoever was in dire need. One might expect the nuns' cultivation of awareness of God's presence through prayer to stop there. Time for prayer was over; the time for work had come. But the other secret of their survival arose in just those moments. The second secret was to stay in touch with the inner silence even as the nuns began their work of serving the poorest of the poor. This secret involved continuous prayer, and this discovery was the most impressive surprise of my trip.

The nuns prayed as they climbed into their rattling vans, and as they drove, and as they stopped, and as they assisted the needy, and as they drove them to the home for the dying, and as they arrived, and as they carried them inside, and as they cared for their needs. They used simple prayers they could recite from memory, like "Lord, make me an instrument of thy peace." But the exact words were not the point. The nuns were using prayer to keep their attention focused on the presence of the One who could give the strength they needed for that moment.

Fortifying themselves by continually bathing themselves in this mantra of prayer was the nuns' second secret. This form of living in the inner sanctuary, and not just visiting it once in a while, was a powerful model to me. Calcutta was one of the most stressful places on the planet. So if these women could find the strength to face those struggles each day through their hour of morning silence and their continuous return to prayer, surely I could learn to do the same with my troubles.

And yet, even decades later I'm still just beginning to learn. Setting aside the time to practice each morning is still a personal struggle. And remembering to keep breathing a prayer of the heart as I listen to people in counseling, visit sick people, lead retreats, and go about all the rest of my daily duties still frequently slips my mind. Some of us are just slow learners I guess. But I am committed to the practice, to following the secrets of the Missionaries of Charity. And when I remember, I say, "Ah," within.

Silence is not just a practice for Catholic nuns. Nor is it only intended for Quakers such as myself. In fact, Christians are not the only ones who sometimes come to learn the value of silence for a contemplative life. *Tzom shtikah* was a medieval Jewish practice in which "Jewish mystics refrained from speaking, and, in their stillness contemplated the mysteries of the divine."[5] In silence, these mystics fasted from speaking, but the purpose was not just self-denial. Their silence was a way to encounter the divine by removing themselves from the usual activities of public discourse. They cultivated a higher discourse within.

Mystics in every religious tradition are those people who seek inner communication between self and God. Some use outward silence to facilitate such encounters. Others use outward sounds, like music or chanting, to facilitate inward silence—to open the heart space in which the Divine can be revealed and directly experienced. Whether inward or outward silence or both, that silence can facilitate direct union between our human selves and the Divine.

My own earliest awareness of the value of silence came in my young adult years. A peer in ministry gave me a copy of a book by Thomas Merton called *Contemplative Prayer*. From the very first reading, I was fascinated with the idea of inner silence. Merton was obviously writing from deep experience, and his words spoke to the deep in me. Perhaps I was too young to be ready to practice much silence in those days. But I loved the idea. Only gradually did my being mature enough to become ready to taste what fascinated my spirit early on. When the time came to begin that journey, Merton's words became my first guides.

Stillness

"Be still, and know that I am God."

(Ps 46:10 NIV)

The call to be still, which the psalm writer included in the psalm above, is one translation of a wonderful Hebrew word: *rapha*. *Rapha* also has other enriching meanings, like "relax," "let go," "let it fall," or "cease striving." When the psalm writer shared these words as he heard them from God a few thousand years ago, I believe he was helping us find our way into an inner sanctuary. As he simply put it, being still in this place can help us to know God.

Some people search for God their whole lives, and yet they never learn how to know God. I meet many of these people in my office looking for counseling and spiritual direction. Some are willing to listen to the psalmist's words and even to try to practice them. Some are just not ready.

---

5. Winner, *Mudhouse Sabbath*, 87.

Harry's Story

Harry was one of those guys who was just not ready. When I met Harry through my private counseling practice, he was struggling with panic attacks. I was in my early years of seeing people at an office in his church. He was having physical symptoms that felt like a heart attack, and they scared him enough to send him to the emergency room several times. Harry was not even fifty years old. He had a wife and several kids. He surely wasn't ready to die. Harry went through thousands of dollars of medical tests trying to find the cause of the problems. Finally, his physician gave him the news: "There is no physical cause of these symptoms. It's stress." Harry was a little relieved. Yet he was also disturbed by this news.

In our counseling sessions, he revealed his desire to learn how to deal with stress. Though he attended church, he also felt alienated from God. He had asked God to help him with his stress, but he believed God had failed him by not responding. He was frustrated because he had tried very hard to get God to fix the problem for him.

You can imagine his consternation when I proposed that he might have come to the place in life's journey where it's time to let go of striving, become still, learn to relax, and surrender to God. This would mean no longer treating God as a servant to be called. The word "surrender" just did not compute to Harry. For a man who had spent his whole life troubleshooting in his job and his family, the psalmist's message meant next to nothing to him. "I hear your words but I don't get anything out of them," he told me.

His face showed even more anger and frustration after that. He changed the subject, finished the conversation, and never returned. Harry was not even ready to hear the words about letting go and surrendering, much less to take the time to learn to practice them.

Julia's Story

Some people are more than ready for the "be still" message. Julia was one such person. She was a counselor from out of state who attended an Into the Stillness retreat I was co-leading on a chill autumn day in the 1990s. She came after feeling a kind of constriction across her chest, saying it was "like a tight band." She privately admitted she believed the tightness was really her guilt and shame for some immoral behavior in her past.

My co-facilitator, Sister Janet Franklin, and I introduced the psalmist's message in the day-long silent retreat we hosted at the convent grounds for her religious order, the Sisters of Saint Joseph. We selected that site for its natural beauty and quiet setting. Old live oaks with massive branches reaching to the sky draped with Spanish moss surrounded the campus. Roses still bloomed. Blue jays sang to us. Only an occasional passing car disturbed the stillness.

Julia's expression slowly changed throughout the day. She began with tension, anxiety, and stiffness in her movements. Then she began to enter into the silent stillness. She participated in silent sitting, letting go of troubling thoughts, reflecting on sacred writings, listening to peaceful music, learning yoga stretches, and practicing walking meditation around the grounds of Sister Janet's convent. She was wandering between one-hundred-year-old live oaks, eating a simple but delicious meal, quietly journaling any messages she received from God, and finally sharing what the day had been like, speaking for the first time in many hours. Her face communicated ultimate serenity by day's end.

Julia learned how to "be still" and know God that day. She will forget her lesson and have to learn it again and again. We all do. But for that day, as she left, she said the tension across her chest had disappeared. She didn't have to tell us, as her beaming face spoke for her. Some people *are* ready to learn a secret that turns their life around. We can thank the psalmist for providing such simple guidance in the message to be still. Or better yet, we can thank the One who made us for revealing the instructions in such a simple form.

If you want to pause here to experience an exercise of practicing the call to "be still, and know that I am God," turn to the chapter 5, titled "Practicing the Presence." Look for "Beginning Stillness: An Exercise."

It may have taken half my life to learn the secret of being still, but I have learned it now. I do not plan to lose my way from here. But I will. When I do, I'll just start over. That's how it works. I have committed to practicing stillness, relaxing, letting go, and ceasing my striving every day for the rest of my life. Do I forget or get too busy some days? Certainly! But when I do, I just start over again. The sense of wellbeing that comes flowing in is worth the commitment. The chance to feel closer to God's presence and wisdom and guidance deserves some time each day.

Why was such an important psalm, or song, included in Hebrew Scripture in the midst of a longer passage of songs? Reading through, you could easily miss it. In this way, the power of these words seems almost hidden. I frankly have come to believe that this invitation is a kind of secret prescription recorded for us all as a source of serenity. However, the message is for those of us who are *ready* to receive it, ready to discover it hiding there. Are you ready?

You can be sure the serenity of resting in your inner sanctuary is ready for you. The refreshment of that safe place wants you to find your way in. Is this your time to begin?

Solitude

"When you pray, go into your inner room, and when you have shut your door, pray to your Father who is in secret..."
(Matt 6:6 NASB)

Solitude was a regular practice for Jesus. He knew the secret of pulling away from others and going within, where God lives. Notice that solitude includes both movements, withdrawal from others and turning into the interior of our beings. Both movements can help us encounter the inner sanctuary.

In the above passage, Jesus is responding to his disciples' request: "Lord, teach us to pray" (Luke 11:1). His response is a clear and simple invitation teaching us how to pray. I find it immensely instructive that Jesus speaks these words about going into oneself as a primary form of prayer. *Tamieion* is the Greek word translated as "secret inner chamber." The word has also been translated as a "private closet," or "inner room."

So it seems that the founder of the Christian faith placed major emphasis on connecting with God through inner solitude. He, like the psalmist, left us a prescription that many people miss. When we hear the word "prayer," many of us think of times when we heard someone speaking out loud to God. When our pastor asks one of us to lead in prayer before a United Methodist worship service, we never even think of the possibility of leading by silently going into the secret inner chamber.

For Quakers such as myself, there is another way of praying that does not involve speaking words. When we gather in our meeting for worship on First Day (Sunday), we do not come with any program of prayers, songs, or sermons. No one has prepared anything. We like it that way. You might say we want to practice Jesus' words literally. We have not come to hear what others have to say. We come to listen for an Inner Voice who is God.

When the clerk walks in and sits down in the circle of metal folding chairs, we know it is time for us to gather, sit, become silent, and gently move into the secret inner chamber for an hour. We have come to pray, but no one says a word. We are practicing a way of praying in the inner sanctuary that Friends have used for more than 350 years.

Quakers do not use a magical formula. We have no agenda. We just sit still and begin to collect our thoughts. This does not mean we control our thoughts. But we do begin to open our hearts to anything God might want to bring to our attention. When thoughts about the weather or some such matter enter, we gently let those go and return our focus to a simple listening for any "leading" that might seem to come from God.

Occasionally, one of us will express a few thoughts out loud, if we feel led to do so. That is, if we feel compelled from within that some message is not for our ears only, but might serve as a vocal ministry for others too. When we break the silence in this way, words are briefly spoken, and then the silence resumes. No one answers with more thoughts or words, unless they too feel led to speak after an appropriate period of reflection. The focus of the hour is always on inner listening.

The fact that we gather would make most people question what all this has to do with solitude. But remember that inner solitude is an important aspect of prayer. This turning within can be done in the presence of others, and can actually be helped by their presence if they too are turning within. There is a kind of critical mass that can occur spiritually when a gathering of people all seek to enter the inner sanctuary simultaneously.

But there is also another solitude, one that does involve withdrawal from others. In this solitude, we need space from the distractions of others. We need focus. We need undivided attention. Sometimes we find that we cannot encounter the inner sanctuary unless we can pull away from exterior activity and look inside.

In our world there are many voices clamoring for our attention: television shows, commercials, emails, movies (crammed with ten previews of other movies), telephones ringing, pets barking, children crying, friends dropping by to chat, radios, CDs and DVDs, salespersons, magazine articles and ads, bosses' demands, spouses' requests, and on and on. Listen to all the voices in a day, and you hear an awful lot of noise and distraction. It's hard for the Creator of the whole universe to get through to us with any guidance at all.

Thankfully, there is one voice which is patient, willing to wait silently for the chance to show us how to really live. This voice is ready to fill us with everything we need if we can take but a few minutes to visit the secret inner chamber, the sanctuary of the soul.

When we follow Jesus' prescription for prayer, when we finally come inside, we are joining the psalmist in a most heartfelt expression: "My soul, wait in silence for God only, For my hope is from Him" (Ps 62:5 NASB). Silence is not the only way to pray, it's just that we can get out of balance when spoken words are the only way we pray. Eventually we might join the writer of Ecclesiastes and realize, "There is a time for everything . . . a time to be silent and a time to speak" (Eccl 3:1–7 NIV). We might also be faithful to the spirit of the text if we added "a time to gather with others, and a time to be alone."

Waiting in silence can feel like a waste of time, whether we are alone or with others. After all, nothing is really happening. We are not accomplishing anything. And in America, inactivity is a great sin. The purpose of this silence is not just to be quiet, and it is not a way to be lazy. This silence is for a listening of the heart. Kathleen Norris expressed it this way, "'Listen' is the first word of [Saint] Benedict's *Rule* and of course it is silence that makes listening possible."[6]

Jesse's Story

Jesse was a church member who wanted to talk to a pastor about his spiritual life back when I served as an associate pastor as well as a therapist in private practice. He had only known prayer to be a one-way communication in which we talk and God listens. Jesse was like many of us. He got a little spooked by all the talk of prayer as "listening to God." To Jesse, prayer meant talking out loud to God in a church service while others listened. Lately, he had heard too much about that business of silent prayer. It frankly made him a little edgy.

He had been telling God what to do all his life, and that seemed to work just fine. Jesse reminds me of a most convincing quote from centuries ago. Isaac of Nineveh, the Syrian monk, said, "Every man who delights in a multitude of words, even though he says admirable things, is

---

6. Norris, *Dakota*, 185.

empty within."[7] Jesse needed to keep talking to protect himself from the emptiness within. Spoken words are reassuring. Silence can be frightening. It can cause us to feel out of control.

So you might imagine Jesse's irritation when he was in a group meeting that began a time of prayer as follows: "Tonight God does not need our instruction or guidance. As you pray in silence, listen for what God wants to say to you about your prayer concern. Maybe God wants to show you God's compassion for the need of that person. Maybe God will reveal how God is already at work in that person's life. Whatever the case, let God be the speaker and you the listener tonight." Jesse was not a happy camper that night.

Jesse isn't the only one who finds Jesus' teachings on prayer difficult. He just gives us an example of what Jesus' instruction for prayer might sound like if we authored the words from our place of resistance, which might go something like: "When you pray, say a lot of flowery words that make people think you are close to God. Presume God doesn't know how to handle your situations. Tell God what to do. Be specific. If God does not follow your instructions to the letter, get mad at God and keep repeating the commands, or presume you just didn't believe hard enough when you made the request. Keep trying harder. God will listen sooner or later!"

For Jesus, prayer was much simpler: "When you pray, go into your inner room." Jesus teaches us to enter into solitude, to go inward, to step away from people when we pray, and to commune with one who is like a loving parent, bidding us to "pray to your Father who is in secret." Unless times have changed since Jesus' day, most parents are not waiting for their kids to instruct them. I could be wrong, but I don't believe that Jesus' Father needs much guidance either. For Jesus, it's better to enjoy the company of the parent and to await guidance like a child.

What I learned from Jesus is that prayer often requires solitude so that we can really focus our attention on inner hearing, inner sight, and inner communion. What I learned from Jesus is that prayer happens like this: *regardez et ecoutez*, meaning "watch and listen." You will find a poem by this title in chapter 6 hinting at this kind of prayer.

---

7. Quoted in Merton, *Contemplative Prayer*, 30.

Christ in the Desert

I can still picture the scene when I first drew away for a day of solitude at the Monastery of Christ in the Desert in the 1980s. The Benedictine community living there is situated in the Chama Valley north of Santa Fe, New Mexico. Their austere adobe buildings match the surrounding landscape at the end of a thirteen-mile dirt road. The ruts in the road were so bad I think we broke a shock absorber on our little yellow Toyota Tercel. But the trek was worth it.

My wife and I had driven to Santa Fe for a weekend trip and set off for the monastery early on Saturday morning. We arrived in the serene stillness on a cold morning, wandered around a bit, and then found our way into the beautiful simplicity of a chapel with windows looking out into the adobe cliffs nearby.

We were just in time for a late-morning prayer service, followed by an invitation to share lunch with the monks. After lunch, the guests were invited to walk the grounds of the monastery or work alongside one of the monks doing daily chores. I joined an older Brother with a long white beard, kind of a Santa Claus-looking fellow, to help split wood to prepare for the approaching winter.

Then in the middle of the afternoon there was another brief prayer in the chapel, and we were left free to wander again. Carol and I strolled around on our own in silence. The high desert landscape, the variety of adobe colors, the barrenness of the scene, and the chill in the air on a cloudless blue-sky day were striking. The stroll through that world, so far from the busy setting where I served as a hospital chaplain in those days, was a delicious taste of solitude.

I could not have told you in those days what I was searching for, or what my soul needed, or why an adobe monastery in the middle of nowhere seemed so appealing. But over time I came to know that I need more than my daily twenty minutes or even the occasional hour of solitude. Sometimes I need to withdraw into the secret inner chamber for a day or even a week so that I can practice the simplicity of being, watching, and listening.

There is something invigorating to the soul in airing things out, letting go of our usual responsibilities, slowing down the pace of our lives, and settling into the mode of just being. I think this kind of shift is like letting our souls catch up with us when we have been speeding through life for too long. I believe such solitude is necessary as a kind of reset button to the soul, where priorities can shift from what seemed ever so important before to find a larger perspective on our lives.

I visited that first monastery during a time when I was on-call for hospital emergencies in addition to the full-time job of walking the halls greeting patients and sharing prayers and making friends with hospital staff. In those years I was often overwhelmed with the late hours, waking up in the night to a beeper, and never knowing what to say or how to be with people in a way that would really help. Even in my late twenties, something in me was already sensing a need for silence, solitude, stillness, and simple being beyond what I could verbalize. Some inner guidance was already calling me away toward that unknown something we sometimes meet when we retreat. I have shared more about this need in the "Practices" section on retreats in chapter 5.

Searching for a Sanctuary Abroad

"Too late have I loved you, O Beauty of ancient days, yet ever new! Too late I loved you! And behold, you were within and I abroad, and there I searched for you... You were with me, but I was not with you... You breathed odors, and I drew in breath—and I pant for you. I tasted, and I hunger and thirst. You touched me, and I burned for your peace."

—SAINT AUGUSTINE[8]

Saint Augustine penned these words centuries ago. They may sound archaic in form, but they are words of intimate communion, for they offer insight into the nature of the inner sanctuary. Sometimes we might need to go away for a bit of solitude, but we need to embark on the journey within regularly.

"Too late have I loved you" reminds us that it can take a long time, maybe most of our lives, to learn to release some of our self-focusing and to turn our attention toward love of the One who has always loved us. The lover of our souls has been around a long time, but in the personal encounter every meeting is in the present moment: "O Beauty of ancient days, yet ever new!" Each new day finds us like a beginner, starting all over.

"You were within and I abroad, and there I searched for You... You were with me, but I was not with You" reminds us that despite our

---

8. Foley and McCloskey, "August 28: Augustine, Bishop and Doctor," 257–58.

tendency to look out to the external world for God (as well as for peace, fulfillment, and getting our needs met), the One we search for is always within. Perhaps we have to search elsewhere first, as I did by traveling to Calcutta, India. Eventually, with grace, we find that the Source of our life was with us even when we were not present ourselves.

Stepping through the Door

When I was thirty and flying to Bangladesh and India, I had a day of layover in London. At the time my cousins were in Birmingham, England, studying to serve as missionaries to Egypt. So I took the 100-minute train from London to Birmingham to catch a brief visit with the family overnight.

I had never been in the Birmingham rail station, and I was feeling extremely jetlagged. So when I arrived in the station and followed the signs to where I imagined I was supposed to meet my family, I got completely lost. I wandered back and forth near the exit door where I looked for them for over an hour. My eyes strained to catch a glimpse of their faces in the crowd of travelers passing by. Moment by moment I became more frustrated. That sense of being lost is a terrible feeling.

Finally, near despair, I noticed that the door I had been standing beside for so long was an exit. I had been afraid to go through it for fear that I would get even more lost on the other side. I gathered up my courage and stepped through. Within a moment I saw the faces I had so longed to see. I was exuberant with relief. I had found the people I was seeking.

All that time they had just been on the other side. They were not allowed to come through that same door because they were not passengers. They were waiting, hoping, perhaps even straining to see my face come through the door, from the opposite side. They wanted to see me as badly as I wanted to see them. But they were prohibited from pushing through that door. I had to step through to find that they were right there all along.

Saint Augustine tells us it works the same way with the One who longs to be with us. We go searching all over the place. Sometimes we travel around the whole world. We go abroad looking for the One who is already at home. And we so often miss that One because the door only works in one direction. We're afraid to step through that inner door, for fear we'll become even more lost.

When we finally take that simple step, open that inner door, and greet the One we love with a deep fulfillment of longing after an extended absence, we too might say, "Too late I loved you." In more modern language, we might admit: "I waited too long to step through the door, to find you there waiting for me all along. Now, having found you, I so wish I had stepped through sooner."

But there is no need to waste time scolding oneself for taking so long. That's like going back to standing on the other side of the door. We need only enjoy the blessing of having found the One we were searching for. And we renew our commitment to step through the inner door sooner next time, now that we know the way.

Here you might want to pause to try a related exercise. If so, turn to chapter 5, "Practicing the Presence," and look for "Stepping through the Door: An Exercise."

"You breathed odors, and I drew in breath—and I pant for you" reminds us that mystical encounters, sensing we are closer to God than our breath, may be rare. But once we have these encounters, we long for more—we pant for God. I am not content to have occasional contact with God. I want to be in touch most every day. I long for it, and I can no longer settle for less. Perhaps you too have experienced the closeness of God. Perhaps you too have later missed the connection and longed for it again.

"I tasted, and I hunger and thirst" is to say that spiritual hunger and thirst do not end once we experience a moment of quenching. They return. They are renewed each day, just as surely as are physical hunger and thirst. One taste of spiritual experience does not end the search. This is one of the reasons why we need a spiritual practice that we can return to each day.

"You touched me, and I burned for your peace" speaks to me because since finding the location of peace of mind, I am not able to put up with periods of anxiety for very long. The touch of peace creates a longing that cannot be easily satisfied by substitutes. Perhaps some people can go most of the day, or the month, or years without peace of mind. I cannot. Maybe peace is my addiction. Maybe it's just a wonderful gift I do not want to give up.

Carol's Story

There was a time in my married life when I craved peace of mind, when I could not carry on without it. That time began about six years into my marriage to Carol, when she was pregnant with our first child. The pregnancy had gone smoothly for seven months, and then problems began. By the time Carol's symptoms had been diagnosed, we were being admitted to the hospital to deliver our son five weeks prematurely. That was only the beginning.

After delivering our four-pound, fourteen-ounce boy, Carol's symptoms did not resolve. A biopsy confirmed that she had glomerulonephritis, an autoimmune disease in one kidney. It was only working at twenty percent of normal function. The other kidney was not there. It had never fully developed—only a remnant of its formation remained. Needless to say, this diagnosis did not allow for much peace of mind. Then the news got worse.

Carol's nephrologist offered a poor prognosis, and so did a second opinion. My twenty-eight year-old wife, mother of our premature son, was told her one kidney would fail within a year or two at the most. Her only options were dialysis, transplant, or death. Within a month, our security was shattered. We had shifted from the exciting anticipation of new life to the terrifying anticipation of her health failure.

This was too much reality for me. As a young father, I was suddenly imagining what it would be like to raise our son alone. Much to my embarrassment, thoughts of having to find another wife came flooding into my awareness. After all, what did I know about raising a baby? I could not imagine carrying on alone without my beloved wife, so I guess my imagination was coping by creating an alternative reality in which I would need a new partner if I lost her.

Over time, the fears of whether today would be the day when my wife's kidney would suddenly fail resolved into a questioning denial. What if the doctors were wrong? One year had become two, and nothing had changed. Then Carol found an inner gift that I had only hoped for. She approached me one day and simply said, "It's going to be okay." I asked if she meant the kidney disease was going to be cured. She replied, with a great sense of serenity, that "whatever happens, it's going to be okay." She had found a secret of rest within the inner sanctuary.

In just a few words, Carol had stated the essence of peace of mind. Peace is not ever based on circumstances. Peace does not say, "If things go as we wish." Peace is deeper than circumstances. Peace requires the first part of Carol's discovery: "Whatever happens." Without that acceptance, the "It's going to be okay" is just wishful thinking. But in that awareness that the worst *can* really happen, true peace is really possible, though never in our control.

After that, we still waited and wondered if this would be the year her kidney would fail. In fact, we waited for ten years. Every year, her doctor would say, "It looks like it will be this year or the next." A decade passed before that dreaded day came.

The day Carol's kidney began to fail came suddenly in July of 1994. Within a month, my vigorous wife had lost most of her strength. During that same time, her family hurriedly underwent tissue testing to see if anyone was a suitable match for a kidney transplant. Both parents and both sisters were immediately, without question, ready to put their lives on the line and offer Carol a kidney. Soon we learned that Jan, her older sister, was the best match and would undergo surgery in August.

The stress of those days was immense. I tried to continue my counseling practice as best I could, but by the week before my wife's surgery, I no longer had the emotional energy to even return phone calls. My counseling supervisor gently confronted my attempts to work beyond my limits. He humorously suggested I might want to practice what I preached about honoring human limits. Thankfully I listened, hurriedly cancelled my appointments for the following week, and admitted to my clients that I could not be sure when I would return.

The day of the kidney transplant surgery arrived. Everyone in the family felt the tension. Without speaking the words, we all knew that two lives hung in the balance. We pinned all our hopes on a successful surgery, a modern-day miracle of removing a kidney from one person and attaching it to the blood vessels of the other. When the doctor came out to tell us that the kidney had responded immediately, we were tremendously relieved. After many years of performing transplants, our surgeon actually seemed excited about how that little kidney was working from the first moment he attached the blood vessels and let the blood flow through.

Peace is never dependent on circumstances, and so my attempt to find peace in a successful surgery was snatched away two days later. That was the day that the surgeon came to us with the bad news. Carol's new kidney could go into failure any day for the rest of her life, without warning! We would just have to take it one day at a time. A sinking feeling overtook my stomach. A terrible uncertainty lodged itself deep in my gut. That same sense of not knowing what will happen next has never left. It has been many years now.

Uncertainty, anxiety, the ultimate what-ifs, can dominate our lives. They can control our thoughts, rule our moods, and even dictate our behaviors. Living in that kind of prison is not quite living, it's more like existing. Life is too precious, too sacred, to settle for just existing. I had to learn a way to let these consuming worries become passing thoughts. I had to find a quality of serenity that was deeper than what might happen today or tomorrow. I had to learn a practice that could sustain me through whatever happens. In learning to enter the inner sanctuary each day, I believe I found that practice, that place, and that spiritual home.

Carol found her way into the sanctuary more as a natural outcome of lifestyle. She had grown up in a home where contentment was the norm. There was no scurrying about to keep up appearances. No trying to have as much as others. Her family found it natural to accept life as it came. There was a closeness, a family love, and a stability that held a family together.

God was central in Carol's life from the time she was small. Trusting God to lead the family through hard times or good times was her family's way. So when Carol's health crisis arose, her family did not see it as God's punishment or God's fault. They thought of the Holy One as a comforter, a supporter, the One who stood with family through anything and everything. The realization of God's peace was not as surprising to Carol as it was to me. She found the peace as a gift to be cherished, but did not feel responsible for creating it.

Carol knew to be receptive to peace. She knew there were times to say yes to requests and times to say no. There was time for togetherness but also plenty of time for solitude. She did not allow stress to control or ruin her life. There was always time to take a long relaxing bath. Carol found her peace in dedicating herself to living her life as a parent, prioritizing raising our son over all of life's many concerns. You might say her consistent motto was to keep life simple. Simplicity and contentment, these were Carol's companions. They opened the way for peace to come and visit, be it midnight or brightest day.

More than a year after Carol's transplant, as we began the winter, a deeper peace had begun to settle in. One evening, after the family had gone to bed, the words of a poem titled "Holding Near the Deep

Presence" came into me expressing what we were experiencing. That poem is included in chapter 6.

Carol's way of cultivating peace of mind has always seemed to be a natural part of how she crafts her life. She doesn't overcommit herself. She focuses on one thing at a time. She creates a peaceful rhythm of balancing time for work and time for rest, reading, and relaxing.

For me, the art of relaxation has been an ongoing challenge and a fundamental part of learning to slow down enough to encounter the inner sanctuary. My ongoing education has been enriched by meeting several experts in relaxation and mindfulness. Dr. Herbert Benson's research on the relaxation response and Dr. Jon Kabat-Zinn's work on mindfulness became a solid platform from which to deepen my understanding and experience of the inner sanctuary. The following sections explore their research and what I, and others I have counseled, have learned about the art of cultivating relaxation and mindfulness.

Relaxing

"When the mind quiets down, the body follows suit."

—Dr. Herbert Benson[9]

"True silence is rest of the mind, and is to the spirit what sleep is to the body, nourishment and refreshment."

—William Penn

"I was brought up all my life among the Sages, and I have found nothing as good for the body as silence, and it is not study/explication that is the essence—but the practice/doing."

—Simon, son of Rabban Gamliel[10]

I guess it took a medical doctor from Harvard to help me realize that teachings like William Penn's and Simon's about the health benefits of practicing silence were literal and could be proven by medical research. Sometimes the doubting mind needs some data to reassure us that what

---

9. Benson and Stark, *Timeless Healing*, 127. In this book, Dr. Benson details the medical benefits of the relaxation response.

10. *Pirke Avot* 1:17, quoted by Rabbi Simkha Y. Weintraub, CSW, "Jewish Spiritual Healing Practices" (presentation, "Spirituality and Healing in Medicine V" Conference, Harvard Medical School, Houston, TX, March 23, 1998).

we believe to be true is factually true. Research will never prove there is an inner sanctuary. But the work of Dr. Herbert Benson and others comes close.

Living in the inner sanctuary is surely not a phrase Dr. Benson would use. He is a professor at Harvard Medical School and Director Emeritus at the Benson-Henry Institute for Mind/Body Medicine at Massachusetts General Hospital. He has focused thirty years of research on the relaxation response, documenting the physiological changes that occur when we relax. He has also studied how eliciting this response can improve or even cure some stress-related illnesses. More recently, Dr. Benson's writings and national conferences on "Spirituality and Healing in Medicine" have introduced many people to the spiritual aspects of relaxation practices.

For example, Dr. Benson notes in *Timeless Healing* that many people have spiritual experiences of a loving presence as a result of relaxation, even when they are not seeking such encounters or even necessarily identify as religious.[11] He recommends that his patients dedicate two daily periods of twenty minutes to eliciting the relaxation response.[12] These two twenty-minute periods parallel Father Thomas Keating's recommendations for centering prayer.[13]

Dr. Benson suggests that his patients use a two-part formula to relax. First, focus the attention on a sound, an image, a comforting word, or a prayer word like "God," "Jesus," "love," "peace," etc. Second, gently ignore any other thoughts. He even encourages awareness of the breath as an option for a mental focus,[14] just as Dr. Jon Kabat-Zinn does in his Mindfulness-Based Stress Reduction Clinics[15] and as centering prayer facilitators and yoga instructors have done for years.

Dr. Benson is now internationally famous for showing in his research that the body needs daily periods of relaxation to still the over-stimulated monkey mind of modern life.[16] He reports that during the relaxation response, the body shifts gears into a natural state wherein multiple body systems become balanced and rejuvenated, even more than when we are

11. Benson and Stark, *Timeless Healing*, 152–57.
12. Ibid., 136.
13. Keating, "Theological Foundations," 1.
14. Benson and Stark, *Timeless Healing*, 134.
15. Kabat-Zinn, *Full Catastrophe Living*, 51. In this text, Dr. Kabat-Zinn shares the birth of his programs of mindfulness-based stress reduction.
16. Benson and Stark, *Timeless Healing*, 128–31.

asleep.[17] He and his staff teach medical patients how to elicit the relaxation response to improve or cure many stress-related illnesses.

After listening to Dr. Benson and his peers presenting their research over the course of a three-day conference in the late 1990s, I began to teach the practice to counseling clients who might benefit from it. Two of my counseling clients, Mary and her stepdaughter Sally, both found the relaxation response to be a powerful tool for managing anxiety and phobias. Their stories follow.

Mary's Story

Mary was a very tense woman in her late forties. She had been successful in her profession. But lately her anxiety had been getting out of control. She had become a workaholic. Even after driving herself hard all day long, Mary could never seem to feel she had done enough. She could not turn her mind off in the evenings, and by bedtime she would feel frantic. Her sleep was always restless. She would awaken throughout the night and often couldn't get back to sleep. When her husband brought her in for counseling, Mary was feeling hopeless.

In our first session, Mary related the story of her mounting anxiety. In the second session, she agreed to practice eliciting the relaxation response. So we tried it together in my office. She was amazed. She said she had never felt so peaceful. She was so excited that she agreed to keep practicing on her own. When she returned for her third and final session, Mary looked like a changed woman. She was smiling. She had been sleeping. She was learning to let things go that had been worrying her incessantly. She had found what she was looking for, and she no longer needed my help.

Sally's Story

A few months later, I received a call from Mary's husband. "Was Mary having trouble again?" I wondered. "No. She's doing fine. This time it's my daughter Sally. She's been having panic attacks. Would you see her?" he asked. I answered, "Of course," and we made an appointment.

Sally came in and told me that she was suffering from more than panic attacks. She was eighteen, pregnant, unmarried, and experiencing overwhelming phobias. Sally was afraid of needles, which are hard to

---

17. Ibid., 132.

avoid when you're pregnant, and of dying during childbirth. She had a paralyzing fear that while going into labor she might suffer a heart attack without warning. As these scenes flashed before her mind's eye, she would begin to experience a panic attack. It was like her mind did not know the difference between her imaginings and reality. So the chemistry of high anxiety would flood her body and she would feel sensations much like a heart attack.

We decided to start with her fear of needles since she was due to have blood work. Sally was quite willing to learn to use her breathing as a source of relaxation. Frankly, she was willing to try anything to stop her panic attacks. As she closed her eyes, Sally gradually became still. She felt her breath with each inhale and exhale. She released worrying thoughts as they came. And she relaxed. Her relief was evident in her face and her whole demeanor, and I felt I could see relaxation overtaking her.

This success gave Sally the courage to go in for blood work the next day. As the nurse began to draw her blood, Sally began to feel nervous. Her pulse rate was increasing. We had discussed this possibility, so she knew what to do. Explaining her phobia of needles, Sally asked the nurse to give her just a minute. She closed her eyes and practiced her gentle breathing. Peace began to replace high anxiety. Soon she told the nurse she was ready.

She was surprised when the nurse said, "I already started." Sally opened her eyes to see the needle in her arm. She had not even felt it going in. Sally could not believe that she could look directly at the very source of her fears. She had used the relaxation response to conquer her phobia, so much so that she told the nurse, "Take your time and get all the blood you need."

Sally returned for her follow-up appointment with a sense of assurance. "I'm ready to have that baby now," she told me. I asked her what she meant. "I know how to face that fear now. All I have to do is go in there and breathe. I think I can do that." I congratulated her for her success. I love it when a treatment plan works and people get better.

At his "Spirituality and Healing in Medicine Conference V" in March of 1998, Dr. Benson and his peers in the medical community confirmed that serotonin and endorphin levels do rise during the relaxation response. In my own experience of the relaxation response, endorphins often seem to flow freely in my body, and as I slowly breathe in and out, a visceral sense of wellbeing comes into my chest. This feeling can be addictive if I try to control it, or use it to escape reality, or try to *make* it happen when I practice. So I let go of efforts to control my thoughts and feelings as best I can, just keep breathing, and let come what may. This letting go is central to most relaxation practices, and in my opinion it is a fundamental spiritual attitude.

The amazing physiological responses described above helped convince me, as Dr. Benson seems convinced,[18] that God made our bodies to be nourished by taking time to let go of all thoughts and just rest in simple awareness. This practice is like a mini-experience of solitude. For many of us, this means resting in God's presence in the inner sanctuary where relaxation resides. I believe there is a direct connection between the kind of letting go that elicits the relaxation response and the spiritual attitude of surrender that helps us drop down into the inner sanctuary.

Perhaps the time has come when physicians will contradict the words of Ben Franklin: "Prayer is a healing power that cannot be prescribed."[19] In the very near future, I believe we will see some bold physicians literally prescribing prayer. I can even see groups being established to teach these simple forms of prayer in physician's offices. Perhaps such instruction will be offered alongside classes for diabetes education. I predict that the principles of relaxation, the health benefits of prayer, and the actual practice of meditation and prayer will become part of the medical model.

Why will all this happen, and soon? The facts are in. The field of medicine is opening its eyes to the research of Dr. Benson and others. And when enough research accumulates, the medical community can finally be convinced that even physiological problems can sometimes have spiritual remedies. Dr. Benson has convinced me that we were made for this simple spiritual practice. Our minds, bodies, and spirits need these periods of relaxation (letting go), of solitude (going within), and silent prayer (surrender) every day.

Once we have learned this practice, we can continue to stay in touch with the reservoir of serenity we have cultivated as we go about our work each day. We do not have to exhaust ourselves by separating the workday from our time for nurturing the spirit. We do not have to work out of the depletion model, pushing ourselves past our limits until we collapse into a hospital or a vacation once a year. We can nourish our beings even as we go about our daily tasks, as I will explain further in chapter 3.

One of the most-quoted founders of pastoral counseling, Dr. Wayne Oates, explained how to incorporate spiritual centering into counseling

---

18. Ibid., 306.

19. Quoted in Benson, Herbert, "Spirituality and Healing in Medicine V" Conference, Harvard Medical School, Houston, TX, March 22–24, 1998.

sessions in his book, *The Presence of God in Pastoral Counseling*.[20] His model informs the way I practice my professional pastoral care and counseling: staying near the breath in my awareness and opening my heart to God's presence as best I can, all while listening to the person's concerns. In this way, I seek to integrate work and attention to the inner sanctuary.

Perhaps this business of being in touch with the inner sanctuary while at work sounds like a fairy tale to you. Perhaps you are already saying to yourself, "Sure, maybe you can find peace at your job. But that's impossible for those of us who work in the *real* world." So I remind you where I learned the model of working with serenity: Calcutta, India.

If nuns laboring in the slums of Calcutta are using this practice to center themselves even as you read these words—if they can face the homeless and dying in the streets by continuously praying themselves into a state of serenity and compassion—then I believe you and I can do the same. Whatever terrible stresses we face, rest assured that they do not surpass those taken on each day by those caregivers of Calcutta.

Are you desperate enough to be willing to learn what they know? Can you trust Dr. Benson's thirty years of research as a solid enough foundation for establishing your own practice of the relaxation response each day? Do you need peace of mind badly enough to give it a try right now? If so, settle in to the practice called "Prelude to the Inner Sanctuary: A Relaxation Exercise" in chapter 5.

Commitment

"Only that day dawns to which we are awake."

—Henry David Thoreau[21]

"Our lives unfold only in moments."

—Dr. Jon Kabat-Zinn[22]

It took an eight-day retreat for healthcare professionals with Dr. Jon Kabat-Zinn and Dr. Saki Santorelli at the Omega Institute for Holistic Studies to finally help me commit to practice entering into the inner

---

20. Oates, *God in Pastoral Counseling*, 40, 69, 81.

21. Thoreau, *Walden*, quoted in Kabat-Zinn, *Wherever You Go*, 1. Kabat-Zinn's book explains the essence of mindfulness with great clarity and is filled with practical mindfulness exercises, many of which we have used with great success in our classes.

22. Ibid., 4.

sanctuary each day. The retreat taught mindfulness meditation practice for stress reduction. We practiced mindfulness from 6:00 a.m. to 6:00 p.m. each day, attending presentations on mindfulness research at night. This prolonged daily practice was the direct experience I needed to strengthen my foundation for lifelong practice.

The attitudes, principles, and practices of mindfulness were try-it-this-way practical and very helpful. For me, the encouragement to focus awareness on the present moment throughout the day fit in with Thomas Kelly's invitation to keep returning our awareness to the inner sanctuary. What's more, the mindfulness training's use of the breath as a place to rest the attention taught me a simple step that I had lacked up to that time.

In practicing mindfulness, I learned to *be* in the present moment with my awareness much of the time. I learned the call to cultivate inner stillness as a physical, mental, and spiritual practice. I learned sitting meditation, walking meditation, eating meditation, and yoga. I committed to extended periods of formal practice each day, and to informal practice throughout the day.

Formal practice means setting aside a period of time each day to become what Dr. Kabat-Zinn and Dr. Santorelli called a "silent witness," to quietly observe whatever thoughts and feelings appear without getting lost in them. During this time, I just pay attention to the experience of my breath as it comes in and goes out. I use this attention to the breath to hold my awareness in the present moment. I do not judge my thoughts or feelings as they come to me. I do not strive to accomplish anything, including trying hard to relax. This is a time for doing nothing, which helps me remember to just be myself. These attitudes of non-judging, non-striving, and non-doing are central to the practice of mindfulness in the present moment, as I will explain in further detail in the coming pages.

Informal practice means continuing to practice mindfulness throughout the day. When we resume our normal, daily routine, our minds tend to go on automatic pilot. We tend to lose awareness of the present moment. Thoughts start to race between past events and future possibilities to everything in between. Without focusing our attention, we can pass through a whole day, or lifetime, without knowing where we have been.

To avoid the tragedy of missing our whole lives, we use informal practice. We simply pay attention to the breath during the day. We seek to keep our attention in each present moment. When we notice that we have lost our focus, we simply guide our awareness back into the present. In this way, we notice what is happening with ourselves and with those we encounter, and so we have a chance to make wise choices in how to respond. This is the opposite of reacting to situations or people unthinkingly and unfeelingly. I had been seeking peace of mind throughout my life, but I also sought wisdom. Even when I was too young to be wise, I still needed a higher wisdom to know how to live my life and how to serve others. What if the inner sanctuary turns out to be the place from which wisdom arises?

Wisdom's Source

After several decades of studying myself and observing others, the truth became clear that many of our decisions are not based in wisdom. Reactions often rule our relationships. A reaction is an action that comes without thought. Often they are too quick for any wisdom to arise. Reactions are usually unconscious. They arise from preconceptions or beliefs we have about the way things must be. And most of us are deluded about what we need in life and how to go about satisfying those needs.

Wisdom, on the other hand, comes from the depths. Wisdom comes in a response. Responses are choices. They are conscious. If a reaction is a thoughtless, unconscious reflex, a response is more like a wise path chosen after careful deliberation.

One of the many benefits of spending time in the inner sanctuary and of living in the present moment with mindfulness is taking the time to allow wisdom to arise. Myrna's story taught me more about the difference between unconscious reactions and the spring of wisdom that flows through mindful responses.

Myrna's Story

Myrna was a participant in one of my eight-week training workshops on mindfulness as a strategy for stress reduction. I was teaching what I had learned from Dr. Kabat-Zinn and Dr. Santorelli after several years of additional practice. One day during our mindfulness training, Myrna spoke of an upcoming trip to see her family. She said that for years, she had gotten a nervous stomach every time she visited them. She always heard messages of "You don't measure up" from her family. Being true to herself was not good enough. Myrna developed an unconscious reaction to protect herself. She would draw down into herself and go numb. She said it was like she wasn't really there when her family hurled insults and criticisms. The numbness seemed safer than conflict. After a while, it just happened automatically, and numb became Myrna's norm.

At other times, Myrna would react with anger, defend her position, contradict her relatives' opinions, or blow up and quit speaking to them all for years. Her explosion of anger would lead to a kind of emotional cut-off that also seemed safer than direct contact. These were her gut reactions. She did not know how else to survive.

But then Myrna began learning another way to live. She began to practice yoga. She found that sense of inward balance that comes from the gentle movement from one posture to another. She was beginning to *be* breath, to follow the breath as it flows in and out, and to use her simple breathing as a way to calm her very being.

Myrna was also learning to honor her limits by listening to her body. When she stretched and her muscles began to tense, she paid attention and eased up. She let her body teach her how far it wanted to turn in each direction. She stopped pushing her body past its limits. She quit trying to whip her body into shape. Straining was no longer part of her physical vocabulary. Gentleness, paying attention, and accepting the way things are became her new vocabulary for how she wanted to treat her body and herself.

As Myrna eased into her yoga postures every other morning, she practiced non-judging. She might have had critical thoughts about her body for its inflexibility or feelings of not measuring up. But Myrna started noticing those thoughts. She did not become slave to these thoughts by pushing or punishing herself. She just let them go and returned to breathing, and gently attended to the body's teaching.

These attitudes of gentleness, acceptance, honoring her limits, finding balance, listening to her body, learning to just breathe and be herself without judgment—these are the practices of yoga. And as Myrna learned them from yoga she began to learn them in the rest of her life.

As Myrna prepared to see her family, the old automatic tension began to return. She wondered if she would need to go numb again. She wondered if she would be able to honor her limits and avoid family fights. She wondered if she had accepted herself enough to handle verbal attacks and just let them be, without having to judge herself or her family members. If her anger arose, would she be able to wait for a wise response, to breathe, calm herself, and let silence be her ally. She wondered if she was ready.

Yoga is a patient teacher. And Myrna had become a willing student. She was awake and staying in the now as best she could. I never heard the outcome of her visit. But I believe she encountered her family with the ability to just appreciate each moment for what it is. I like to think she was able to be mindful and did not have to go on automatic pilot out of habit. She might have reacted with numbness or with anger, but her practice was growing strong. I believe she responded with wisdom. That was my hope and prayer.

Over the years, I too studied yoga and seated meditation to learn to focus on my breath. I learned to be still and breathe, to let relaxation flow into my body, and to let tension release. I learned the value of feeling balance physically. And this helped me be in touch with inner balance. I too learned to honor the limits of my body without judging, straining, or striving to control it. In the process I learned that the body is a wise teacher. All this and more came from the simple practice of breathing and stretching called yoga.

Paying attention to the present moment by noticing my own breath has been an ultra-simple way to *be* in the inner sanctuary, whether sitting at home alone or sitting with counseling clients in the office. This has become a way to stay in touch with my own soul, the font of wisdom, during counseling and spiritual direction with others. It is a way for me to remember the sacredness of the moment with each client. It is a way to be fulfilled throughout the day instead of being constantly depleted by my own efforts as a caregiver. I tried giving pastoral care, counseling, and spiritual direction from my own strength for a long time, and the way of depletion did not work. Now I try another way.

I am immensely grateful to Dr. Kabat-Zinn and Dr. Santorelli for their training in mindfulness, and for their help in learning to integrate mindfulness into my work as a caregiver. One particular experience at their retreat stands out as an example of beginning to learn to "be in the present moment," as they called it.

During an early morning session on the fifth day of our eight days of training, we were invited to take the usual break for breakfast in silence. I was immersed in inner silence by that time and decided to stay behind as the room cleared of the 175 doctors, nurses, therapists, and other healthcare professionals who had come to the "Mindfulness for Professionals" seminar.

A light rain was falling. All the doors of the meditation hall were open so that the sounds and sights of the outside world were near. The dripping sounds were almost mesmerizing as rain fell onto the hillside outside our room. An inner stillness descended upon my being. The heart of peace was there. As I sat in meditation, simply being aware of the present moment, a sense of oneness with everything around me emerged. For a little while, I became a mountain in the rain.

I do not mean that I just liked sitting on the side of a mountain in the rain. It was like the sense of separation between myself and my surroundings had disappeared. For those moments I *was* a mountain in the rain. The oneness was complete. What a gift! I will never forget that morning. You will find a poem I wrote about being mountain in rain in chapter 6.

Since that day, I have known what it means to live in the present moment, to not get perpetually lost in thoughts of past occurrences or expectations of future events. No, I cannot keep my awareness in the present moment all the time. Mindfulness is a practice, so I just keep practicing.

Clearly, mindfulness of the present moment is an essential aspect of finding peace of mind. What a treasure to have spent a week with a group of beginners who learned the art of peace from two masters— not that we can master peace, but that we can master a practice which opens and prepares us for whenever peace may come to visit. So now when I teach meditation classes, I start with the foundational practice of cultivating mindfulness. I want to share the gift of mindfulness with others so they can move into opening the heart to the presence of God, the source of peace.

Simple Being

"What our souls really need *is* available; it has always been and always will be available. It is given, being given, all the time. All it takes to recognize and appreciate this gift is to ease our frantic striving to make it happen."

—Dr. Gerald May[23]

In the spring of 1992, I attended a five-day retreat in Maryland led by Dr. Gerald May and the staff of the Shalem Institute for Spiritual Formation called "The Spiritual Life of Spiritual Leaders." Their contemplative spirit calmed and invigorated me at the same time. I saw and

---

23. May, *Simply Sane*, 136.

experienced what Dr. May writes about so effectively: that it is really possible to learn to "just be."[24]

I loved watching Dr. Gerald May, the Reverend Dr. Tilden Edwards, and Sister Rose Mary Dougherty as they humbly led us through each contemplative experience. The humility was so real, so deeply human. The retreat leaders demonstrated a peaceful flow of movement from one event to the next. They were internationally famous from their writing and conferences, but in person they were as regular, simple, and human as any of us. They were relaxed, at ease. And seeing this simple way of being was a moving invitation. It said, "Be yourself, as you are right now. What you are looking for is right here. You do not need to work hard to find it. Ease up. Let go. Let what you need find you."

One particularly moving moment came as we left our several days of silence and began to speak again in small groups. Because we were in a retreat center without phones or television, we had spent the days of silence cut off from the outside world. Upon first speaking, we learned that James, one of our small group members for the retreat, had walked out to get a newspaper. He was quite disturbed by what he read.

James's Story

James was a Presbyterian pastor. His congregation was multiracial. They had been praying for some time for a healing outcome to the trial of the police officers involved in the beating of Rodney King in Los Angeles, California. The newspaper brought no good news. The headlines and photos revealed that riots had broken out in south Los Angeles after the police officers were all acquitted.

James was disheartened. We all were, but James was in tears, and he was angry. He challenged Dr. May with a question meant for God: "What good does it do to pray? All this time we have pleaded for God to help justice prevail. We've prayed for healing to come between the races, for some resolution that will bring people together, and now this happens."

Dr. May listened patiently. He did not become defensive. He did not rush to come up with an explanation for human suffering. After a time of silence, he comforted James with these simple words: "I bet God is thankful that you are all joining him as he agonizes over this suffering." That was all. No other words were needed.

24. Ibid., 28.

We all sat in silence for a while after that. It was a powerful moment. It was a comforting thought: What if we are not alone when we suffer? What if we are just joining God, who is already suffering for us? What if the Source of Life is not a magician who is on the verge of some magical trick to erase the reality of suffering? What if the nature of God is to sit in silence and suffer with us, to simply be with us until our suffering eases?

The inner sanctuary may be a place of profound peace at times. But it is most assuredly not a place to escape reality. Suffering does not pass us over because we are in that quiet place. When we become still and quiet in our being, everything that is in us comes to the surface—our doubts, our fears, our sorrows, our joys, our thoughts, and feelings that we're too embarrassed to share with anyone. If you want to escape reality, there are plenty of addictions to try. But not the inner sanctuary. You will be miserably disappointed. Days of silence had not protected us from the harsh realities of the world, and it cannot offer you escape either.

A common misconception is that people who enter contemplation, like monks and nuns, are avoiding the real world. One of this past century's best spokespersons for contemplative prayer, or interior prayer, was Thomas Merton. He was a Cistercian monk who died in 1968. Merton noted that when you enter a monastery (that is, when you dedicate your life to interior prayer), you bring all the world with you.[25] It was his way of saying there is no escaping reality, not even in a monastery.

Though time spent in the inner sanctuary cannot help us avoid reality, it *is* helpful in allowing us to face the very things we would prefer to escape. Wisdom truly seems to arise from contemplation, from looking within. Looking deeply into the nature of suffering is an essential part of finding freedom from our suffering. As I mentioned earlier, my wife Carol did not find peace with whatever happens by pretending that nothing bad would happen. The courage to keep looking within is a necessary part of living in the inner sanctuary.

For most of us, this courage is impossible to find by ourselves. We need helpers, friends whose commitment to live this way supports our own intention. I was not able to sustain regular contemplative practice by myself. For years, my times of sitting in silence were sporadic at best. So I followed the suggestions of Dr. May and the Shalem staff in forming several contemplative prayer groups in our area during the years following that retreat in 1992.

---

25. Merton, *Contemplative Prayer*, xvii.

The first group included therapists who wanted to explore personal spirituality and how to integrate that practice into their counseling work. The group lasted a year. The next group included a priest, several nuns, a pastor, a therapist, and some lay caregivers.

We shared our spiritual lives and struggled to maintain a regular practice of contemplation together. We committed ourselves to helping each other practice Dr. May's phrase: "Simply be who you are, completely. Better yet, just realize that you *are* being who you are, right now, completely. That's all."[26]

We gathered for an hour and a half each week and eventually continued on a monthly basis. We consecrated our intention to just be and kept encouraging each other in this direction for eight years. We grew close. We developed trust in each other to share our intimate struggles and to ask for prayer. We admitted our resistance to the work of silence in our lives. We learned what it is like to be prayer, helped somehow by the silent presence and being of each other.

For me, this being involves a practical kind of giving up. I often fail to manage my own life very well. So I have to keep giving up on trying to control everything. And I am barely beginning to learn, in the smallest way, to just *be* the being I am (which turns out to be what God wants anyway, in my opinion).

In this sense, entering the inner sanctuary is not so much an entering at all. It is more being where I already am, both when I am alone and when I am with clients and friends. It is noticing that the inner sanctuary is here all the time. Everywhere, all the time, I want to continue just being with this inner sanctuary, this holy of holies. But I am human, and I forget all the time. So I just keep practicing as best I can. I try not to judge myself too harshly for being a beginner. I remember what Dr. May wrote: "In all things, above all, be gentle with yourself."[27]

This gentleness of being, this simple way of life, can be cultivated every day. In fact, it is a practice that needs daily cultivation. The outer pressures and inner impulses of daily life can be too intense for simplicity to rule our lives. So most of us could use some help in this area. One of the best ways to nurture a daily life of simple being is through the practice of centering prayer.

---

26. Ibid., 103.
27. Ibid., 105.

The Way of Centering Prayer

> "Contemplative prayer is the opening of mind and heart—our whole being—to God, the Ultimate Mystery, beyond thoughts, words, and emotions ... Centering prayer is a method designed to facilitate the development of contemplative prayer by preparing our faculties to cooperate with this gift."
>
> —Thomas Keating[28]

"Centering prayer" is a fairly new name for a very old form of prayer. The term was coined by Father Thomas Merton and popularized by Father Thomas Keating, Father Basil Pennington, and other monks in the past century. In this form of prayer, we select a word, phrase, image, or even awareness of the breath as a place to focus the attention for a moment when our thoughts are carrying us away. Because it is prayer, we both center our attention and open our heart to God by saying yes to God's presence and action within. We might say we center ourselves in God. And when other thoughts come along, as they always do, we gently disregard them and return our focus to God, who is in our hearts already.

One of the best things I learned from Father Keating is that even for monks who spend much of their day in quiet prayer for years, thoughts and feelings always keep coming. They bubble up from the unconscious. This never stops, but it does not mean we are doing something wrong. It does not mean that we do not know how to pray. It does not mean we are not sincere in our desire to pray. This is just what thoughts and feelings do. The mind just works that way.

My understanding of Father Keating's teaching is that this bubbling up of thoughts and feelings is the way the unconscious mind cleanses itself. It is a kind of letting go of whatever is inside of us. The unconscious apparently needs this release just like it needs dreams. This is not a problem unless we spend undue time trying to fight off thoughts or to rid ourselves of feelings. This bubbling up only becomes a problem if we keep judging ourselves for such natural occurrences, which can distract us from our goal: centering ourselves in God.

The solution Thomas Keating proposes to all this distraction is amazingly simple. Leave the thoughts and feelings alone. Let them be. Pay as little attention to them as possible. Treat them as what they are: thoughts and feelings. They do not define us. They are temporary visitors.

---

28. Reininger, *Centering Prayer in Daily Life*, 130.

When we are engaged in opening our hearts to God during centering prayer and busy thoughts arise, we just let them pass. Then we return our focus to the One who is with us beneath all those thoughts and feelings. We rest in simple being. We do that by using the sacred word, or breath, to express our intention to once again say yes to God's presence and action within us.

The regular practice of centering prayer is a way to nurture our awareness of our true home, the place our souls belong. Our souls yearn for a deep belonging that cannot be lost. Beneath every longing, every need, I believe there is a longing to be at home with the One who made us. That longing for belonging is described in the following story.

Mike's Story

A homeless man got off the streets of New Orleans for a while to seek treatment for an alcohol problem in the years when I was working at the psychiatric hospital. Mike, a friend who ran a residential treatment facility for recovering alcoholics and addicts, told me his story in the mid-1990s. The man was admitted to Mike's halfway house.

Mike was leading a spirituality group one day and asked the participants one of his favorite questions: "How would you define the difference between spirituality and religion?" Several group members took a stab at answering with flowery definitions. Most of them had negative views of religion as judgmental and held positive views of spirituality as accepting and loving. As everyone took a turn, the disheveled older man in the corner bided his time. He kept his head down. Mike couldn't tell if he was even listening.

Eventually, Mike turned to the man and asked him, "Jake, how would you define spirituality?" Jake paused for a minute, looked Mike straight in the eye, and with a small, toothless grin said, "Belonging." The room went silent. Mike's eyes watered. It was a holy moment, too special to speak. In one word, Jake had reduced the whole discussion to the heart of the greatest longing we can know: the desire to belong. Just telling Jake's belonging story was enough to bring both Mike and I into a tearful awareness of holiness.

Father Keating's words taught me that centering my attention on the presence of God inside my own being is the ultimate belonging. We might visit other houses, but nowhere else is *home*. Religions create codes of morality and belief systems. But that longing for spiritual belonging is more profound than any dogma and seems to be lodged in the human heart.

I don't want to have a separation between the inner home I experience in the morning quiet and what I experience when I am working. I want to stay near that sanctuary all the time. Does that sound like too much navel-gazing? Perhaps so, but it's what I want to learn. I'm not willing to only be an occasional visitor to the inner sanctuary anymore! It is where I belong.

Thomas Kelly teaches that we can live life on two levels at the same time. First, being aware of what is happening around us in mindfulness, and second, worshipping all the while at a deeper level of the soul. I have committed my life to living in this inner sanctuary as best I can, whenever I can remember to be present. In fact, I am breathing that air right now!

This experience has become the basis for the founding of our School for Contemplative Living. Now, we can gather others who want to belong in the inner sanctuary. Would you care to join us? If you want to learn more about the secret that has come to mean so much to my life and work, turn to the exercises called "Entering the Inner Sanctuary: Three Ways" in chapter 5. These are ways of practicing simple being.

If you walked into one of the rooms where we gather for contemplative practice, you wouldn't necessarily be able to tell what was happening inside us. We are likely all sitting in silence and stillness, being washed back and forth between our own stray thoughts and God's presence in the inner sanctuary. This ebb and flow is the norm among us. We are messy contemplatives, beginners, and ever shall be. The following chapter is filled with real stories of our unfolding journey as contemplative pilgrims seeking to practice the presence of God in the world.

3

Stories of Practicing the Presence

CATCHING SIGHT OF A MONK

The contemplative missionary, as a monk in the world, wears what Dr. Thomas Moore called "invisible robes" in his book of *Meditations*.[1] There are no shaved heads, orange garments, special rings, or secret handshakes among us. If you look around New Orleans for these monks, you won't know how to recognize them because they are all just regular people. So here are a few hints of how and where to locate a contemplative monk in the wild world of New Orleans.

One monk spends part of her retirement doing taxes. It's not the job itself but the way Liz serves that makes the difference. After her daily centering practice, this devout Catholic widow prays for the clients she will serve that day. Liz begins to unite her presence for God and her presence with others. If you could see into Liz's heart, you would know her contemplation and her action are already one, even before she brings God's presence to the people she sees each day. She keeps her heart open for inner guidance as she practices the presence in each face-to-face encounter. She might not name herself as such, but she is our kind of monk, for Liz unites her contemplation with her service of the world.

Another of our monks is a philosophy professor, another is a sociology professor, and another gave up her job as professor to teach high

---

1. Moore, *Meditations*, 41.

school English in a local all-girls school. Three others teach in suburban public high schools. You could say that most teachers care about their students, so how would you know that a teacher is a contemplative monk? Again, you would need to see into their heart.

You might catch any one of them in that pause when a student asks a question, a moment when each of them are leaning into the spiritual heart—hoping for a response to come up from the source of wisdom within. Or you might see them inviting their students to practice periods of silent reflection before writing journal entries on their inner experiences. The focus is not so much on how perfectly they accomplish their goal, but the fact that they have the goal of bringing God's presence into their service as teachers as best they can.

One monk is a hand therapist, centering her compassion into patient's broken hands. There is something spiritual going on when she takes time during a hand exercise to remember to pray each person's hand and life into God's care. Contemplative presence for her is not a substitute for technical advancement in hand therapy, but it permeates her therapy. She has invited the Healer to use her as a vessel for the healing process.

Another monk uses her hands to form sacred objects from clay. She begins by centering herself, sliding her hands into the mud and water, shaping and molding, glazing and firing to create holy beauty. Then you might be dismayed as she uses those same hands to break some of her pottery into pieces, revealing the sacredness of human brokenness, and invites others to take a piece into their hands to represent their own holy brokenness. Her practice of the Presence of God with clay can reveal the beauty of wholeness and brokenness together, the very essence of the human condition.

Some of our monks are pastors from several denominations, and some monks serve the world as spiritual directors. All of them are hoping to practice the Presence as companions to others on their spiritual journey. Their work has a more obvious connection to the religious and spiritual, but these practitioners are no different from our other monks in that we all seek to bring God's presence into our way of caring for the world. They do the same tasks as most pastors and spiritual directors. What might be unique is our commitment to actually practice the presence of God for our own transformation first, which can't help but bleed over into how we sit with others.

One example would be the wise lesbian contemplative who is following her call to offer spiritual guidance to those who are just finding the courage to come out of their closet. They need God's acceptance and compassion, and she knows how to offer it. She committed herself to spending several years learning the art of spiritual guidance from the contemplative staff at the Shalem Institute for Spiritual Formation in hopes of being a vehicle of healing, guidance, and restoration. After knowing the frequent rejection experienced by the LGBT community, she seeks to enter the ground of being as a source to sustain her work of caring for others on the journey.

A number of our monks are healers of various types: physicians, nurses, physical therapists, psychotherapists, and others in the medical profession. These are the servants who care for those broken in body, mind, and spirit, including the grieving, the anxious, and the depressed. As contemplative missionaries, they seek to bring the practice of the Presence into the healing arts. You might see them closing their eyes as they reach out to touch their patients. They are pausing for a moment of sensing the Presence within the patient.

Or maybe you will hear these healer monks asking their patients how they are doing mentally, physically, *and* spiritually. Their next prescription might even include a form of meditation to put patients in touch with their own deep source of healing and wholeness. Even in the hurried pace of modern medicine, the contemplative healer wants to be a vessel for helping patients know their deepest wholeness beneath all the human brokenness.

Years ago I read a fascinating chapter on "Doing Good Badly" in Wayne Muller's book, *Sabbath*.[2] In this chapter, Muller describes the many ways people launch into projects to do good without taking time to seek a higher wisdom on *how* to work. So you could say the contemplative missionary is taking classes on how to do good wisely. One of the best resources for this task is found in the simple booklet called *Contemplative Service*, which is part of the Contemplative Life Program created by Contemplative Outreach.

One of these healers is looking for ways the Presence is already at work in people's lives, and she is hoping to get into step with that spiritual flow. Another is resisting the profound urge to fix people's problems, seeking wisdom as he leans back into the spiritual heart, as Tilden Edwards

---

2. Muller, *Sabbath*, 157–64. Muller's collection of stories and suggestions inspires us to actually practice Sabbath as lifestyle.

suggests in his book, *Embracing the Call to Spiritual Depth*.[3] In such ways our monks hope to *be* love, and to learn to love wisely and well.

If you want to know which residents of New Orleans are monks from our school, look for Merry, the retired French teacher who enters the stillness as she uses her talent for calligraphy to pen love notes in support of friends. When she expresses her longing to share love in a way that will last over time, you can tell she has been in the Presence and wants to share that gift with others.

Or watch for Julia, the photographer who heads out into the city early in the morning to catch the first light of the Creator as she bathes her creation from the farthest horizon. There is something in Julia's way of seeing that tells you she has known the Creator within, recognized sacred footprints in the natural world, and wants to capture those traces of Spirit in an aesthetic that will inspire others.

Or pay attention to the young man rebuilding storm-struck and dilapidated houses who keeps breaking away from his labor to pray for personal guidance at Saint Joseph's Abbey across Lake Pontchartrain. Something about being in contact with those Benedictine monks helps him remember to be a monk in the world himself. And some longing in him wants to bring the Presence with him into his work, to learn how to integrate prayer and service.

If you are hoping to catch a glimpse of a contemplative missionary, don't pay attention to their clothes. There is no uniform. But you might examine the behavior of our volunteers in the Good Samaritan/Open Table ministry, which meets at the local Mount Zion United Methodist Church on Tuesday afternoons, as they stand together in a silent circle, holding hands with their homeless friends.

They are praying that the Great Love might dissolve each person's suffering today. They are hoping to serve *from* the Presence within, not from some misguided desire to fix people's problems. As they are learning from this time spent with the poor, poverty is always more complex and deep-seated than our futile efforts to change it. The volunteers hope to be *in* the One who transcends the circumstances of poverty, who is *in* the poor already.

Just last week I was reminded to listen closely to our poor friends as they led a vocal prayer after the group's silent prayer. Murray, a man in need of shelter, mentioned afterwards that one of his friends shouldn't

---

3. Edwards, *Embracing the Call*, 10.

refer to everyone as "homeless" as he had done in the preceding prayer. I asked him to tell me more. Murray said calling people homeless boxes them in. He explained, "Everyone here is in transition; they are on their way to finding a place to live." Murray went on to describe how important it is to speak from the faith of where we are heading so we don't get locked into where we have been. Murray shared a great insight with me that day. It led to a decision to rename the ministry the Good Samaritan/Open Table ministry so as not to call it "homeless hospitality" any longer. That kind of careful listening is an example of what you will see our monks attempting.

Another view of contemplative service might come from watching the way one mother nurtures her gay son with compassionate smiles and simple words of blessing that arise from the source of all compassion within her. She has been practicing the Presence for years, and that inner communion has guided her time and again in supporting this young man as he blossoms into his full being in God.

Monks in the world might just be found wherever people of all colors are embracing as sisters and brothers in the knowledge of their full equality. For practicing the Presence dissolves the artificial barriers that often separate God's children from one another. Contemplative monks are also likely sharing leadership and exchanging the roles of teacher and learner from moment to moment. Time spent in God's presence tends to dissolve hierarchies and break down our human tendency to categorize people into the kind of boxes Murray warned us about.

When the School for Contemplative Living gathers, you won't know who the clergy are and who the lay people are. You will know that they have enrolled in the school by their air of inner stillness, and yet see they are barely beginning the journey. Try asking who in the group seems to be living the contemplative path, and everyone will point to someone else. You will never find a graduate of our school, since this kind of learning never ends, but you might hear a learner exclaim, "I think I finally see that contemplation and service can be one!"

You will know you are in a room of contemplative monks when it just doesn't matter whether the people in it are Republican or Democrat, black or white or Latino or Asian, young or old, gay or straight, male or female, Christian or Jewish or Buddhist or Muslim. You will have found the monks of the School for Contemplative Living when you realize they all know they don't have the answers. They will say things like, "I am getting more and more comfortable with knowing less and less," or "I am uncomfortable around people who have all the answers," and you will know that you have found the monks of our contemplative community.

THE WAY OF THE CONTEMPLATIVE

One contemplative group was kiddingly nicknamed the Know-Nothing Society, to which everyone cheered their approval. In an insecure world filled with self-help books to answer all our dilemmas, what kind of transformation is going on when people can relish the limits of their own knowing? Contemplatives are following the long tradition of what is called the Way of Unknowing.[4] As practice of the Presence deepens, trust in the unseen grows.

But we should not romanticize this Way of Unknowing, for it is extremely difficult to live life in the reality of not knowing the way ahead. It is a major commitment to keep opening up to the presence of a Spirit Guide within. It is uncomfortable to experience a sense of some spiritual answer coming for a question we are not even aware of asking. And all of us know those periods of self-doubt when there is no apparent guidance at all. Such are the challenges of seeking the Spirit who is never under our control.

Every gathering of the School for Contemplative Living draws a new mix of participants. A typical collection of these fledgling monks might include a few United Methodists, Lutherans, Presbyterians, Episcopalians, Catholics, Baptists, and Quakers. On a good day, a Jewish brother, a Buddhist sister, and a few spiritual seekers with no religious affiliation will join the circle.

You see, contemplatives are really modern-day mystics who care very little about competing doctrines or theological battles. These mystics care about experiencing the Divine in daily life together. Everyday mystics are not otherworldly or set apart from their peers in any way. They just treasure the appearance of the Sacred in all her forms. They want contact with the Holy by any means. So the way of the contemplative is the beginners' path of orienting all of life around seeking the Presence.

Contemplatives are seeking the blessing of having eyes to see God's kingdom all around them, noticing the Presence within people from every possible category of life. Actually, contemplatives don't tend to be big

---

4. Bondi, *Love as God Loves*, 98–100. Dr. Bondi inspired our community with her delightful explanation of ways postmodern churches can adopt the attitudes and heart of the first monastic communities.

on categories in the first place. But they do care about spreading the tent wider, inclusively opening the Lord's table, and seeking to create places where Jesus and *all* his friends will be welcome.

So if you wonder who the monks and missionaries of the School for Contemplative Living are, look for the ones who have difficulty defining what it means to be a contemplative. That's most of us. Yet you might stand near Dick, a man with a PhD in marine geology, whose journey led him through scientific skepticism to believe in the existence of a numinous universal consciousness and a "God field" underlying all of our space-time dimensions. Now this scientist practices meditation to seek oneness with that consciousness.

Or spend some time with Joan, the human resources consultant who is hoping to start a new meditation group with cancer patients. It's been her passion for some time, and she knows that someday the walls of medical institutions will come down and the doors will open up to such healing practices. She might be a contemplative missionary because she hopes to gather people with cancer together to help them find their spiritual center. But she would never call herself a monk or a missionary, or possibly not even a contemplative. This way is just not about titles or terms that capture what it means to seek and follow the Source of our very longing.

Notice when Anna Maria, the seasoned social worker and psychotherapist, invites a group of caseworkers to pull away from their service with mental health crisis units around town so they can engage in spiritual practices together. In her efforts to bring centering spiritual experience to these first responders, you know there is something different about how she serves. She knows the difference we can make in other's lives when we base our own lives in the wisdom of the Great Love. And she would like to call other caregivers into that sacred space.

Walk alongside Mark, the retired oil company businessman who now drives several hours a day to simply be a loving presence for his granddaughter. When he brings his inner sense of God's presence into her world, cultivated by years of contemplative practice, he is also serving as a missionary for a way of life she will remember years later. But ask him to define the way of a contemplative and he will probably answer, "I don't know."

Pay attention when my pastor friend, Rev. Irvin, risks disapproval by introducing a mid-week contemplative service to his congregation. He knows people get comfortable with saying, "We've always done it that way," and yet he hopes to bring them into contact with the Spirit who blows wherever the Spirit will blow. So he tells stories of the first monastics among Christian followers, desert fathers and mothers like Saint Anthony. He uses words from the desert monastics to call his people onto the way.

Then Rev. Irvin hosts a candlelight service and a period of silence much longer than most people's usual comfort zone allows. Surprisingly, the initial core group who answered his call sustained itself and then expanded over time. In this way, Rev. Irvin is another contemplative missionary, sharing the way he is led to practice himself.

In the summer of 2013, our School for Contemplative Living hosted a session for participants who could attend on a Saturday morning. I shared with the group the contemplative pledge included later in this chapter. I asked them to read the pledge and then, if the words spoke to them, to sign it.

Anna Maria spoke up and suggested that we hold fellow participants accountable to each other. She invited each person to respond to our open invitation by sharing at least one example of how he or she is contemplative. I was taken with the idea of having all of us define the contemplative life for ourselves. Everyone jumped in until together we had shared twelve ways to be a contemplative. Several people humbly protested, as usual, "I am not a contemplative." But then even they proceeded to say how they *were* contemplatives.

So on that hot and steamy Saturday in August, our school consisted of a contemplative fabric artist who weaves God's presence into symbols and words. We also had a contemplative who gathers friends to share book discussions on contemplative living. One woman said she is a spiritual seeker who has found a good fit on the contemplative path, where there is room for questions of faith. A psychotherapist spoke up to say that she seeks to be a contemplative in her parenting and in her work with grieving clients. A pastor spoke of thinking contemplatively, praying Scripture in *lectio divina*, and using life's distractions to seek God.

Another therapist defined her contemplative path as seeking to overcome the illusion of separateness with an open heart. One mother's way of being contemplative was feeling a sense of Presence she had known as a child and using that understanding as an adult seeker and as a painter. A retired engineer said that as an introvert, he was finally moving from solitude into contemplative community. Another contemplative told us that she was just seeking to be closer to God through any means she could find.

I told the group that I am a practitioner of oneness. A contemplative widow said that since losing her husband she has been seeking to find God everywhere. And a retired professor told of being drawn from the intellectual world of academia into communion with God like a bicycle tire beginning to turn true on the wheel. The group agreed that no particular title fit them as a whole, but did agree that everyone there was on a contemplative path in their own way. They affirmed the sense that God was not waiting until we become more worthy to be a part of our lives, but was already infused in us all.

We started this adventure several years ago as a handful of seekers gathering to learn how to practice being in God's presence from each other as a community. We decided to quit having discussions filled with our thoughts about other people's thoughts. Such conversations are rarely transformative, and besides, intellectual discussions were not our goal. We needed something more enriching than thoughts about thoughts, something more sustaining than rational conclusions or theological formulas.

We chose instead to share from our life experiences of what it is like to long for a Presence that cannot be grasped. We admitted our failures to sustain a daily practice of quiet time on our own. We confessed our need for each other's help in following the way of Christ. We saw how Jesus needed to retreat from the crowds to practice the presence of God, and we read of his return to service filled with powerful compassion. We wanted to source our lives in the Great Love as he had done, and we knew we couldn't stick with it unless we were standing beside each other.

Now, our weekly and monthly groups, classes, and workshops have begun to spring up all over town. Our annual speakers might draw anywhere from twenty-five people to hundreds of local seekers and pilgrims from other states. Over three hundred people joined us to hear Richard Rohr in 2011. We were all encouraged by his wise guidance, and most of these regional participants ask to be added to our email list for upcoming gatherings. The hunger seems to be growing and spreading, one person at a time.

But at heart we are still a handful of contemplatives who still grasp for words to define the contemplative path. We still feel inadequate and unsure of how to proceed. We can barely see the next step in the unfolding of our School for Contemplative Living. So we meet, center ourselves in the Presence as best we can, face the multitude of competing thoughts in our minds once again, and keep opening towards the heart-center as best we can.

Seeking out this uncertain unfolding is the guiding task of monks in the world. Our wandering is sometimes like that of the early monks on the foggy coasts of Ireland, who also made the practice of the presence of God their first priority. Our guiding light comes from within personal practice, no matter how foggy our surroundings. We seem to be led to practice the presence of God as our first priority in our daily lives. And that practice probably looks different for every one of us, but a gentle tug from within invites us to gather as a supportive spiritual community wherever and whenever we can.

After practicing the Presence individually and in groups for several years, I began to feel called to serve the larger world as a contemplative missionary. I believe others among us feel drawn to a similar path. Being monks in the world means bringing our practice of God's presence out into the world wherever and however we serve.

This means we invite people to come join us in a school where we are both learners and teachers, both followers and guides. We are evangelists of what Dr. Dwight Judy has called a "quiet Pentecost,"[5] by which the Spirit uses us to welcome all seekers to the Lord's table. We create opportunities for our mutual spiritual growth and welcome anyone who is hungry for the something more Spirit is offering. Each of us, in our own way, invites others to come and see.

ON CONTEMPLATIVE EVANGELISM

If you heard the invitation above, if it came into your being as a simple urge saying, "I'd like to be a part of that," then you just got a hint of how contemplative evangelism works. Spirit moves in the contemplative heart like a stream of living water (John 7:38), and by nature that spiritual stream wants to flow out into others.

There is something in the direct experience of the sacred that calls for sharing. The movement from thoughts about the Divine into knowing the Divine in a given moment is a story just waiting to be told. Wise contemplatives seek to be careful in this sharing in several ways.

Enthusiastic sharing of spiritual experience can be contagious, or it can be off-putting. Pride can slip in, as though we somehow did something right to allow the experience. And if there is pride in the sharing of

---

5. Judy, *Quiet Pentecost*, 15. Dr. Judy's collected stories of spiritual formation in faith communities reveal the national emergence of a quiet Pentecost.

the story, others will hear that in the telling. Enthusiasm can also engender guilt in the hearer, making listeners wonder why they have not been having such experiences.

Enthusiastic sharing can also be premature if the recipient of a grace-filled moment has not allowed himself or herself time for the full meaning of the experience of the Holy One to do its transformative work within. A gift shared too soon can lose its impact in becoming a story to tell before it has finished its good work *within* the one who first had the experience.

But there is a time and a place for everything, according to the author of Ecclesiastes (Eccl 3:1). So when spiritual experience has brought the healing, wholeness, comfort, guidance, direction, humility, gratitude, or love it was given to bring about, the time will come for the experience to be shared. Here a contemplative experience becomes evangelism—an invitation to the next person to come home, a welcome into God's good company, an offer to meet loving-kindness face to face.

If such moments of sharing are graced, the original gift of that stream of living water can move forward to help quench the spiritual thirst of another. The story can inspire, offer hope, lift spirits, and encourage the hearer to open his or her own heart for such an experience. An example of contemplative evangelism happened in an encounter with a woman living on the streets. I will call her Sadie. Sadie is one of many people in need who have become our friends in the Good Samaritan/Open Table ministry each week.

I shook her hand as she sat waiting for the opening prayer before the offering of shelter vouchers and other services would begin. Sadie had been there every Tuesday with her snaggletooth smile for over a year. One day, when I asked her how her day had been, she beamed that same open-mouthed smile and said what so many street people say: "Blessed."

I told Sadie that it always surprises me to hear that word, since life on the streets can be so very hard. She said, "Well my life *is* blessed. I made it through the day. I'm about to receive this food. I have a place to stay tonight. I *am* blessed." Sadie's appreciation of her blessings even while living on the streets of New Orleans moves and inspires me. Even in such dire circumstances, she can still get her needs for food and shelter met. And even being asked about her life is, for Sadie, an experience of the same grace that sustains her through the day. Her dependence on the Divine is immense, and her willingness to share how her life is blessed brings a sense of God's presence to me.

Contemplative evangelism can be paradoxical for those who enter the process with a contemplative, open heart. The roles are reversed all the time. One of the greatest mistakes of Christian evangelism is the frequent presumption that says, "I have the salvation, you don't, and it is my job to get it to you." For contemplatives who are seeking the presence of God at all times, any conversation can be a moment when *we* will be shown that Presence. Reverse evangelism happens frequently as others become the revealers of the Presence to us.

On the other hand, there are times when the contemplative is the one who is called to share a story that offers another inspiration (the Spirit breathing in). This too can be contemplative evangelism.

For instance, I was facilitating centering prayer with the group of mostly African American senior adults at the Mercy Endeavors Senior Center one day when I felt led to share a few words of Scripture before we practiced. I related the Jeremiah passage where the Lord says, "You will seek me and find me when you seek me with all your heart" (Jer 29:13). I invited the group to practice the actual presence of God with me by simply seeking God with our hearts wide open in the silence of our prayer. So we did our best to seek God with all our hearts.

I rang the handcrafted metal Tibetan singing bowl three times by lightly touching its side with a small wooden mallet. This is an instrument I often use to begin and end a period of silent prayer. The quiet sound trails off into silence as a form of invitation for us all to do the same. As we moved into the inner stillness together while seated near a noisy kitchen with the ice machine whirring and the staff starting lunch preparations, I believe we actually entered into the presence of God, at least for a moment as we practiced. That belief is based on the inner sense of stillness I felt in that room despite all the background noises. We never know for certain what is happening within others during the silence. There is only a sense of our group connection, a spiritual bond that comes through the heart's awareness more than the mind's.

My sharing of the invitation that day was nothing profound. It was not a planned speech or an insightful lecture. It was a simple expression of the belief that we could all settle into the Presence right there if we could seek God with all our heart as the prophet Jeremiah said. This form of evangelism is a way of passing on our personal discovery that we can seek the presence of God everywhere and always. And in graced moments we also sense that presence.

It is my experience that contemplative evangelism is best kept simple and brief, for it works better with as few words as possible. The cliché that says less is more surely applies to contemplatives sharing words about spiritual experience. Our own practice of the Presence, and bringing that presence with us into the rooms of our lives, is potentially to open a vessel for the stream of living waters to come flowing in. Words are optional, and lengthy explanations are often a hindrance.

Finally, when we do speak of our spiritual experiences, speaking from a sense of inner guidance is essential. Quakers are invited to practice a similar discernment in unprogrammed meetings. In these extended periods of silence, we are taught to listen within to see if there is some sense of vocal ministry arising within us. If some movement of the Spirit comes to us in the silence, we listen with an obedient heart. If there is some inner leading to share that truth we are experiencing within, we are invited to ask the Spirit if this is for us alone or something meant for the larger group. If we feel guided to share, we are cautioned to speak with concise clarity. We call that brief sharing vocal ministry, and anyone present is equally free to share.

Contemplative evangelism becomes a few words reflecting real experience that we feel led to share for others' benefit. We rarely know what the Spirit might intend to do with our sharing. And we could be wrong in our sense of rightness to speak in the first place. So with all humility, we seek the courage to tell a simple story or relate an experience of the holy with the hope that the Spirit wants to use those words to help another find their way into the Presence.

Contemplatives experience the presence of the Great Love in their inner being and, when so moved, speak up to tell that story. The speaking is done so that Love will find her way into the hearer's life in some new or expanded way. Our evangelism is just telling the story and then trusting the Spirit to take it from there wherever it is needed.

If you wanted to see contemplative evangelism at work, one of the best places to look would be in our weekly classes at the school. As we go through some text on the contemplative life, we are invited to share from experience more than thoughts. A weekly question is, "How does this passage speak to you?" Or we might invite one another to relate where the author's idea touches our own life experience. We are at our worst when we just analyze whatever we did or didn't like about what some author wrote. We are at our best when we relate our own journey.

You could say we are evangelists for each other in those most personal means of sharing. We are inspiring each other with our real stories of where and how we do, and do not, experience the sacred. Since we are all learners *and* teachers, guides *and* followers, whether we know it or not, we evangelize each other when we speak truth from experience. It will happen again in tomorrow night's group. It is what I hope for every week and month as we gather and examine our next text on contemplative living.

For example, during one session we looked over Tilden Edward's ideas on gifts for contemplative living in his latest book, *Embracing the Call to Spiritual Depth*. We remembered some of the phrases and exercises he led us through when he came to visit, and then we shifted into sharing how they spoke to our own lives and experiences.

One of us might disagree with an author's wording, but that person is invited to focus on how his own spiritual experience can teach us all. Another learner might denigrate herself by sharing her concern that she may never reach the heights of spiritual experience she believes others have known. She might go on to explain that her thoughts keep interrupting her desire to know God directly. The group might respond by reassuring her that we all struggle in that area, but at least everyone is sharing experience, not just opinions.

It is this sharing of direct spiritual experience—the good, bad, and ugly of it—that makes these groups potentially transformative. Spiritual transformation is the goal of contemplative evangelism. We seek growth in becoming love, and we know this will be a lifelong journey. We also know that just saying words about our thoughts on spiritual subjects is rarely able to offer the kind of transformation we seek.

If you come by one of our weekly growth groups, you might feel our humility, our struggles with the false self all of us have, our need for surrender of spiritual expectations, and our desire to know the One who loves us just as we are. Hearing our sincere sharing, our foibles, our ways of laughing at ourselves, and our honest spiritual desires might help you hear the call to join us as we birth a School for Contemplative Living together. Or if you live elsewhere, maybe our sharing will inspire you to create your own contemplative community.

This is our hope, for none of us wants to journey alone. In fact, we gather because we have learned that the contemplative way cannot be followed well in utter solitude. Perhaps there have been rare monks over the centuries who could eventually move from community life into total solitude, but that is not our way.

We are being called to come together and share the contemplative path as fellow mystics, seekers of the presence of the Divine, beginners who both learn from each other and teach each other by simply sharing our stories of practice. When the moment is graced, the Spirit shows up in our midst, and we are blessed to find a true spiritual home in community. Once we find our home, we have something remarkable to carry with us out into the crazy, frantic world called America. This is our fundamental mission: to create contemplative communities who practice the presence of God for personal transformation and radical engagement with the world. Won't you come join us sometime so we can seek to be monks in the world together?

ON THE IMPORTANCE OF DAILY PRACTICE

"Submit to a daily practice. Your loyalty to that is a ring on the door. Keep knocking, and the joy inside will eventually open a window and look out to see who's there."

—Rumi[6]

"Sit in your cell and your cell will teach you everything."

—Abba Moses[7]

I don't stand a chance of finding the inner ground of my being when my life is consumed with obsessive doing from daybreak until dark. How can I possibly make wise decisions about *doing* when I have spent no time this day in the deep source of my *being*, when I have not stopped to listen for the wisest Voice? The Sufi poet Rumi, writing many centuries ago, clearly understood the importance of a daily practice as seen in his quote above.

Sixteen hundred years ago, Abba Moses, one of the first Christian monks in the desert, advised followers of Christ to sit in our prayer cells—our private places of prayer where the heart and mind are united in one act of devotion. With our mind and heart together, we can voice our private need and longing by saying, "Show me the way." Abba Moses' simple guidance was to let the place of private devotion teach us everything. To receive such wise guidance, we are finding that we must take time each day to listen for the voice of God in our cells.

---

6. Rumi, *Essential Rumi*, 101.
7. Quoted in Bondi, *Love as God Loves*, 98.

For contemplative monks in the world, the commitment to a daily practice in our prayer cell is not optional. It is not a situation of "If I get around to it this week," or "Maybe next year I will start." We have tried engaging the spiritual journey without a daily practice and found it both unsatisfying and impossible. We have tried serving the world without first sourcing our lives from the power and wisdom to serve wisely and well, and the result was usually some form of doing good badly.

How are we to undergo our own transformation into beings full of loving-kindness if we find no time or place to practice the presence of the Great Love this day? Who do we think will transform us if we are spending no time alone with the Transformer?

If a friend told us he was heading out for a drive through the desert wilderness with no gas in the car and no gas stations on the map for hundreds of miles, how might we respond? After laughing at the absurd joke or worrying about our friend's mental health if he was being serious, we might insist on doing whatever was necessary to stop him from such a foolhardy journey.

Yet we have attempted a similar spiritual journey through many a wilderness ourselves and wondered how we got lost, or why we felt empty and alone. We might have blamed ourselves, or our parents, or God, or our spiritual leaders for this feeling of being lost in the wilderness. But blame does not get us anywhere on this path. For slow learners like ourselves, there might be many years of frustrating spiritual journeys ahead of us before we learn the simple principle that we must return to our prayer cell—our spiritual gas station—every day. When we do not return, we soon run empty.

One of the earliest participants in our school was Rev. Callie, a pastor who established her daily practice many years ago. She created a personal rhythm of getting up and dedicating the first two hours of her morning to her own prayer and study from 5:00 to 7:00 a.m. She has repeated this story through many years of service, telling us, "I don't know what I would do if I didn't have that time every morning."

She is not trying to be self-righteous, or super spiritual. She does not set aside that time so anyone will think better of her. She discovered her own need for inner stillness, study, and reflection to give her the spiritual strength to oversee hundreds of lives in the church she serves. She practices out of need, not duty. And Rev. Callie's own form of *lectio divina* helps save her life each morning as she spends time caring for her own soul.

You can imagine what would happen to Rev. Callie's congregation if she stopped practicing the Presence in this way. How can a sermon inspire if the preacher has not taken time to find her own inspiration? How can she bring compassion during hospital visits if she has not been in touch with the Source of compassion herself?

I confirmed my need for regular spiritual practice when I was entering graduate school for the second time in 1989 while working fulltime to support my wife and three-year-old son. I will share more about my final commitment in 1998 to practice every day in the coming pages, but within the first year of my four-year program I was getting frazzled with the many directions I felt pulled in. When should I study, when should I work, when should I be with my wife, and when should I play with our son? Lord knows I hardly had time to wonder when I could be with myself.

After many years of feeling guilty for having been told in religion that I *should* have daily quiet time, I finally came to a place where my sanity required that I find some inner stillness to sort things out. I started a sporadic practice of spending time in my daily prayer cell in my mid-thirties. I did not begin this commitment out of guilt, or duty, or a self-serving desire to be seen as super spiritual. No one else knew what I did in the early morning hours anyway.

The pull toward so many different responsibilities every day was what really pushed me into an awareness that I needed alone time for connecting with the inner stillness at the center of my being. To be honest, I am not sure if I knew I needed to be in God's presence in those early days or if I just knew I needed to *be* each day. I suspect the practice was a mixture of all of the above.

One thing I did learn in those years was how fragmenting the American way of life can be. Not everyone is attempting to cram their schedules with fulltime graduate school and a fulltime job, but many of us can identify with the mother whose children need her every single waking moment, or the working dad who feels torn in body and mind between obligations towards work and family every single day. And God help the working single parent who feels these fragmenting tugs without the help of a partner.

For several years of my own version of fragmentation, I would gather friends into small groups to encourage each other in sustaining regular spiritual practice. Fellow therapists, physicians, nurses, pastors, and nuns would commit to a daily time of centering ourselves in God's presence through some form of meditation. We would meet weekly, or sometimes only monthly, to practice the Presence in silence together and share our spiritual journeys.

In June of 1998, my experience of professional training in mindfulness-based stress reduction finally cemented my commitment to daily practice. After reading about a commitment by medical patients to practice daily mindfulness for at least forty-five minutes and after experiencing the guidance of Dr. Jon Kabat-Zinn and Dr. Saki Santorelli over our eight-day immersion in mindfulness practice, I decided I was ready to commit to my own practice of centering for at least forty-five minutes each day. After all, if medical patients in terrible pain could make that commitment, perhaps a regular guy who just needed to find his own center each day could do it too.

Some warnings should be included here. If anyone ever tells you that daily spiritual practice gets easier over time, you should run the other way. They are either lying, fooling themselves, or have never actually tried it. One's commitment to spiritual practice is tested every single day. Even now, I'm tempted to let my efforts to write about this practice take the place of actually practicing today. There are always a million other tugs from within and without to do most anything else instead of finding the inner stillness.

There are discomforts with encountering the sense of emptiness that can sometimes arise. There are feelings lurking down below that we might not want to visit. We may wish to numb them with distractions. There are the million things to do that demand our attention. There will be phone calls to answer, chores to attend to, spouses or kids asking for our attention, Facebook pages or emails or texts calling our name. The list of potential interruptions is endless.

Through all of these distractions, we will find the strength and courage to sustain a daily practice of the presence of God for one reason: *We need it*. And if we are answering a call to be a monk in the world, we have probably tried chasing all the other fragmenting calls long enough to know that lifestyle just makes us crazy. Enough already! A day comes when we learn we simply need to be in the Presence every day, as best we can. And when we forget, we just need to begin again.

The daily call to the prayer cell is our spiritual gas station, our source of wisdom for service and also our source of creativity. While there is some tendency in human beings to get stuck in ruts of repetitive behavior, we also possess an innate desire to be creative, to try new things and new ways of being in the world. The prayer cell is a metaphor for the daily need to source our creativity in the Creator's energy.

How do we think we can participate in the Wild Divinity who works throughout the universe, if we do not take the time to connect with that Creative Source? Do we not know that there is a Divine Artist within us, just waiting to be consulted? I need only take a moment to look at the intricate details in the purple spots arrayed across the white petals of the orchid on my desk to appreciate the divine artistry of the Creative Source.

A day will come when we are ready to tap into that Divine Artist and her unbelievable skill in making all things new. In her beautiful guide to creativity, *The Artist's Way*, Julia Cameron has inspired many of us with the call to invite the presence of the Divine Source each day with practices like morning pages (writing about any subject for at least three pages each morning) and a hundred other ways to cultivate the connection with the Divine Artist within.

In this artistic way, as we seek wise service and energy for the day's spiritual journey, we do not practice being in the presence of God because we are holier than others, ultra religious, or duty-bound to do the right thing. We engage in daily practices because we need them.

Coming to her Creative Wisdom for daily guidance out of an awareness of our need is quite a different motivation than religious guilt (less-than thinking) or a sense of spiritual superiority (more-than thinking). Monks in the world finally come to an understanding that we need to be in the presence of God's Majesty for our own sake. We cultivate this connection with whichever daily contemplative practices work for us and with the hope of staying near that Presence as we enter our daily lives in the world. We are not being perfectionists, just practical. Monks simply need to be with the Presence each day.

That need brings up another warning about daily practice. When the need we feel for the presence of God turns into an inner clamoring, we are in trouble. If we try too hard to get what we are longing for, our very striving can get in the way. I will illustrate this problem with two stories about my grandson, Sam, who is nearly five.

We drove seven and a half hours this past spring to watch Sam play in his first year of tee ball. To our amazement, our young grandson showed an intensity and passion for playing ball we had never seen before. Even though he and most of the other boys could barely keep that massive glove on their hands, when a ball hit the field he and every one of his teammates would dash after it like Black Friday shoppers chasing a bargain. Even boys standing on the far side of the field would fling themselves on the pile of players converging on the stray ball. I guess their parents had taught them to go after the ball, but none of them had learned that their teammates could also go after the same ball.

When Sam didn't get to that ball first, even if it had hit the ground next to his teammate all the way across the field from him, Sam would throw himself onto the ground, drag himself across the green grass (Why in the world do they make white baseball uniforms for boys?), cross his arms, and pout. He would do it every time a ball was hit into the field!

Sam was demonstrating an incredible desire to get that ball. He wanted to be the one every time. And if he didn't get to it first, his dashed hopes would wreck his world. It was like he might as well just die right there on the field because life was over. Thank God, in a few seconds he would get up, sometimes with the encouragement of his coach, who was immensely patient with Sam's outbursts of emotion, and start the whole process over again. I guess his desire to get that ball the next time helped him shake off the disappointment of not getting it the last time.

Seeing Sam and his four-year-old buddies stampeding after that little white ball reminded me of what it often feels like for spiritual seekers like me. We also go scrambling all over the place trying to catch God in our little mitts. But in spiritual life as in tee ball, trying too hard can get in the way.

We try going to church faithfully every Sunday in hopes of hearing a word from God, or we take time off work to go on that spiritual retreat that promises to give us time alone with God. We read our Bible regularly, attend Scripture study groups, agree to serve on church committees, offer to teach vacation Bible school to the kids even though we know we don't have time, or give God a tip in the offering plate. All this clamoring for God's attention can distract us from finding the thing that will put us in touch with God.

If we are really adventurous we take a trip to India, or to Sedona, Arizona, or to some other holy place in hopes of having a transcendental experience. If we are really desperate to find the holy, we might even join a weekly meditation group, or shave our heads, or buy some prayer beads, or buy a CD or DVD on yoga, or actually commit to attending a class. It's not that any of these things are wrong in themselves, but there's a danger in trying to force spiritual experiences. This is why I have to warn you about turning a daily practice into clamoring. Trying to control spiritual experience and expecting to do it perfectly every time never works—any more than trying to catch that little white ball every time works for Sam.

But there is another way to find the presence of God. It involves dropping our kooky expectations of how and when spiritual experience should come and instead opening to however the Presence finds us. I will say a bit more about willingness and openness in the section on "The Core Contemplative Attitudes" later in this chapter. I have experienced Sam's being in my life in a way that can offer a hint of how openness to spiritual experience can work.

When we are visiting our son, daughter-in-law, and grandson, the morning starts early for me. Sam wakes up before everyone else in the house and finds his way to my bedside. Sometimes he just stands there staring at me with his face about a foot from mine. I am a light sleeper, so it only takes a few seconds for me to sense Sam's expectant presence. On some treasured mornings, he gently lays the sweetest little kiss on my cheek. I am pretty sure this experience is heaven.

This is a real, bona fide practice of the presence of God. But I am in no way in control of what happens. I find that when I am open to that early morning awakening for that moment of treasured tenderness, I am able to receive the gift of the very presence of God. The moment comes as it comes. It is not my job to clamor for it or to try to create it. It is not a reward for being extra dedicated or doing my religious duty. It is pure gift.

So let this be a lesson to all of us. Instead of clamoring across the spiritual tee ball fields of life, chasing spiritual experiences and crying every time we miss the ball, we might ease up and simply open ourselves to experience the sacred moments in any way they come. Our daily practice is our openness, not any attempt to make something happen in a certain way. After all, who could control the coming of heaven through a kiss on the cheek?

BRINGING PRESENCE INTO THE WORLD

"As thou art in church or cell, that same frame of mind carry out into the world, into its turmoil and its fitfulness."

—Meister Eckhart[8]

The monk who is imperfectly practicing the presence each day, who is undergoing the slow-motion transformation from daily contact with God's Majesty, can hardly hide those changes from the world. Having

---

8. Quoted in Kelly, *Testament of Devotion*, 3.

spent time in the Great Love this morning, how could I avoid the outflow of that love toward my wife, son, friends, and strangers during the day? Having been sometimes blessed with a taste of "the peace that passes understanding" (Phil 4:7), how could I help but bring a measure of that peace to work with me? In reality, the act of bringing God's presence with us into the details of our days isn't always easy to remember.

German theologian and mystic Meister Eckhart wrote of bringing God's presence "into the world, into its turmoil and its fitfulness" in a very different time. But his call still rings true today. We should take notice of his verbs: "As thou art" is a statement of being. Here we see that being comes first. "Carry out" is a statement of expression, a kind of doing. Doing follows being.

This is an important order. Contemplation comes before action, and then interpenetrates our service in the world. For a monk in the world, this order is especially important.

Meister Eckhart's "As thou art in church or [prayer] cell" is a phrase that, for the contemplative, speaks of the experience of oneness, of union with the Divine, of the experience of devotion. At our best, contemplatives are *mystics* seeking to experience the Presence and *missionaries* seeking to bring the Presence into the world.

The mystic doesn't stop being a mystic when he or she walks away from private prayer practice. Mystics bring the same desire to experience the Presence into their daily life. Of course, the mystic will sometimes forget to look for he Divine throughout the day. But when the mystic remembers, he or she pauses inwardly, opens the ears and eyes of the spirit, and seeks the next unfolding moment of encounter.

When a contemplative professor takes time to hear a speaking Voice during a meditative walk in the park, the words he hears can become a kind of mantra throughout the workday. Yes, this professor will get caught up in the tasks of getting the kids off to school, giving lectures, grading papers, and all the rest. But the word will return. Because it was spoken from the ground of being, the word will come looking for the contemplative in a moment of awakening later in the day. The Presence will find us out in the world.

Contemplative monks in the world continue to be mystics throughout their day, and because we carry our attention to the Presence within us, we have an innate tendency to share that Presence during the day. We don't have to memorize an evangelistic formula. We don't have to manipulate conversations in some pre-ordained direction. We are missionaries because we are conscious of the Presence while in the company of others, and that presence changes our relationships. There is a kind of resonance as the Presence within us reaches out toward others.

Bowing School

"You must have gone to some kind of bowing school," the chaplain queried. The group facilitator asked him what he meant. "You bow slowly with a sense of real reverence," the chaplain answered. The group's leader was in the middle of a continuing education event for chaplains. He was, in fact, teaching a practice of bowing in reverence towards each group member as a way of communicating, "We see the divine radiance in you."

But the facilitator was not trying to convince the participants to believe in bowing. There was no prepared curriculum to make the class agree that bowing was the right thing to do. The group was being offered the experience of bowing in reverence through practice. It was learning by experience, a way of finding that knowledge which is discovered in the union of heart, body, mind, and soul.

One could say the experience of reverence was simply expressing itself through the facilitator, and the chaplain noticed. There was a resonance between their beings. Resonance is one way a mystic becomes a missionary. Of course, there are as many ways to be evangelistic as there are ways to be monks. But the source of the evangelism, the faith sharing, is the same Presence within. Despite all the negative versions of being evangelistic, an evangelist is really just a messenger of God.

If my contemplative friend Susie has practiced being in the Presence while she is out walking her dogs in the early hours of the morning, she just might pay attention when that Presence nudges her to fix a meal for a sick friend that afternoon. When my pastor friend, Rev. Susan, gets caught up in a Scripture phrase that shimmers off the page during her *lectio divina* practice in the morning, she just might find the very guidance she will need as she offers spiritual direction to a parishioner that afternoon.

Lou established the practice of meditating on a scriptural phrase throughout his week in hopes that his social work practice might be transformed as his attuned spiritual heart senses that his counseling client needs something deeper than a temporary fix. Because Lou has practiced the Presence and brought the Presence into his work, his clients may actually experience transformation through the encounter. He is contemplatively searching his own depths all week long, and in this way becomes an agent of transformation for clients who also need to go deep.

These are just a few ways our monks might appear to be graduates of a bowing school. The chaplain was saying he felt an inner shift from being in contact with reverence. Reverence in one of us will have an effect on others, since we are all interconnected. And Lord knows we all need a lot more contact with inner reverence in this frantic and often violent world. One way of bringing God's presence into our daily lives is to practice bowing in reverence and letting that reverence resonate from us through the day.

SUFFERING WITH COMMUNITY

As Meister Eckhart wrote, there is a lot of "turmoil and fitfulness" in this world. There are orphans living in the streets of New Orleans who have never known real compassion. Their stories too often end in a jail cell or even early death. Another form of orphans are those who have never known any kind of personal relationship with their Maker, never experienced the Divine Presence as their true home. The orphans of our world come from all walks of life. They could be anyone you meet, and any of them could be blessed by an encounter with the Presence through a centered monk in the world.

The contemplative monk is called to see the needs of the world and not look away. The call of this way of life is to be present with one's own suffering as well as that of others. In this unflinching encounter with suffering, monks become brothers and sisters. If they stay near the Presence within, the suffering does not have to overwhelm them forever. The Presence actually gives them the strength to see the suffering as it is without turning away. But entering their own suffering is often painful and resisted by everything in their being.

One of the toughest and darkest times in my life came when I entered high school. I had been part of the same social groups at church and school for most of my life, especially during my junior high years. Although most of the girls I had known from junior high were sent to the same high school I would attend, my guy friends all happened to live in another high school's district. So on the first frightening day of my freshman year, I went looking for the people I knew at lunch. Looking around the cavernous high school cafeteria, I could not see anyone I knew.

Finally, I spotted a group of familiar faces—whew! I pulled up a chair next to all the girls I had known. But being the only boy at a table of fifteen girls felt discomforting. Having always been part of the *in* crowd during junior high, this new situation left me with a terrible feeling of not belonging. For the first time in my memory, a judgmental voice arose in my head saying, "Dude, you don't belong here anymore."

I had never before felt that keen sense of not belonging. And no one had to say it. There was simply an innate understanding that things had changed. Rather than finding the courage to venture into that daunting lunchroom to make new friends, I opted for wandering outside with my little brown lunch sack and eating alone.

I did it again the next day, and the next. Soon I had established the pattern for the daily lunch break: being alone. I was not self-aware. I did not see what I was doing. I expect no one else knew what I was doing either. My fear of going into a room filled with strangers and having to start over in making friends drove me out the door time and again.

That was the start of a very bleak time, my first experience of the depressive mood that comes to some of us when we feel completely alone. A stranger might have seen me sitting down at the end of the parking lot by the bayou and thought, "That guy likes to be alone." But I was really falling into a dark hole each day. I had lost the connection I had always needed. I was learning for the first time what happens on the inside when we lose our sense of belonging. I would call those days suffering without community.

Reading this little vignette might remind you that there are many kinds of suffering worse than a high school kid feeling like he doesn't belong. But suffering is not a contest. And that particular suffering of mine has a point: I do not want to feel alone. I want to belong. In fact, connecting with other people has become a fundamental need of my life.

I now see that within my mission of creating contemplative community is my own need to belong with the human family. I seem to have a powerful desire to experience oneness, union, interconnectedness, and belonging. When I can gather the courage to voice my own struggles, doubts, fears, and needs with someone or with a group, my loneliness begins to heal. My need to be a part of others' lives is met. And perhaps within both of these situations my need to be accepted, valued, and loved as I am also begins to be satisfied.

It might seem a lot more heroic to say that I help to create contemplative groups because it is good for others—and that might be part of the truth. But beneath that, I gather people to practice the presence of God because being with nonjudgmental and accepting people is healing for me. Maybe there is some altruism in there, but I need it as much as anyone who attends.

Communities that share their suffering and their human imperfections have a chance of finding communion: the oneness that heals the soul. Sharing suffering in community is dangerous in a way. We are always risking that someone might press us with advice or criticize how we handled a situation. The group might become uncomfortable hearing our pain and fall into an awkward silence where no one knows what to say. But we also might be embraced, nurtured with comforting words, and reminded that our suffering is exactly why we belong in community with each other.

The men in my weekly ManKind Project group, where men support each other in our inner work, were examining our personal resistance to living our own missions. I realized in my work on myself one evening that what keeps me from sharing my love of contemplative experience, even what inhibits this very act of writing about it, is the mistaken belief that no one else will care about the things that matter the most to me.

A critical voice in my head speaks this lie all the time as though it were truth. It says, "Nobody in this culture cares about cultivating inner stillness or practicing the presence of God." These lies come in many forms, but this critical inner voice has the power to land me on my back, saying, "You see, you really don't belong." I think that voice might have been born in my head when I was going through those dark days of high school, and it has never left.

Recently I was telling my new friend, Dr. Elaine Heath, about my desire to write these stories about contemplative living. We were sitting in the airport waiting for her plane after she had led a weekend workshop. I told Elaine that what shuts down my writing is that sense that nobody in this culture cares about the thing I love the most. Elaine looked at me with the saddest eyes. She didn't get defensive and try to talk me out of that feeling or belief. She just looked at me with sympathetic understanding and never said a word.

It was a painful moment, maybe even an awkward moment, but it was also a blessed moment of suffering in community. I think Elaine's look said she knew what I was feeling. Maybe she knew from her own experience what it is to feel like you don't belong. Maybe she felt compassion for me. Maybe she was joining God in seeing me with sorrow, pity, and simple love. I just know it moved me deeply to be heard and seen in that moment, and a little bit of my own suffering was healed through that sharing.

Suffering in community is not magic. There is no quick fix in giving words to what ails us. There is no mysterious formula for saying just the right words to make everything better. That is why I told you about that little moment with Elaine. It reminds us that it is enough to just be heard and accepted. Acceptance validates and soothes. Understanding and compassion heal. And we do not bring our suffering into community to get the answer. Whether we know it or not, I believe we are wired with a need to commune, to know union in common, and to experience our interconnectedness as the balm of knowing we are not alone.

Participants in our school's classes, practice groups, workshops, and retreats share our lives and our spiritual journeys with each other, suffering in community and expressing our joys to one another. Our community practices God's presence together, is silent together, and tells our stories together. This sharing is at the heart of our adventure in contemplative living.

TWO PLACES WE BELONG

There are two places contemplatives belong, and I got to visit both of them in one day during the fall of 2013. It was a warm and sultry N'awlins Thursday. The morning started out like many mornings in that I started doing emails and attending to some work matters on the computer before I took my time in the stillness of the inner sanctuary. That is always dangerous for me because I can get lost in trying to fit in one more activity before contemplative practice. I finally got to that quiet place, but I only squeezed in about fifteen minutes just before heading out to offer some pastoral counseling and spiritual direction at the office.

I found myself in the first place contemplatives belong from lunchtime until mid-afternoon, as one of the guests invited for an ongoing community-building event on "Faith, Race, and LGBT Social Justice Issues." I had been at a discussion table the first week with a transgendered Italian male who struggled with coming out about his Christian faith in the LGBT community, a gay black male who was a non-theist concerned for LGBT people of faith, a white lesbian friend who is a beloved member of my church, and the black mother of a gay son. This week I sat with a white Jewish lesbian who has a wife and young child, an older white lesbian, a bisexual white female pastor, and a straight black clergywoman concerned about racism, sexism, and LGBT prejudice. There are so many labels we use to describe people, and although I have just used quite a few of them, none of these labels tells you who these new friends really are.

So where, exactly, is the first place contemplatives belong? The answer is: Wherever there are people who have been excluded by others. A Christian contemplative seeks to follow the Jesus who always preferred to spend time with the outcasts of society. Aren't there enough gospel stories showing how outcasts were his closest companions? And didn't Jesus manage to also get himself excluded and eventually killed by the religious people who were doing the excluding?

Christian contemplatives who spend enough time living in the presence of God will invariably find themselves being led by the Great Love to seek out these excluded people. We will find them sooner or later and begin new friendships. My example above is simply one version of the story, one collection of the excluded. The excluded can be the elderly, introverts, the lower socioeconomic classes of the American capitalist caste system, the disabled, people who are too fat, too thin, too tall, or too short, people of any color besides white, people of any other religious faith, people of no particular faith, people of any sexual orientation besides straight, people with odd hair, strange faces, or just about any distinguishing feature that isn't the norm. I could go on and on.

So why do Christian contemplatives belong wherever these outcasts are found? In short, because of our ongoing conversion. Jesus is just not done with us yet. There are plenty of Christians who are content with their belief in Jesus. They might think their initial salvation is the end of the story. They got their salvation, so what else is there?

But the Christian contemplative is a long way from being done. We have just started cooking in God's pot, and she has barely begun to turn up the heat. She's just got so much to teach us and so many layers of transformation to bring us through. If Jesus is still hanging around on this planet, and I believe he is present in the form of the Christ Spirit, then a Christian contemplative wants to be in those places where Jesus and *all* his friends are welcome. Forming those friendships with the excluded alongside Jesus is right where our transformation can happen. It was so very clear to me in these last few weeks that the mix of people from every possible background I found at the "Faith, Race, and LGBT Social Justice Issues" event is exactly where the Christ Spirit will be showing up. That's where I want to be.

So let's be careful and clear here. I am not trying to create one more exclusive group. I am not saying Christian contemplatives are superior. I am not saying that we all need to be seated around the LGBT table as though this were the only table. But I am saying that if you find yourself as a Christian strangely drawn towards some people who are usually excluded by others, you just might be a Christian contemplative.

Why are friendships with excluded people an indicating trait of the contemplative? Because we just can't be in the presence of God, the Creator of all of God's children, day in and day out, without gradually seeing how all of God's children are part of us too. And if we keep spending time in the presence of Love, which flows into us and through us over and over, then that Great Love will lead us into loving relationships with those who are ignored or mistreated by others.

A Christian Scripture says this most simply and clearly: "God is love. Whoever lives in love lives in God, and God in him [or her] . . . If anyone says, 'I love God,' yet hates his brother, he is a liar. For anyone who does not love his brother [or sister, elder, person of color, gay, disabled, poor, etc.], whom he has seen, cannot love God, whom he has not seen" (1 John 4:16–20 NIV). So, when you find yourself loving your excluded neighbor, you are engaged in loving God. The first place contemplatives belong is where we can love the excluded, wherever we can find them and in whatever form they exist.

Then where is the second place contemplatives belong? That was the other place I visited that day. A small group of young adults gathered a few weeks ago to begin a weekly contemplative practice group. They met in a rundown old manor house with fading white plaster and large green shutters at the edge of the French Quarter, where the sounds of prostitutes calling in the streets mingled with the wail of faraway sirens and the nearer noises of locusts chirping and the breeze rattling the palm trees on the back porch. These young people had invited me to lead the gathering for centering prayer for the evening. Now, I have to say the word "lead" kind of throws me when it comes to the practice of contemplation, because the practice is really about letting go of striving, surrendering our efforts, and turning our heart into a welcoming space for a living God. I believe leading this practice means saying as little as possible about it and entering into the actual practice of the presence of God. Then, once we have practiced for at least twenty minutes, leading for me means inviting the group to share their experience.

So on this rainy afternoon, I said a few words about my own practice, and these young contemplatives shared a bit about the formats they had experimented with so far. Then we began. As usual, I focused on my breath as my sacred word—that is, the focus I use to bring my attention back to opening my heart to God when my thoughts try to skitter off to their usual distractions. I treasured the simple feel of the breeze. I noticed again how we can feel a spiritual consciousness of God's presence and a sense of oneness with the group even while our minds also notice the birds, locusts, sirens, and calls from the street. There is an ebb and flow of attention to thoughts and sounds, letting that awareness go for a second, and then noticing them again.

This is the second place where a contemplative belongs: sitting with others in an imperfect practice of the presence of God, and then if the group chooses, sharing the experience with the group. One of the guys said his experience felt like being a baby dipped into water, symbolizing how we are not in control and that the Divine is all around us. One of the young ladies explained that she finds the presence of the others makes it easier to practice than when she tries meditation alone. I shared my favorite quote from Thomas Kelly, which reminds me that "deep within us all there is an amazing sanctuary of the soul,"[9] and how it relaxes me to remember the simple home of God is already near.

Soon it was time to go. The rain had stopped. The locusts were singing sweetly. The prostitutes still called out in the street, but in our state of contemplative communion, they may as well have been saying, "Remember we are God's children too." So there you have it, a day when I got to visit both of the places where contemplatives belong: making friends with some of God's excluded children and practicing the presence of God with other imperfect contemplatives. Not a bad way to spend a warm and sultry Thursday in the city called N'awlins.

THE CORE CONTEMPLATIVE ATTITUDES

Perhaps it is time in this story to explore what it means to be a contemplative in another way, the way of cultivating contemplative attitudes. Contemplative communities can start getting a grasp of how to be contemplatives by practicing a core set of attitudes adopted through the centuries by contemplatives who came before us. I discovered the following attitudes through an extensive study of select Christian mystics in writing my dissertation on

9. Ibid.

the subject in 1992. This list of core contemplative attitudes is not intended to be exhaustive, but remains open for additional reflection:

Seeking Union: Spiritual communion, or seeking oneness with God's presence, is the central spiritual attitude for contemplatives.[10]

Spiritual Awareness: Spiritual awakening and awareness of the Presence involves being ready, expectant, and attentively listening without grasping or striving to control.[11]

Willingness/Openness: We surrender our will and open to God's will and presence, which centering prayer refers to as consenting to God's presence and action within.[12]

Honesty: We summon the courage to face ourselves, God, and reality in the light of truth.[13]

Humility: We accept the truth of who we are.[14]

Simplicity: We singularly focus our hearts on God.[15]

---

10. "It is not Thy gifts that I seek and desire but Thyself, and I can be content with nothing less" (Brother Lawrence, *Practice of the Presence*, 92). "Lord, God, when you send me elsewhere than into your presence, give me then another you; for you are my comfort and I want only you" (Eckhart, *Meister Eckhart*, 48).

11. Contemplation is "essentially a listening in silence, an expectancy" (Merton, *Contemplative Prayer*, 90). "God is present to us. But are we present to Him?" (Pennington, *Daily We Touch Him*, 15).

12. "For those who have surrendered themselves completely to God, all they are and do has power" (de Caussade, *Abandonment to Divine Providence*, 60). The essence of contemplative spirituality is "the courage to open oneself to mystery" (May, *Will and Spirit*, 32).

13. "No one has known God who has not known himself—fly to the soul, the secret place of the Most High" (Eckhart, quoted in May, *Man's Search for Himself*, 222). We should visit "the room of self-knowledge" in the interior castle because "His Majesty wishes us to take the means and understand ourselves" (Teresa of Avila, *Interior Castle*, 3:73).

14. "One cannot begin to face the real difficulties of the life of prayer and meditation unless one is first perfectly content to be a beginner and really experience himself as one who knows little or nothing" (Merton, *Contemplative Prayer*, 37). We come into solitude "in the presence of our Lord with empty hands, naked, vulnerable, useless, without much to show, prove, or defend" (Nouwen, *Making All Things New*, 76). "If you are humble, nothing will touch you, neither praise nor disgrace, because you know what you are" (Mother Teresa, *Jesus, the Word*, 191).

15. "A simple reaching out directly towards God is sufficient" (Johnston, *Cloud of Unknowing*, 133). "It is not necessary to have great things to do. I turn my little omelet in the pan for the love of God" (Brother Lawrence, *Practice of the Presence*, 81).

Classical and contemporary contemplative authors have emphasized these core spiritual attitudes to define the nature of the contemplative life. These attitudes are intertwined. They move in and out of each other organically. For example, in practice I cannot cultivate honesty, seeing myself as I really am, without humility, accepting myself as I am. To do so would be to stir up self-judgment. Opening to my own spiritual awakening and the discovery of God's presence within does little good if I am not also moving toward an attitude of willingness to follow the lead of that Presence. Otherwise my attitude might be telling God, "Thanks for showing up, but I don't really need your help in how to live my life."

The contemplative authors also use two primary metaphors to describe the spiritual dependence of the divine-human relationship: the parent-child relationship and the giver-receiver relationship. Put simply, this relationship is like saying, "Thanks for showing up *and* boy, do I need your help."

As a contemplative community, we can use these attitudes as touchstones for our own practice as contemplatives. Without judgment, we might ask ourselves simple questions like, "How am I seeking oneness with the presence of God today?" and "How am I bringing the Presence with me as I serve in the wild world?"

We cannot force mystical or even spiritual experiences, of course, but we can practice the attitudes that help us be ready when the Presence comes near. For Albert Einstein, that included a fundamental stance of wonder and awe in life.[16] We can also engage in the spiritual practices that help us live in readiness for the Holy to come find us. I may be so bold as to say no one will encounter oneness with the One regularly who does not have a steady practice to help them hear the knocking at the inner door.

BEING IN THE PRESENCE: LISTENING IN STILLNESS

"When you pray, go into your inner room . . ."

(MATT 6:6 NASB)

In our early years of forming a School for Contemplative Living we adopted an informal motto to summarize our calling: "Listening in

---

16. As Einstein explained, "The most beautiful and profound emotion we can experience is the sensation of the mystical . . . He [or she] to whom this emotion is a stranger, who can no longer wonder and stand rapt in awe, is as good as dead" (Einstein, "The World as I See It," 3–7).

stillness, serving in joy." We felt the way God was calling us involved two primary facets: contemplation and service. So the following sections offer a hint of what this union of contemplation and action, of prayer and work, means to us.

Practicing the presence of God is a fundamental in the call to be a contemplative. This is not some command or law that no one can keep, or just another rule dictated by a demanding God. Practice is an invitation to come and see, to experience the Sacred in daily life. So our choice of practices that are not burdensome, but which fit our own personalities, needs, and spiritual receptivity, is very important.

As the Sufi poet Rumi says, "There are hundreds of ways to kneel and kiss the ground."[17] So it is that there are endless ways to practice the Presence. The question is: What practice most helps me be present to the Presence? In recent years, our still-forming contemplative community has shared the following practices: *lectio divina* (sacred reading), *scriptio divina* (sacred writing), *visio divina* (sacred seeing or art as prayer), *audio divina* (sacred hearing or music as prayer), *conversatio divina* (sacred conversations), walking meditation through labyrinths, and nature mysticism through walking meditation in nature, dance (body prayer in the spirituality of movement), sacred yoga (another form of devotional body prayer), and centering prayer. Some details are included in the section on "Ten Ways to Meditate" in chapter 5.

The ways of practicing the presence of God are important in that they need to match our own personality and need. But the main thing is that we do practice praying in that secret, inner chamber. When his disciples asked him how to pray, Jesus gave clear instruction in telling his disciples, "When you pray, go into your inner room." First he presumed we *would* pray, and then he pointed us inward. Whatever specific practices we select as our way of being in God's presence, it seems that the main thing for Jesus was knowing that we need to come to God in the inner room–a secret or private experience.

---

17. Rumi, *The Essential Rumi*, 36.

BRINGING PRESENCE: SERVING WITH JOY IN THE WILD WORLD

"Whatever you did for one of the least of these brothers of mine, you did for me"

(Matt 25:40 NIV)

Practicing awareness of the Presence brings us into the heart of God. This means we will sometimes be encountering the Great Love like waves lapping at the shore. A contemplative cannot help but be filled at times with this Great Love, and thus cannot avoid sharing that love in travelling through the wild world. Fullness, even in our human emptiness, brings a quality of joy into daily life. This lifestyle is a long way from trying to serve in our own strength, burning out, and going empty and dry, as caregivers so often do.

On this contemplative path, we are being filled by the presence of the love, joy, and wise guidance we all need. So we seek to serve with our sisters and brothers from that place of fullness. Our calling is twofold: First, to be in the presence of God through formal and informal spiritual practice, and second, to share that presence as we walk about and serve the world. But this sharing isn't necessarily saying words about God. On this path, we seek to be in the Presence and to simply bring this inner Presence with us in joyful service.

This brings me to the five principles of contemplative living and service that have emerged from this lifestyle of living in stillness and serving in joy. I believe these principles can be applied to any arena of service. We begin in the practice of sourcing. "Sourcing" is my word for drawing our life's breath, radiant energy, inner direction, wise guidance, and compassionate action from the Source of Life within us. Sourcing is returning to the ground of our being to be in the Source of Life for a few moments. This is an experience of oneness. I believe serving in joy requires sourcing *before* we take action. This is another way of saying contemplation comes before deeds. That is the first principle.

I also have come to the awareness that to serve in joy, I need to source as much as I serve. That is the second principle. This means I am not able to serve the world with joy if I only spend a few minutes in God's presence every once in a while. In stressful times, the wise servant spends even more time practicing the Presence than usual. I know this seems impossible, and for this reason the second principle calls for the third principle: I need to practice my sourcing *while* I am serving.

Let's say I work a forty-hour week. It would seem absurd to say I need to source as much as I serve, for that would imply that I needed to meditate forty hours a week as well. While that might be possible for some hermit monks within a monastery, I have never met a monk in the world who could come close to that many hours of solitude. So our best practice is to continue sourcing our lives in God's presence *while* we are serving.

When I am listening to a friend named Willie, who lived on the streets for two years, as he describes his joy over receiving his own apartment through government-subsidized housing and seeing his happiness in getting off the streets for the first time in two years, I want to pay attention to him. But I am also keeping my heart open to God's presence within him and within me. I am listening with the ears of my heart. I am open to any guidance that might arise if God wants to teach me something through Willie. I am keeping my inner ears open for some guidance about how to respond. I am seeking God's presence in the midst of this ministry moment. I am *sourcing while serving*. In my best moments of practicing this way, sourcing and service become a seamless, continuous stream.

Paradoxically, the fourth principle involves the Great Walk-away. If I stand any chance of serving in joy, I also have to learn to *walk away* from other people's needs on a daily basis. I have seen far too many caregivers who are perpetually burning themselves out by working six or seven days a week, working overtime, or agreeing to a hectic pace of constant emergencies. I have tried that lifestyle too. I have had too many interrupted conversations with friends who are doctors, nurses, social workers, chaplains, and other caregivers who believe they have no permission to speak without a beeper dictating their every moment. The same has been true with some pastor friends for whom the office email or cell phone is always the first priority.

In the principle of the Great Walk-away I must establish ways during my day of service to let go of the needs of others. I must eat a meal without answering other calls. I must stop and take a few long breaths. I must pause and say a prayer, or light a candle, or step into a chapel, or create a ringtone on my phone that plays a hymn, or set my watch to chime on the hour so I remember to drop what I am doing to just be for a moment. In a hundred ways, I simply must step away from the needs of the crowd to tune back into the One True Voice, the voice of wise guidance. If I do not practice walking away for moments through the day I will still be serving, but it will not be from joy, and my resentments will likely be secretly growing as I wear myself out.

The fifth principle of serving in joy is learning to live on the *liminal threshold*. The term "liminal space" comes from Celtic spirituality. This is a term for sacred spaces both on the planet and within. We are crossing a liminal threshold when we awaken to the sacredness of a moment after we had been lost in thought. Maybe we were in a conversation, and someone's words finally caught our attention. We realize we had not been present. But suddenly we are there and engaged in the special meaning of what is happening. A moment becomes holy.

We are also crossing a liminal threshold when we enter a place and the setting speaks to us of something holy. Lighting a candle can be a simple way of experiencing liminal space. When a group gathers for centering prayer and someone lights several candles, this symbolic gesture says, "We are entering sacred space." When our men's group prepares to begin our evening of sharing our life experiences, we take time to cross over into sacred space by facing the four directions as well as the sky, the earth, and the space within. We light a bundle of sweet grass and pass the smoke across our bodies to initiate our awareness of sacred time.

Mystics take this practice one step further. We want to live our lives *on* the liminal threshold. We want to stay in touch with the sacredness of the moment as often as we can. We want to be open to mystical moments *while* we are serving the world. In this way, we are seeking to awaken our spiritual sensibilities so that anywhere we walk can become holy ground. Perhaps we will have the opportunity to visit special places in the world one day and experience their sacred significance. But the fifth principle is to treat the very ground under our feet right now as holy, this moment of our lives as sacred, and this opportunity to be in service as a liminal threshold—a home of the living God.

To review, the five principles of contemplative service in joy are sourcing before serving, sourcing as much as serving, sourcing while serving, practicing the Great Walk-away, and living on the liminal threshold. Contemplatives do not use these principles as just one more impossible standard. These are principles we hope to practice as best we can, when we can, though our hope is not always our reality. When we do remember, some simple and wonderful moments of serving in joy can appear.

Stories of Serving in Joy

"To postpone my dream no longer
But do at last what I came here for
And waste my heart on fear no more."

—JOHN O'DONOHUE[18]

Today, my Buddhist friend Shannon shared her *metta* (loving-kindness) chants as a kind of call and response in our Christian worship service at Parker United Methodist Church. She sang a phrase with her quiet, pure voice, and then we imitated. The phrases were about ideas like cultivating loving-kindness, and showing reverence, and being a world community. How delicious is that—a pure-hearted and loving Buddhist leading a group of followers of Jesus in a call to compassion?

My friend was doing what our monks aspire to: serving in joy. There was something so right about letting Shannon lead us with a heart that was as open as a child's. For despite her PhD and her brilliant mind, as she told us, "The way is a heart thing." She was being a heartfelt child leading adults, as it should be. She was a follower who was being a leader. She was the insecure one showing her courage. She was the quiet one giving voice to the heart.

Some voice of the Divine Joy was guiding her to overcome her fears, to transcend her sense of inadequacy as a Buddhist, to put aside the worrisome nag of a mental critic telling her she had no right to speak about either Buddhism or Christianity. She let me read quotes from Jesus and Buddha and ask her questions about the parallel meanings. In those moments, joy was winning the battle with the critical voice that lives in all of our heads. And doesn't this world need more victories like that?

So what would happen if we all let the Presence of an inner joy guide us into leading and serving in the world? What would happen if you took that next step in answering your calling because Joy said to start now?

Alisha, our contemplative friend, brought her joy among us when she offered to share a liturgical dance in a worship service for the first time in years. Here in our little rag-tag band of inadequate followers, Alisha found the courage, despite her fears, to blossom in the middle of her new friends. She toyed with the idea for some time. She mentioned

---

18. O'Donohue, *Bless the Space*, 9. O'Donohue's collection of poetic blessings serves as a guide to the sacredness of daily life, especially the lines above taken from "A Morning Offering."

it in passing in an email to me with a subtle hope that I wouldn't catch it so she would be off the hook, and yet she felt that longing to share something beautiful if I did. She postponed doing it for a few months and put the intimidating image of dancing in public on a slow simmer. But over time, the passion of her courage arose. The Joy stood up and said, "Let's do it now."

Alisha served in joy, and the words and music of the song she chose by Christian singer Larnelle Harris, her fluid and expressive movements, and especially her sincere heart reflected in her face all brought me to tears from the moment Alisha began. At first it was a trickle of tears, but before long I was weeping. In case you haven't been through this, it is very messy to try to stand up and speak to a group when your eyes are too wet to see straight, and your voice is cracked, and your nose is running like a faucet.

What had me by the throat? It was overpowering joy. Joy is like a benign infection: It spreads from the inside of one person to another, and soon it can even infect a whole group at once. Beauty had me in its grasp. Alisha is a beautiful woman, but the beauty in this dance was the joy that lit her face and the raw courage I saw in someone who had spent months trying to work up to sharing her gift.

This kind of beauty is that of a rose when it spends months preparing to unfurl when the time is just right. This beauty is what happens in spring when the cypress trees just outside our window pull the life force up from the roots of winter's dormancy to bloom in rich iridescent green fronds. Such was the unfurling beauty of Alisha as she let joy dance freely among us.

Another form of serving in joy from the same Sunday worship hour at our Parker United Methodist Church was much more subtle than singing *metta* chants or dancing. Lou had a light bulb go off in his head months before when he envisioned a Christian worship service to honor the presence of the Dalai Lama in New Orleans in the spring of 2013. Lou had proposed that we host a Christian-Buddhist dialogue for the weekend when the Dalai Lama was in town, and so we did.

When Lou offered to read a children's story written by a Jewish rabbi who had captured God's true name as the One in her story, I hesitated. I feared we were cramming too much into a single worship service. After all, going over our usual hour meant some people would have to leave early to rush off to their next engagement or that others might complain at having so much of their valuable time taken up.

Lou hung in there until a little nudge came to my ears saying, "A reading on God's oneness is perfect for a day of celebrating the aspects of oneness between our faiths." Lou had found a wonderful joy residing in a very creative story, and it turned out that reading fit our service like a warm hand holding another in friendly embrace.

The real joy to me was in Lou's wisdom to pass out the copies of the story, read it to us from the story book with picture illustrations, and then just sit down so we could let the closing truth of God's name of "One" sink in. He knew our time would be limited. He knew my concern about sliding into a lengthy discussion as we usually do with a poem or piece of art. So he just offered his gift, resisted the temptation to add more words to the story, and sat down.

Lou sat down as a service of joy. Joy does not have to hog the limelight like preachers in churches usually do. Joy does not have to plumb the depths of every possible meaning or have the answer to every question. Sometimes a service of joy means offering less instead of more, like writing those "shitty first drafts," as Anne Lamott calls them,[19] and then creatively carving away half of what we might have said. Sometimes joy keeps things simple by speaking up and then just sitting down, leaving time for a quiet inner response.

On a very special day, Shannon, Alisha, and Lou all served us in joy within a single worship service, and it just made my heart want to burst open. I just sat there saying to myself, "How did I get to be here in such a fascinating, diverse, imaginative, gifted, and inclusive spiritual community?" Joy was welling up in my heart throughout the service and the divine joy is still with me now as I write these stories for you.

Here are a few more examples of serving in joy. Millie sat with me at a coffee shop on a bright summer morning and asked my blessing for her to adopt a ministry to animals as her mission in life. She had seen invitations in our church bulletin to serve with our homeless hospitality ministry or children's ministry and was feeling guilty that she was not interested in such things. She wondered whether service to animals would be an acceptable ministry in the world. Maybe the real question underneath it all was whether God loves us for being the beings we are, or if we have to be like others to get God's approval.

When Millie started describing her joy in caring for chickens in her backyard, in loving her family dog, and in connecting with the local

---

19. Lamott, *Bird by Bird*, 21.

SPCA to attend to the needs of stray dogs with her youngest daughter Emma, she was demonstrating what it means to serve in joy. Service is not supposed to be drudgery, duty, or guilt-based determination to make ourselves do what we *should* do. Service is God's gift to us as we discover unique ways to help the world in ways that also bless us. Service is about mutuality and spreading the joy all around.

Elizabeth noticed a couple at her Catholic church who remained in their seats as everyone else went forward for the Eucharist week after week. Eventually Elizabeth sensed that something must have been preventing the couple from taking part in communion. Elizabeth's intuition told her they were trying to honor one of the church's rules about who can and who can't partake of the Lord's body.

This loss hurt Elizabeth. She prayed for guidance in case a day might come when the way would open for her to invite the couple to come on forward and join in. Soon she bumped into the man she had hoped to see. Without hesitating, Elizabeth spoke from the joy inside saying, "I noticed you all weren't going up for communion. You know that is the Lord's table, and he would be so very pleased if you joined in the celebration. He welcomes everyone."

The man mumbled a phrase of embarrassed explanation that Elizabeth couldn't quite catch. She thought it was something about having been divorced. But within two weeks she saw the couple go forward to taste the body and blood of their Lord. This brought great joy into Elizabeth's heart. As she told our small group the story, you could see the radiant joy in her face. Even the telling was bringing the radiance from that first moment of joy into the group. This was Elizabeth's latest form of joyful service, a moment when she spoke up and offered the Lord's invitation to everyone, regardless of any denomination's rules about who is worthy.

She reminded me of my encounters with a patient named John while my wife was undergoing radiation for breast cancer. John was at the end of his latest round of radiation to treat metastatic bone cancer. Not much else could be done to stave off the cancer's advance since John had already been through four years of surgeries, bone marrow transplants, chemo, and radiation. He had decided to spend his last days living his life, not being incapacitated by more treatments.

John had enjoyed a long career as a truck driver until the pain from bone cancer treatments caused him to quit work and file bankruptcy. He had loved life on the road and told me about when he drove a large tank of hydrogen onto the grounds of the Kennedy Space Center. Giving up that work had been pretty depressing for him. But his weakness and pain had left him no choice.

John responded to my interested questions, as if he liked being able to tell his story. He went into detail on the various phases of his treatments, what had gone wrong, how he had survived infections, and even once woken from surgery on a respirator. It was natural to admire his warrior-like nature in agreeing to undergo so much for the chance to live, and I told him so. It was easy to feel compassion for John and his courageous decision to quit the treatments so he could live out the rest of his days in peace. He spoke of gaining the strength to take walks in our parks around New Orleans and the joy of seeing the trees and flowers again.

I waited for John on the morning that was to have been his last radiation treatment. I was looking forward to connecting with him one more time. I asked God to use me if there was any simple way I could offer him one last blessing on his big day. I looked for John at the regular time, but he was nowhere to be found. I never found out what happened to John, and I was sad that I couldn't connect with him one last time.

I wondered later why that was. Why had those random encounters with a stranger in a radiation waiting room become important? I guess there is a kind of simple joy that emerges when two human beings share the stories of our lives. The interconnectedness of our beings becomes a felt reality, and that seems to let the joy arise. I think the sadness from missing John on his last day and missing the chance to wish him well or to celebrate the finishing of a long, hard road was one more proof that we need each other. That is the kind of joyful service we aspire to.

Willie was one of our homeless friends who appeared to be on the verge of finding a place to live through a Section 8 housing program. Willie wore a broad smile that beamed out from an obvious internal joy. How could a man with persistent mental illness and no place to live still keep such a reservoir of joy inside? Willie did just that. He could probably teach a course in living with joy no matter the circumstances.

When I would ask him how things were going that week, Willie would always say, "First, how is your wife?" Because I had shared prayer requests about my wife's cancer treatments, many of our homeless friends who we saw each week through our Good Samaritan/Open Table ministry wanted to know how my "madam" was. But why did they care? When they had nothing, and every single day they lived with the question of where they would sleep that night and what they would eat, how could they care about the wife of a man who has all he needs? I certainly didn't know why Willie wanted to put my own family concerns before his own.

So here is my theory: I think Willie and some of his friends learn to find a security deeper than circumstances as they travel the streets of New Orleans every day. I think they develop a profound faith based on the experience of contentment with so little. Some of them have developed character from many days of learning what really matters in relationships and a kind of joy based in the freedom to decide how to respond to whatever life throws their way. The bottom line is that people like Willie actually *know* God face to face, in radical trust, and this knowing is a source of great joy larger than anything else in their lives.

If we were wiser, we would appoint people like Willie as our teachers. Instead of treating him like some poor man who needs our help, enlightenment might lead us to bow down in his presence like students to a master. This is not some romantic notion, some imagined dream that overlooks Willie's serious difficulties. It is looking beneath the surface to see a teacher of true joy beneath the scruffy clothes and the obvious hunger for food and shelter. This is joyful service in reverse, seeing the innate dignity under the indignities of a hard life on the street. This is realizing that we have so much we could learn if only we could switch roles and receive the gifts of the teachers of joy.

Serving without Joy

But just to be clear about how disastrous things can be when joy is not leading our service, I better tell you one more story that happened in our school's ministry with homeless friends. Men and women from several denominations gather each Tuesday afternoon at the Mount Zion United Methodist Church to make friends and offer services to our poorest neighbors. We are people from several races and ideologies all working together. We do not always respond to people in the same ways. We are all learning about love and service, and that includes some of our homeless neighbors who serve alongside the rest of us.

Sam really lost it one week and the results weren't pretty. Sam leads a group of African-American friends from the Mount Zion church. They dispense the shelter vouchers purchased for our poorest friends from the streets, and sometimes they also hand out new donated socks or underwear. Most of the cost of the shelter vouchers, toiletries, food for two meals a month, and donated clothing comes from the Rayne United Methodist Church. All told, the people from that church donate about $1,500 each month for these services. They are very generous, and some even cook meals and serve them too. On other weeks, people from other churches prepare meals, help serve food, dispense toiletries, and occasionally bring used clothing. People from Mount Zion donate another $400 a month for additional shelter vouchers in addition to offering their building and paying the utilities for the ministry.

Sam has a passionate desire to serve the needs of our homeless neighbors. But on his bad days Sam can get caught up in standing against the same poor people we are serving if he thinks someone is being ungrateful or trying to break the rules. He can be amazingly playful one minute and can become angrily reactive a minute later.

One week we were nearing the end of distributing shelter vouchers, meals, and toiletries with our homeless friends when Sam was helping to put things away because he does not like for our other poor neighbors who have a place to stay to ask for anything but the leftover meals. These neighbors come in after the homeless people have been served. Perhaps out of the fear that the whole neighborhood would come to his church asking for aid, leaving none for the people without homes, he gets a bit indignant when locals with even a temporary place to stay ask for anything else.

Alvin came in with the second group of people who did not need shelter vouchers. For the first time in many months he had found a temporary place to stay with an acquaintance, so he was just very hungry. He possessed nothing else but the bike he used to ride around town. Not realizing he had just become part of a different group in Sam's mind, Alvin asked Sam for some of the clean socks.

We had brought Sam a hundred pair of new socks to share, and he had many pairs left. He hoped to save them for other homeless friends the following week. But Alvin had just crossed an invisible line by having a place to stay, and Sam felt he no longer needed new socks as much as others might. In his passion to protect things for the homeless, Sam's joy had left the building, and he became indignant that Alvin would dare ask for those socks. Alvin became just as indignant that Sam would not spare such a simple thing as a clean pair of socks.

Soon their voices rose enough to draw my attention away from the conversation I was having with Willie on the other side of the room. I excused myself and walked over behind Alvin, a tall African-American man with diabetes, a broken ankle in a cast, and a persistent mental illness always brewing just under the surface.

I put my hands on Alvin's shoulders, taking a risk that he might just turn and elbow me in the face. I whispered in his ear to calm down, as he was practically shouting back at Sam. Alvin kept on. Sam kept on. Things were escalating as Sam came out from behind the table as if he wanted a fistfight. Can you sense how there was no joy to be found between them?

Like a parent separating two children before things get worse, I gently placed my hands on Alvin's shoulders to guide him towards the door. He let me guide him but kept looking over his shoulder to say, "I can't believe this man won't even share a simple pair of socks!" Halfway across the room, a volunteer from our school saw the situation and came over to place a plate of food in Alvin's hands, which is what he had really come for to start with.

As Sam's anger escalated he made a nonsensical threat, saying something sarcastic like, "I am the devil." Alvin asked me, "Can you believe he said that?" As I got him to the open door to exit, Sam threw in one last taunt and called Alvin a name. Then he criticized me for not snatching the plate of food out of Alvin's hands and accused me of making things worse.

In a miraculous moment, Alvin did not throw his plate of food in Sam's face but just yelled out in total exasperation, "Can you believe this devil of a man would call me that in his own church?" He let me keep guiding him outside until we found a place where he could put his food on one of our clothing tables to eat. He began to simmer down. Alvin kept voicing his dismay over the next thirty minutes until he was settled enough for me to step away and help to close down the ministry for the day.

Maybe we have to encounter the terrible feeling of the absence of joy to know how gifted we are when humans can gather in shared joy. I did not know what would happen when we would all gather again the next week. I do not run the universe. But I do know the rugged path of serving where there is no joy, and it is in no way pretty. I was praying that violent words would not turn into violent actions in a city already overrun with acts of violence every day.

I wondered if I would find the courage to sit down with Sam and discuss what happened, ask some questions, listen, humbly admit my own frailties, and speak truth about our common need to serve from joy. Service gets messy sometimes. It's obviously not all sweet-smelling roses and pretty green cypress fronds. I wondered if I could cultivate enough of the presence of Joy to let it lead me as I had that conversation.

The spark of God is in Sam, and Alvin, and me. So if I had become all self-righteous like I wanted to, I would have been missing the spark in Sam (although that was happening in my mind through most of my meditation and yoga the following morning, for I had a strong case of "See how I am right and you are wrong" infecting my thoughts). If I had gone limp and passive, then I would have been missing the spark of God in me too. And passivity invites bullies to keep ruling the world.

Right in the middle of that mess I wished someone could tell me how to bring the joy into that follow-up conversation. Just writing out such stories does not mean I have the answers. I truly don't know how to invite joy into the midst of conflict, how to bow together in reverence when the situation usually aggravates the tension already present. I don't always know how to stand in truth, speak truth, and still have some fun in the process.

Monks in the world are not necessarily people with answers. We question ourselves as much as the next person, and maybe even more so. But we are seeking to ask good questions, like "How do I stay near the joy when I meet with Sam?" In that case, I was also asking a hard question for a man who does not like to rock the boat. Would I be the guy to speak up in saying that we would not let this great ministry turn hateful? Would I surrender the whole situation into the hands of a Power greater than myself, who just might have plans bigger than my own? If I did, if I let go of the outcome as best I could, I was hoping the Great Joy would find a way to do her good work in us all.

When I called Sam to discuss the event, he did not want to meet with me in person. Over the phone he said he appreciated my concern to know how he was doing after the drama of that event. He felt things would simmer down by the following week. He agreed to treat Alvin with friendship if he should show up the next week, though he doubted Alvin would return. Sam believed Alvin was the kind of guy who liked to break the rules and then get upset with people.

Who knows, as a former principal from the New Orleans public schools, maybe Sam sensed a troublemaker in Alvin. Maybe he wanted to keep Alvin from getting out of control. All I knew is that I didn't want the whole ministry of hospitality to turn into a street fight. I wanted us to work together to create a safe place where love and simple joy could lead us. I spoke my part and Sam spoke his part, and we carried on the following week. Regardless of the outcome, seeing Sam's encounter with Alvin reminded me of the importance of serving in joy, for to do otherwise is to do good work badly. I try to keep this in mind throughout my daily practice.

More on Contemplative Service

Service as a contemplative can take a million forms, and you can see many of these forms of serving in the world in the people who come into our school. Yet there are some distinctive characteristics of contemplative service we can use to guide us. By following this path of service, we might avoid some of the pitfalls of trying to do good in ways that end up causing harm.

Contemplative Outreach, the international organization created to help spread the practice of centering prayer, has created a series of seventeen helpful booklets called the Contemplative Life Program to guide contemplatives in various aspects of seeking the contemplative path. I would highly recommend reading the booklet on contemplative service, for I believe it captures some important principles for serving the world in joy, and our group benefited greatly from studying it together in the fall of 2013.

One of the first principles of contemplative service is Thomas Keating's statement that "the effectiveness of every action depends on the source from which it springs."[20] To me, Father Keating is saying we will do little good in the world if we are not first sourced in God. He expressed the same idea as follows: "Action and contemplation have to go together so one doesn't get ahead of one's inner resources."[21] When I get ahead of my inner resources I become irritable, often toward the very people I want to serve. This life is not intended to be straining, draining, overworking, over-doing, or violent to our own needs.

Another principle from the *Contemplative Service* booklet concerns the importance of cultivating true humility as we seek to love our neighbors. Contemplative service means our role is that "of [a] servant . . . We

---

20. Quoted in Fitzpatrick-Hopler et al., *Contemplative Service*, 29.

21. Thomas Keating, interview by Rich Heffern, "Rewards of 'Divine Therapy,'" *National Catholic Reporter*, July 22, 2011.

no longer need to be seen, to be first, to be recognized, to be useful or to be in control."[22]

Thomas Merton offers especially wise guidance for contemplatives who want to share their experience or lifestyle with others. This form of contemplative evangelism has been discussed elsewhere, but Merton offers remarkable insight which bears reading:

> The best way to prepare ourselves for the possible vocation of sharing contemplation with others is not to study how to talk and reason about contemplation, but to withdraw ourselves as much as we can from talk and argument and retire into the silence and humility of heart in which God will purify our love of all its human imperfections. Then in His own time He will set our hand to the work He wants us to do, and we will find ourselves doing it without being quite able to realize how we got there, or how it all started.[23]

Since the authors of the contemplative service booklet tell us that "the greatest obstacle to service is the desire to be successful,"[24] Merton's guidance fits perfectly with the call to go to the Source of Life and Love who is God before we venture out to serve the world. We let go of outcomes and keep seeking inner guidance of the Spirit who knows what is needed far more than we do.

We seek our own transformation through our daily consent to God's presence and action within. In so doing, we can be blessed with opportunities to radiate divine love even when we are not aware that is happening. As Father Keating says, "If one is transformed, one can walk down the street, drink a cup of tea or shake hands with somebody and be pouring divine life into the world . . . Transmission is not preaching as such. Transmission is the capacity to awaken in other people their own potentiality to become Divine."[25] Keating's words form a pretty clear expression of our overall goal as a contemplative community. Yet the goal is clearly not attainable by even our most dogged efforts—it will come as a gift.

The Contemplative Outreach booklets have a lot more to teach on contemplative service, but I will close this section with their beautiful

22. Merton, *New Seeds of Contemplation*, quoted in Fitzpatrick-Hopler et al., *Contemplative Service*, 15.
23. Ibid., 26.
24. Ibid., 29.
25. Keating, *Mystery of Christ*, 81.

words of instruction, which you might consider making into your own mantra: "Using the practice of attention/intention, intend to radiate Divine Love today as your silent service to others."[26] As contemplatives, we do intend to radiate Divine Love as best we can.

CENTERING, MUDDING, AND CANCER

In the first days of the summer of 2013, I am looking out over the Mississippi River from the fifth floor of the Gayle and Tom Benson Cancer Center in New Orleans as my wife begins the preventative phase of her breast cancer treatment. It has been a long year of too many impossibly difficult days: a messy, muddy time that also brought lessons that took us to our depths.

This southern part of the river gets muddied as it nears the Gulf of Mexico. For reasons unknown to me, my mind is making connections between wet mud, centering, and cancer. Maybe all of them are messy containers of beauty.

I am picturing the muddy hands of several of my friends who serve the world by centering and mudding. Mudding is my imagined word for what potters do when they throw a lump of clay on the wheel in hopes of creating beauty. Enter the world of the potter with me, and see the connections between the centering necessary for both transforming messy clay into pottery and being transformed by the messy journey of cancer.

My potter friends take a hard-packed lump of muddy clay and place it in the middle of the potter's wheel, a circular stone. They wet their hands and pour water over the solid lump of gray clay. They turn their attention inward to enter the center of their own being. When they are ready, they set the wheel to spinning with their wet hands around the clay, seeking its center.

The inner being, the mind's attention, the hands, and the clay are entering into one messy center, and the mudding begins. In case you haven't tried to shape spinning clay in this way, it is impossible without the oneness of being, attention, and hands—an art of centering.

I tried it once, and what a mess! I really thought my practice of daily centering would mean I would be centered enough to shape clay. I was very wrong. My muddy lump spun off the platform time and again. I was

---

26. Fitzpatrick-Hopler et al., *Contemplative Service*, 81.

not even close to being centered enough to get it right, and the experience taught me great admiration for my talented friends Jane and Michele.

As Jane, Michele, and any good potter knows, there is an art to shaping the messy, wet mud into beauty. There is a long process of learning this craft, a period of mastery. And for a year now, my wife and I have been learning there is a similar art to shaping the messy journey called cancer. Both demand an incredible amount of daily centering.

Bringing the body, mind, heart, spirit, and soul into oneness is actually the meaning of the Sanskrit word for yoga, which is translated as "yoking." To practice yoga is to practice yoking all that we are together into one whole. We usually think of yoga as people stretching into physical postures, but we often miss how yoga is an art of becoming one with the breath and all that we are. Yoga is coming into a centered oneness of our whole beings in the present moment.

Centered oneness, or yoga, is what happens when a potter transforms messy, muddy clay into beauty. Centered oneness is also needed if the messiness of cancer treatment is to be transformed into a still-beautiful life. But this is not a lecture on the power of positive thinking. I am not trying to say that terrible things are really wonderful if you just change your perspective. I am reminding you from right here in the middle of our own experience that after this messy life has had its way with you, you can still come to your center and shape the mess toward beauty. For as it turns out, at the center of our being lives the Great Love. I know this from experience. The Great Love can make all things beautiful eventually.

Now I admit this all sounds a bit rosy considering that tough experiences like cancer are anything but that. Yet my wife and I have walked this cancer path for a year now, and we are learning that a person can actually begin to center their being in the Great Love even during cancer. This is one of the hardest times and ways to be a contemplative, but it is possible. So how does such a practice work?

Carol breezed through the first three months of chemotherapy fairly easily, at least physically. Her fears were immense, and her anxiety was unyielding most days. Yet she kept working. She lived a fairly normal life. She handled our move from the suburbs to an apartment in New Orleans so we could be close to the hospital for daily treatment. Then came phase two: A drug called Adriamycin kicked her butt.

The chemo nurses call it the red devil. Carol tried naming the drug something more positive: Christmas, for its red color. It didn't help. Within a month of starting the drug she was flat on her back. She had to quit work, cooking, cleaning, and just about every aspect of her usual activities. I can remember the look in her eyes on the day before Thanksgiving in 2012. It was a look of desperation, of angst, of exhaustion. After trying to work for two hours that morning, she looked at me and simply said, "Take me home."

Carol practically became an invalid for a while. Her brain wasn't firing on all cylinders, and neither was her body. Her usual playful personality and wacky sense of humor disappeared. Her energy was completely depleted by the messy process of chemotherapy. She told it straight to her oncologist: "Adriamycin sucks!"

Carol's double mastectomy surgery was an even muddier mess. The surgeon carved a line from armpit to armpit and removed everything in between down to the ribs. The purpose was to cut away any remnants of the Her2-positive mass still lurking around after multiple courses of chemotherapy. Carol's doctors told us this form of breast cancer is more aggressive than other forms, and so they hit her with everything they could.

As difficult as chemotherapy had been, nothing prepared me to see my wife slashed across the chest or to watch the pain of her healing. I know the surgeons looked upon their work with clinical pride for the infection-free line of staples that would scar Carol from stem to stern, but for us this was as painful emotionally as it was physically. Taking a breath, turning in bed, moving around the apartment, or reaching out all hurt her with the searing pain of knitting scar tissue.

After the bandages were removed, we were ready to try Carol's first shower. I helped her in the tub, since she was still extremely weak. When she was ready, we adjusted the showerhead to bring the water streaming over her head and body. As the water flowed over my wife, the pooling of suffering and compassion that welled up in me was overwhelming. Not knowing how else to express that messy moment, I wrote the lines below on the following morning, and cried my way through each phrase.

MY HANDS GLIDING OVER TERRIBLE SACREDNESS

Yesterday
sacredness was terrible,
my hands gliding
across stitches and staples
that hold your chest flesh together.

Standing together
in your first shower
after the barbaric cutting,
the cancer-killing chemicals,
and just before the burning,

my hands gliding
over terrible sacredness.
Standing in this flood together
I wonder why the monk said,
"Present moment, wonderful moment."

Imperceptibly,
my broken heart
senses the rise
of All Compassion within.
"O," says my heart,
"He meant this."

As if it wasn't enough to poison Carol and slash open her chest, we had to put her through the burning of five weeks' worth of radiation. The scarred skin of Carol's chest began to look and feel like a bad sunburn, darkening into an angry red. Every morning she had to stretch out the stiff ligaments of her chest so that she could raise her arms above her head to receive the burning treatment where her lymph nodes had been excised. How in the world is a person supposed to make it through the muddy mess of life with cancer?

    I tell you the truth from the vantage point of this cancer center overlooking the muddy Mississippi River: There is a way through. Carol found by experience that a contemplative path is the essential art needed for the cancer journey. It takes practice to center oneself right in the middle of the mess. You can't avoid it. The only way is through.

    Stay in touch for a moment with that image of wet hands encircling a spinning lump of clay. Every potter knows that if the artist tenses up during this creative moment, the clay will fly off the spinning wheel with a splatter. Staying in a relaxed and restful posture within and without is essential to the art of shaping the spinning clay into beauty.

Through the loss of all of her energy, Carol was reminded about the beautiful necessity of simple being. If you have never been in this part of the cancer journey, the phrase "extreme fatigue" doesn't begin to express how impossibly difficult this kind of total exhaustion can be. Her mind was saying, "I can still get up and do things like drive, read, watch television, and work," while her body and psyche tiredly insisted, "Don't move. Any stress is too much. You can't even handle bright lights. All you can do is stay here in this bed and sit still."

Not by choice but by force, Carol began to learn more about the art of being. Day in and day out she found her path into that new country. Sitting up in bed and attending to the unfolding of each moment was really all she could do. Carol learned to rest and to be, as best she could.

"Resting" was Carol's word for her daily practice. I would call it "being." Pema Chödrön, beloved Buddhist retreat leader, author, and teacher, has called it "Learning to stay."[27] After losing my own center over those many months of feeling totally overwhelmed, I was fascinated to see how adept my wife became at centering, resting, and being in the moment as the messiness of cancer worked her over. Seeing her form of ultra-simple contemplative practice eventually helped me believe I could recover my own center.

If I could show you what this past year looked like, I would show you a picture of wet and muddy hands circling a mound of clay: centering, mudding, and cancer all united in what we called our life.

This story is just one example of how important a contemplative path can be. In a world and a culture where we try to control everything around us, including life itself, a few of us are taking the road less traveled. This is the road of contemplative living. Our traveling is about resting, being, and staying. Perhaps you will step onto this road with us and we'll travel together. But remember, on the contemplative path none of us knows the way ahead of time. We are all the learners in this walking school. And together we seek to follow in the steps of The Teacher.

THE MYTH OF "I CAN'T"

One of the greatest hindrances to walking the contemplative path is the ever-so-common myth that comes with the territory of trying any form of meditation. Most everyone thinks, "I can't." In actuality, I find

---

27. Chödrön, *Places That Scare You*, 23.

this almost always means that the person in question once spent a few minutes trying to meditate and kept noticing the busy mind and its stream of thoughts.

To jump from one or two hurried attempts at meditation to the myth of "I can't" is about as absurd as believing we should be able to master learning to walk, or ride a bike, or any new skill after only a few minutes of trying. Meditating is so counter-intuitive for most of us that all it takes is a brief attempt to convince us that we can't.

Over my twenty-five years of practicing and teaching many forms of meditation and contemplation, I have crossed paths with hundreds of newbies who have said the same "I can't" for the same reasons. Churchgoers and even pastoral leaders are often so uncomfortable with a moment of stillness and quiet that they print "A moment of silence" in the order of worship and then proceed to allow five to ten seconds before they resume speaking or playing music. The myth of "I can't" is everywhere when it comes to meditation.

Many years ago, I was moved by a choir anthem at our church. I was listed in the bulletin as leading a pastoral prayer after the anthem, but the beauty of the message of the song had deeply affected me. It just seemed wrong to jump up and start talking, even if it was prayer time. So I waited. I sat still. I let the beauty and meaning wash over us for several minutes. That moment of group meditation probably only lasted about two minutes, but it was profound.

After the service, several people came up to me to ask if I was okay. I guess they presumed that if we allowed more than a few seconds for meditation, there must be something wrong. In all honesty, most of the church services I have observed from many religious traditions move quickly from one event to the next, hardly taking time for a breath in between. If you step back and notice, you might think there is an unconscious message in that hurry: We dare not allow a minute for the Spirit of God to slip into *our* service, for who knows what might happen?

These days I have the joy of helping shape worship in a small spiritual community where I serve as a pastor. We set aside a weekly period of meditation as part of the service. Meditation means we actually sit in the silence and stillness. Sometimes there is guidance, and sometimes we are simply invited into God's presence. Of course, there are always people who get uncomfortable after a few seconds. I even suspect one man comes late so he can avoid those moments altogether, for he refers to the experience as our moment of awkward silence.

People speak the myth of "I can't meditate" when they have experienced the discomfort of inner stillness. There are probably millions of reasons why sitting still can be uncomfortable. Thoughts and feelings might arise that have been suppressed for years. Silence and stillness can feel like a loss of control. Even a moment of silence can bring us in touch with the emptiness that is a normal part of consciousness.

The myth of "I can't" is also perpetuated by another myth: I should be able to quiet my mind and empty my mind of all thoughts. Almost everyone who has ever tried even a few minutes of meditation has been influenced by the belief that they should be able to rid themselves of their own thoughts. Since we try to control every other aspect of our lives, we presume we should control our thoughts as well. But let us be clear: This is simply one more myth.

The meditation teacher who says, "I can teach you how to clear your mind," is a newbie. He or she has read or written a self-help book and had little or no actual experience with sustained meditation. A steady stream of thoughts is a normal part of consciousness. Most meditation traditions have very specific teachings on either being mindful of the flow of thoughts or gently releasing the thoughts as they arise, depending on the school of thought. Even in those forms that teach the release of thoughts, there is no effort to control thoughts, for releasing one thought just results in the rise of the next.

Thoughts come and go on their own. Mindfulness training teaches the simple act of observing the stream of thoughts and feelings without any attempt to control or judge them. Other traditions teach the act of noticing each thought, then gently turning the attention toward another focus of attention, such as a mantra or prayer word. In both cases, there is no futile effort to clear the mind of all thoughts.

Meditation is simply coming to our center and resting our attention there. Being mindful of our thoughts and yet staying in touch with the self who is observing these wayward thoughts can help us toward this goal. This can also be done by gently releasing thoughts as they arise in favor of attending to some intention of the heart, such as a focus on love, peace, God, or any other centering thought.

Meditation can be done while sitting in stillness, but that is only one of many ways to practice coming to our center. I will cover a few of the ways we teach meditation through our School for Contemplative Living in chapter 5. Our eventual intention is not simply to meditate, but to come to rest in oneness with the Divine, which has been classically called contemplation.

BELONGING IN COMMUNITY

So knowing there are thousands of ways we can approach meditation, why not just venture off into the wilderness, without or within, and start practicing your favorite form of meditation? I personally do not want to be alone on my spiritual journey, at least not all the time. People who find our small communities often come seeking togetherness. I believe this is because they do not want to travel alone either.

One night in the spring of 2013, I was working on my life in my men's group, which is a part of the international ManKind Project. I was noticing once again how I am always reluctant to attend our meetings. I always have to face my disinclination to show up, so I was thinking again about my own resistance.

For much of my life I have attended church groups, which featured small group studies and discussions. The groups almost always consisted of people saying what they thought about what some author had thought and written. In effect, the groups consisted of thoughts about thoughts. There was a certain comfort in such discussions, but they did not challenge me much. They did not ask me to be real. They did not call forth my struggles, sorrows, insecurities, or personal experience.

When I first walked into a men's group with the ManKind Project, I saw a very different way of relating. Men were sharing their feelings right off the bat. Where else do you see that? These men were looking into themselves to see if they were living with integrity. They began to work on their lives, and that included looking directly at their resistances. My God, what an invigorating experience! I was so moved to hear these men sharing their truths with each other that I decided I wanted to be a part of it.

For years I had been growing discontented with religious groups who pass the time by discussing their thoughts about an author's thoughts, and so I began inviting participants in the School for Contemplative Living to take a different path. I told the group, "I am not interested in our thoughts about some author's thoughts. I want to know how this material moves *you*. How does it speak to your own experience? How does it connect with your spiritual journey?" And then, of course, I would offer an example from my own life experience.

Amazingly, participants did not shy away. They did not need years of knowing each other to get comfortable enough to share honestly. Total strangers began to open up to share their life stories and connect with each other on how the Spirit was part of their journey. I would ask, share myself, and invite others to contribute. Then we would pause long enough for someone else to feel ready to share. Usually this took about a minute of silent waiting, and then the sharing continued.

From day one of inviting this kind of meaningful sharing, people did share. One lady launched into the scary reality of having a daughter diagnosed with schizophrenia and trying to find the guidance of God's Spirit in the midst of that nightmare. One woman shared about coming near the end of seminary and questioning whether she even wanted to be ordained. Was that really where God was leading her? One man spoke of trying to find time for daily meditation when the first weeks and months of retirement had been even busier than his working life.

From week to week, participants in our school's classes explored their needs and longings, their spiritual quests, their struggles with old beliefs, and the joys of finding a few moments of God's presence in the middle of their hectic lives. One of our earliest participants was a blind man who had been recovering from alcoholism for decades. He had always wondered if there was any spiritual group, in addition to Alcoholics Anonymous, that could be a safe place to really tell his story.

One man shared his frustration with trying to teach in the New Orleans Public School system when only a third of his class would show up on any given day. He was trying to apply contemplative living to a situation where he couldn't even get textbooks for his high school classes. One lady described how she tried to stay near God's presence as she worked with mentally ill women in a group home. No, it wasn't easy, but her inner joy was palpable, and you could see how her life was becoming a living example of *ora et labora*, or prayer and work.

One woman cried a few gentle tears as she described how she was following her spiritual longing but had never been in church. She said she didn't really get all the God stuff. And she just couldn't believe God was the big old bearded man depicted in five hundred-year-old paintings. A teacher shared how much she loves the kids in her preschool, and how she believes that it is really God's love moving through her into them. A doctor told a short story about how hard it can be to remember God's presence in a work environment that puts constant pressure on the physician to see at least four patients per hour.

So it is that contemplatives are no longer only monks or nuns cloistered behind monastery walls. Contemplatives are regular people wandering through the wild world of daily life, immersed in a frantic society and yet seeking the kingdom of God right in their midst. Contemplatives are like the monks and nuns of centuries past in that they want to form communities where they can share their lives. Most of our contemplatives get together because we do not know how to practice the presence of God by ourselves, or maybe because we just don't want to try it alone.

Perhaps we are beginning to understand that the spiritual journey is not meant to be lived in isolation. We need a place where we belong, just as we are. We need a community where there is no judgment. We want to gather with people who are also seeking the Presence on a daily basis, as best they can, but who do not need to pretend that this goal is being achieved every day.

We are seekers of belonging: belonging in our own skin, belonging in the kingdom of a God who lives in the real world, belonging in a community of seekers who need each other's help and support. This form of real belonging will never be found in groups where people pretend that they believe all the right things, or feel happy all the time, or have the right answers about religion. Real community will not form between people who are unwilling to share anything but thoughts about thoughts.

What I see happening among us is the emergence of true honesty and humility—people acknowledging that we are *humus* (earth), human, imperfect, and beautiful in our flaws. I see us as people experiencing what it means to be whole beneath all our brokenness. Community is built by practicing honestly facing ourselves as we are and wholly accepting each other as we are. Honesty and humility become the basis for oneness between us. And that is the gift of a God who is present among us.

A person who enters one of our classes hoping to teach all the rest of us how we ought to see things won't last long. That kind of pretention will be gently scolded with something like, "It must be nice to have all the answers, but I personally have a hard time sticking with my daily practice of the Presence." In reality, there is almost never anyone trying to play the spiritual expert. We model a different way, a way of honesty and humility. The pretentious path just seems laughable.

In our emerging contemplative communities, the kind of people who show up are usually people who are spiritually hungry. We want to learn to be open to God's presence wherever she may be found. We want to practice openness to the One who just might show up anywhere, in any way, throughout our days. We just can't be comfortable with keeping God in a box of our own creation. Leave that to religious denominations.

In this way, we are also practicing surrender. We see how straining to control every aspect of our lives doesn't work very well, despite what the dominant culture teaches us about the value of pulling ourselves up by our bootstraps. In a world where the high-achieving, self-made man is praised as the pinnacle of success, we are trying to learn how to turn our lives over to the care of a God who we can't even see.

We are practicing this surrender moment by moment as we release the constant stream of thoughts into God's hands during silent prayer. And we are seeking to learn how to practice Tilden Edward's teaching about leaning back into the spiritual heart[28] as we make decisions in our service of the world. But since we can't do any of this very well on our own, we keep gathering to share the journey in the company of other contemplatives. We just do not want to go it alone.

CENTERING AND TEXTING

In the summer of 2013, my friend Francis suggested we begin a new practice as a form of community-building. His approach would never have entered my mind as a form of spiritual connection, but Francis knew there was an ultra-simple way we could stay in touch with our mutual need to practice the Presence: to text each other when we are centering and invite others to participate as they were able.

This new way of being in each other's company spiritually, without needing to stop what we are doing in our lives, is to use our phones. Although many people are too busy fiddling with their cell phones to connect with the actual presence of those around them, we shouldn't miss the meaning of so many people getting lost in their phones all the time. Our innate need for human connection has simply shifted into a new form: the cell phone.

So why not use this new medium as a source of spiritual connection? Why not take a minute to send this text: "Hey, I am centering. Join me if you can." We just started this practice, so we are at the edge of a new experiment. So far it has been a simple gift to have a friend let me

---

28. Edwards, *Embracing the Call*, 10.

know he or she is in that space of centering. Sometimes I do not get the text until later. That doesn't matter. When I see it come up on my phone, I know where my friend has been, and this reminder helps me in my own practice.

This way of being in community is surely not as fulfilling as when we are actually together. I am not suggesting we stop meeting in person and start texting as our exclusive means of communication. This is an add-on. This is an expression of an honest question, "Why wait until we make time to sit together again?" This is a simple way to remember we are not alone in our desire to practice contemplative living.

Centering and texting is another example of a great truth: We humans do not want to feel so alone. The spiritual journey is not meant to be attempted alone. So why not get creative and discover new ways to join each other on the contemplative path? I have been finding that these little text reminders can help us experience the natural interconnectedness of our beings. A text with a spiritual message may be brief, but it still says, "I am thinking of you. We are still in community with each other even when we can't get together in person."

In a world where being overly busy has become the norm, don't we need new ways to keep in touch spiritually? People now tweet and text about inane things like how their cup of coffee tastes. So why not send a message that says, "I am with you in my heart"? As we adopt each new form of technology as our chosen form of communication, couldn't we turn that next thing into another way to stay united in heart and soul? Whenever possible, we contemplatives gather to be in each other's physical presence. When we can't, let's text, tweet, call, email, or message each other to center together in new ways.

SHE STAYED BACK

She came in late for the hospital's new centering prayer group and slipped in quietly to take her seat on the wooden chapel pew. She seemed to easily connect with our little island of stillness in the midst of a busy and bustling hospital, and settled in with the seven of us as we practiced the presence of God together. Some of us monks have taken to practicing in certain New Orleans hospitals—we take the opportunity of being in God's presence together wherever we can find a tiny oasis.

The lighting in the chapel was low. We could just make out faith symbols on the walls, but we weren't really there to see the room. There was no choir music or sermon, no Scripture study or vocal prayers. But we weren't really there to listen to words. We were in fact seeking an inner room with no symbols or sounds or words—right there in the midst of the American healthcare system.

Molly, as I'll call the latecomer, didn't even receive our brief introduction to the way we were practicing the Presence. She just slipped in late and entered our silent prayer. Like the rest of us, Molly probably had rambling thoughts. It's just what the mind likes to do. But I think she also found that place beneath thoughts where we can just breathe our way into the inner sanctuary. She did not fidget. In fact, no one did. So it was that seven people rested in their own inner sanctuaries together, sitting in a chapel in the middle of a noisy hospital—amazing!

Molly stayed back after the centering group ended. She needed to connect, as is often true of hospital staff whenever they can find a few minutes of quiet intimacy with God in community. Molly wanted to know about the chaplain and his background and ministry. She wanted to share a bit of her longing to be with other Christian believers in the place where she worked helping people overcome strokes and brain injuries. Molly was tired of feeling alone in wanting to integrate her faith and her service.

Molly's need resonates with the reasons why we formed our School for Contemplative Living. We want to unite our prayer and work. We want prayer and service to become one. We cannot walk that contemplative path alone—we need contemplative community.

So watch out for people like Molly in some hospital chapel, church, nonprofit agency, school, or home near you. We are contemplatives in community. We seek to center our service in the ground of our being where we believe the living God dwells. Maybe you will slip into one of our little contemplative communities and join us sometime. You will be made as welcome as Molly was! Or if you live far from our School for Contemplative Living, maybe you will create your own groups.

THE PLEASURE OF CRAFT WITHOUT TOIL:
SEVEN PARABLES OF CONTEMPLATIVE LIVING

"What does the worker gain from his toil?"

(Eccl 3:9 NIV)

Through the following parables, I am seeking to simplify contemplative truths into tiny stories, each becoming a kernel of spiritual reality that might hint at the nature of contemplative living more than all of my lengthy explanations ever could.

A laborer resolved to stop his hard work, and wandered out into a field. There he found a great treasure, but gave all that unlimited wealth away, preferring to treasure a life free of toil. He kept at this craft until he died.

In heaven the angels put the erstwhile laborer in charge of lifting the burdens from other's shoulders so that others might discover his treasure and greatest pleasure: practicing a craft without toil. In heaven, service flows freely from the Great Joy.

A reader put her book down, closed her eyes to the words on the page, and gave up trying to figure things out. There she waited, until a fuller knowledge arose from within, without effort, and her face shone like the sun with inner radiance.

A ripe field of grain awaited the sickle of harvest with joy—slain ambitions waiting to be replaced with the simplicity and gratitude of usefulness.

A creek flowing along in no particular hurry, seeking no other destination, is delighted to offer a place for sunlight to sparkle. She is free of any other purpose than being the being she is!

A cricket's song thrums deep into the cold night, vibrating effortlessly, singing into dark silences just before the great silence comes, and unafraid.

The kitten shows me her way of life: napping, stretching from whisker to tail, lifting her face toward a loving hand, leaning into a stroke, and requiring little more than giving and receiving love—a master of contentment.

Jesus extends one empty hand toward me and offers a bag full of discontentment in the other hand (for any other thing leads only to dissatisfaction). The choice is mine. He hopes I will choose to take his empty hand in mine. Only this choice satisfies.

BIRTHING YOUR OWN SCHOOL

Perhaps you have been reading these stories about contemplative life, service, and community while saying to yourself, "I wish I had a contemplative community like this in my area." No one has a community like this without creating one. That means it is up to you. There is a good chance that if you are one who seeks this kind of community for practicing the presence of God then you will also be the gatherer.

If you would like to birth your own school, or form your own contemplative community, consider the following guidelines. The pages that follow are meant to be like when recovering alcoholics share their experience, strength, and hope. We want to offer you lessons from our own experience that you can test out to see what works for you.

First, before there was any larger gathering, we were a small contemplative community who found we were seeking similar things: support for our personal spiritual journeys, group practice of God's presence, nonjudgmental sharing about our own challenges in establishing a daily contemplative practice, and a sense of connection with peers on a similar journey. We were not all alike, but we had similar longings to practice God's presence on a regular basis.

We started small, with a core group of three to ten people, depending on the week. We asked for an introductory workshop through Contemplative Outreach, the international organization for teaching centering prayer. We followed their recommendation to watch a series of videos created by Father Thomas Keating and the staff of Contemplative Outreach. After that, we all committed to begin a daily practice of centering prayer once or twice a day for up to twenty minutes, as best we could. Over time we invited others to join us, and while attendance fluctuated, the group sustained itself and continues to this day.

The format for that first contemplative group was to gather, chime a bell to begin the silence, practice centering prayer for twenty minutes, sound the chime again to close the prayer, and remain in silence until someone felt led to share some aspect of their experience. Sometimes sharing meant saying what had just happened within us. Sometimes sharing meant telling a story about some aspect of our ongoing spiritual journey. This sharing was never mere random thoughts, but seemed instead to flow out from the silence and inner stillness. No one challenged another. No one focused on beliefs or thoughts about thoughts. We were grounding ourselves in spiritual experience and sharing from that place.

This sharing is one distinctive aspect of creating a contemplative community. The intention is to focus on grounded spiritual experience, not intellectual concepts, doctrines, or beliefs. You could say we gather to practice God's presence and share our experiences around our practice. We also share honestly, since no one will judge our sense of inadequacy in establishing a regular practice. This honest sharing of real experience, in a nonjudgmental environment, becomes a cornerstone of building real community.

Besides focusing on personal experience and creating a safe place for honest sharing, we would sometimes find a sense of universal experience through our sharing. Participants would regularly respond to someone else's sharing with comments like "I thought I was the only one who felt like that, or struggled with that." Although we always left room for everyone's journey to be their own, we also found that we experienced similarities on our contemplative path.

Some of the early group members had known each other for years, which probably helped participants feel more comfortable in honest sharing from the start. There is something about spending intimate time together in silence that seems to increase our sense of connection, to lower defenses, and to invite freedom to just be wherever we are on our own journey.

Another characteristic of our fledgling community was that there seemed to be a lot of love flowing through the group. Entering into the presence of the Source of Love together seems to draw that love into the room, and perhaps increases the group's awareness of the flow of love. This does not mean the group was saying anything about love for each other. There was just a sense of loving connection that would sometimes pervade the group experience.

I first noticed this kind of inner shift when I was privately practicing morning meditation during graduate school. After my usual forty-five minutes of sitting in stillness, I would get up and begin getting my son up for school, preparing a little breakfast, waking my wife before heading out for classes or work, and all my other daily duties. Although these were all normal activities, I would often feel an extra sense of loving-kindness towards my family after practicing God's presence. My time of oneness with the Source of Love nurtured my love for them. The same joy can grow between group members and in the world in general.

I have to say that gathering in community with other contemplatives tends to create a sense of oneness between us. We don't debate issues. We don't try to convince each other of anything. We practice the Presence together and this seems to unite us in spirit. Our differences are just a normal part of relationships. Those differences are not our focus. Even when we share different ways of seeing our spiritual journeys, our unique perspectives offer a kind of multi-layered richness. Each view is an additional outlook, not a matter of who is right or wrong.

Next, let's focus on the unfolding mission of our school to see if our calling might help guide you in the formation of your own vision. We initially envisioned a world where we could gather to practice the presence of God together and stay in touch with the Presence as we served in the world. Our initial statement of mission was "Listening in stillness, serving in joy."

These twin phrases were our way of saying we needed the personal contemplative experience of daily oneness with God. We also needed ways to express that oneness in the wild world around us by serving from God's presence. Our hope was to learn to ground our service in the Presence so that our serving was done in joy, which gave birth to our mission statement on stillness and serving in joy.

Later, as we found that one small community gathering did not provide enough opportunities for all of us around the New Orleans region, we focused on the mission of creating contemplative communities. We saw that our mission was to create contemplative communities.

More recently, we have all been focusing on what outcomes we are seeking in this contemplative lifestyle. To date, these outcomes are personal transformation and radical engagement with the world. So we have begun revising our mission statement to say we are practicing the presence of God to reflect these goals.

Although it may become a mouthful, we want our mission to keep evolving as we evolve. Practicing the presence of God is clearly at the heart of our mission and purpose. So we would invite you, as you explore how to birth your own school in your own life, to keep forming and clarifying your vision and mission. Do not just try hard to think of words or phrases that are interesting or seem meaningful. Instead, I would suggest the following practice.

Envision the world as it could be according to what you feel led to create. Paint your vision with broad strokes and large scenes. Think big and imagine only the best. It is not too big to envision a world where God's love rules. It is okay to be a generalist in your first vision, putting it into words as all-encompassing as "Let love rule." Once you have your vision, gradually seek clarity for details on the way you want the world to be.

As your vision becomes clearer, focus your attention on the main thing you want to achieve with that vision. Begin with the words, "I create a world where . . ." and listen in your heart for the answer. What are you here for at this time in your life? This is a difficult question. Many people go their whole lives without ever asking or ever knowing why they are on this planet. Take your time. Do not rush to fill in the blank. Keep asking. Keep wondering. Keep listening within and slowly craft the words to fit your inner voice.

When the critical voice that lives in everyone's head speaks to you, set it aside. When it whispers, "You don't have a reason to be here—this is stupid—just go back to living your life," you must answer calmly, "Thanks for that," and carry on with listening for your inner voice.

Your inner voice is the voice of what spiritual leaders often call "the True Self." It is your own unique soul speaking, the essence of who you really are. The soul is slow to speak up until we are willing to listen without judgment. Yet our souls are often the source of all that discontent when we do not take time to listen within. In my experience with hundreds of people from all walks of life, Thomas Kelly was right in saying, "Deep within us all there is an amazing inner sanctuary of the soul, a holy place, a Divine Center, a speaking Voice, to which we may continuously return."[29] Practice listening for that voice.

Over time you will find that the mission of your life will emerge from that voice. You will seek details of what you feel led to create. As words and phrases arise and seem to fit, write them down and see if you find an inner sense of resonance. When you find words that resonate, you have your initial mission.

Next you may wish to write out a few steps to accomplish that mission. If your vision is for a world full of more love, then your mission might be something like, "I create a world full of love by . . ." and you fill in that blank. This is an important step to keep your mission from being no more than a pleasant dream. What will you do to birth this vision into reality? What steps will you take? How are you being led to fulfill this vision?

When you have crafted a statement that includes at least a step or two you can take on the path of birthing your vision into reality, you will

---

29. Kelly, *Testament of Devotion*, 3.

have charted a course for your life's purpose. You will begin to have some clarity for why you are here, and you will use that vision and mission to guide you when everything else demands your time.

Birthing your own school will not happen on its own. You could flounder for years if you don't take time to explore your vision and mission. Yet you can't expect that the whole adventure will appear with clarity on day one. You might experience such a vision suddenly, but for most of us there are years of collaboratively crafting a mission worthy of our full attention and effort. So stay at it. Persevere. Your life's purpose is worth it. Your time is worth it. You are worth it.

In the summer of 2013, I was moved to write out an initial expression of a pledge to follow a contemplative path. After calling some words to mind, I felt led to share the pledge with some participants in one of our community-building sessions. Group members signed the pledge one by one. I invited other participants from our School for Contemplative Living email list to respond if they wanted to make the pledge as well. I was grateful that a number of people were ready to add their pledge to mine. I include that pledge below both as an illustration of this unfolding part of our story and as an invitation to begin your own writing of your calling to contemplative living.

A CONTEMPLATIVE PLEDGE

In the early twenty-first century,
a monastery of the heart, a monastery without walls,
a lay, ecumenical, contemplative community
is being born.

We are contemplatives,
simple seekers of oneness with God.
We remember when Jesus said,
"That all of them may be one."[30]
As brothers and sisters of this oneness,
we are gathering in a time when religion is going crazy,
again,
defining itself by who it judges to be unworthy.

---

30. John 17:21 NIV.

In such a time,
we create an open table
to invite any spiritual seeker
to come into the shelter of an inclusive community,
a home for all who are sinners and saints,
a refuge for spiritual seekers
who are wearied by a frantic culture
and an overly-busy church.

In such a time of distress,
we will teach each other how to find our inner sanctuary
and we will learn to serve the world from that True Home together.
We commit ourselves to the mission
of creating contemplative communities
who practice the presence of God
for personal transformation
and radical engagement with the world.

VOWS FOR A CONTEMPLATIVE COMMUNITY

Our pledge was a first step in expressing our common commitment to contemplative living. Through these early years of forming small contemplative communities and sometimes creating a larger gathering of communities for workshops and retreats, we have not yet decided to take the step of inviting our participants to make a formal commitment to live by the same rule of life or to take vows as traditional monastics have done.

Up to this time, even the most basic commitment to practice the presence of God each day has remained an individual endeavor. Yet listening to the Reverend Dr. Elaine Heath, a professor of evangelism at Perkins School of Theology, explain in a workshop the rule of life in the New Day communities around Dallas, Texas, got me to wondering again.

I have wondered about a commitment to a community vow and rule of life many times. When our steering committee discussed the possibility of inviting participants into a shared commitment, several members protested that people in our culture often have too many places where they feel overcommitted already. There has been talk of not wanting to exclude anyone who might just want to slip in and out of groups as they choose. We never wanted to create any form of in-group or out-group.

Nevertheless, the vows below arose in me years ago as an expression of my own inner desire for commitment. They emerged like a vision of a way of life for a community of like-minded contemplatives. I must admit that I still have the yearning to form a circle of contemplatives who seek to live these vows together. Perhaps a next unfolding within our school will be the birth of an Order of Contemplative Missionaries who take these vows to heart and seek to live them out. So what about you? Would you join us? Read the vows below carefully and see if a voice speaks to you about your own contemplative commitment.

The Consecrated Time

We offer one time, set aside each day, for God alone. Let other times be dedicated to sacred reading, reflecting, thinking, writing, communing with others, serving the needs of the world, and other forms of prayer. We give one time for the love of God alone: loving God for God's own sake, breathing our way into union with the Divine, and practicing the presence of God.

We allow no other purpose to this time. We do not seek to receive messages. We do not try to figure out the problems of our lives or those of others. We do not try to fix anything. There is a place in the soul where *we are not broken*. We go to this place of innate wholeness in the inner being.

There we enter the sanctuary of the soul. We bow before the One who has called us into being. We practice simple being for one consecrated time, breathing in the Presence. No need for words with this One. Here begins our contemplative call.

The Consecrated Day

Just this day we give to God: turning all our efforts and cares over to the One who cares for us, serving from more than our own strength, becoming activists under the moment-by-moment guidance of the One who calls us to kingdom activity, working from the Source of Life out of the fullness God gives in each moment.

This day is not about working to exhaustion or frantically striving to save the world while we become empty. We have known that life, and it is no longer fulfilling our calling.

We live our days in consecration now. We do not answer every call to busyness. We do not work outside our personal calling. We keep turning to the Giver of Life, all through the day, asking, "Is this you calling?" As we encounter each new person throughout our days, we keep leaning into that spiritual intuition to learn when to speak and when to keep silent, when to act and when to remain still. Union with the Divine does not end with the first hour of quiet. Herein is our consecrated, contemplative day.

The Consecrated Life

Our decisions are made in union with the Holy One. We cannot rely on reason and logic alone, for they never did contain the greater wisdom we sought. We seek something higher and truer as a source of guidance now. We listen deeply. We listen long. We bring our longing home, and find there the way to a consecrated life.

We seek clearness in our lives in consultation with a contemplative community. We know our judgments can become skewed, our purposes unbalanced. So we turn to each other, trusting that a voice from the inner sanctuary will emerge from group listening.

We regularly gather as a community for prayer, sharing our lives, mutual support of our consecrated intention to live the contemplative life, joyful fellowship, and periods of discernment for our individual and community life. In these vows we have committed our lives to become a community of contemplatives serving the world through prayer and action.

OUT ON THIS VACANT LOT CALLED PRAYER . . . WANTING

Wanting, longing, needing—are these not the essence of prayer? Sometimes what we experience in the inner stillness, coming up from the deep of us, is our own wanting. How counterproductive it is that this experience of longing and wanting is the very thing we so often unwisely seek to avoid. As followers of the way of Christ, what are we to do with our longing? How can we live as wise people, and not be drunk on solutions of our own making, but instead be filled with the Spirit—so much so that our heart sings, making melody in our hearts with psalms and hymns and spiritual songs.

I now know that this is an impossible task. I'm not wise. I still lapse in seeking fulfillment from the wrong places. I've spent many an evening surfing television channels, as you might have. I've spent many days cramming every moment with over-scheduled calendars and ceaseless activities, as you may have. It's a lifestyle that never has worked for me. It probably doesn't work for you either. I still fall down that hole, and only later notice and finally manage to crawl out again.

Any spiritual practice that takes us away from our humanity to avoid this wanting is a counterfeit. Sometimes church people are the busiest people I know, frantically racing around to try to save the world even as we lose our own souls.

So what we are seeking in the School for Contemplative Living is a way of practicing a wiser life that helps us discover the divinity *in* our humanity and the presence of God in the midst of *our* presence, including finding God's presence *in* our inner void.

The willingness to be *with* the wanting, to stop avoiding, and to just *be*—this is one path of the wisdom way. For this reason, in simple trust, with God's help we can say:

> Out on this vacant lot called prayer . . .
> Wanting
> I will bundle up my vast emptiness
> and bring it to *You* now
> and place it on *Your* doorstep
> and wait here outside the door.
> And even if you do not seem to answer,
> somehow this is what I needed today,
> to bring my wanting to You.

When I am longing for this Deep Presence, nothing else can satisfy. I now know this longing is God wooing me, yet it disturbs me. It won't leave me alone. I resist. I try to turn my attention to other things besides the emptiness, or aching, or longing for the One who is my true home. The longing persists. I can turn away, but I cannot hide for long, for it woos me still. I think it is the Great Love calling me, wanting to bring me home.

Finally, I do not know what else to do but sit still, become silent, and let it find me, wash over me, and take me wherever the Great Mystery will lead. The pain is an ache like none other, yet I must trust it to guide my own good, surrender to its mercy, hope for its soothing, and wait for it to lead me home.

Entering into Deep Presence, we begin by focusing on the One who is here with us in the silence. We begin to be present to the Presence, full of longing, leaning in, drawing near, bowing with reverent attention, watching, and waiting. We enter by letting the Great Love within lead us toward love. There we sit, and there we remain. We strive to live in that love. The wisdom way is to feel the wanting and let the wanting lead us into Deep Presence.

I also find in myself a wanting for people like you, a longing for community with whom I can commune by being and sharing myself just as I am, with all my faults and the reality that I am full of wanting. I initially hesitated in sharing this experience from self-doubt. That insidious inner voice asked, "Who cares what I am experiencing? What if it sounds inadequate? I certainly feel inadequate!"

I think an old fear of rejection was lurking underneath the fear of sharing. Slowly I found the courage to share when I sensed that my own wanting might be in you too. Perhaps you have also known the vacant lot called prayer, and been full of wanting without any Hallmark card resolution. Perhaps you too have wished for friends with whom to walk the wanting path.

If so, take my hand. Let's walk this wanting path together. I know I need friends for this journey. Do you? Living in community is another path of the wisdom way. If you cannot come join us in New Orleans, then maybe you will seek out a contemplative community near you—or create your own.

4

The Dark Side of Contemplation

Now we turn to the dark side of contemplative living. Didn't we know there would be a dark side? Did we think this was turning out to be a nice little fairytale destined for a happy ending? Well, we better not even start the contemplative journey if we were planning to avoid an entrance into the shadows. Believe me, I have tried avoiding the dark places, and they always find me sooner or later.

Now we repent of our desire to keep everything neat and tidy on the spiritual path we have chosen. We get pulled into the deep, whether we wanted to or not. We ride the monsters all the way down to the bottom, as Anne Dillard says, in hopes of finding "the unified field: our complex and inexplicable caring for each other, and for our life together here."[1] After all of our avoidances prove to be in vain, we will eventually find that we must meet all that is within us on a contemplative path. In contemplative practice, all that is within us means everything.

I like writing inspiring stories that lift me up as they unfold. In fact, I prefer to have only inspiring experiences. If only that preference could control reality. I also had every wish that if I were to establish a regular meditation practice, I would discover some kind of secret to ultimate peace of mind. People with my kind of personality seek peace as our highest goal. At our best, we occasionally find and share the real thing. At our worst, we simply avoid conflict and any situation that might disturb our search for peace.

---

1. Dillard, *Teaching a Stone*, 94–95.

Now I see that a regular meditation practice in no way guarantees any peace of mind. The closest I have ever come to that is fake equanimity—trying to look peaceful—and I have mastered that for many years. The problem with such fake peace is that no one else but me ever really believed it.

When I use contemplative practices to try to manipulate reality this way, I am entering one of the dark sides of contemplation. Maybe I needed this false motivation to get started on the path. Perhaps I needed to believe that I could achieve peace of mind in three easy steps to help me make a commitment to regular practice. I soon found that wish frustrated.

Peace is elusive and never does our bidding. Peace of mind is a visitor who comes knocking and leaves us in the dust. Even a peace-junkie like me, a person who has tasted some peace of mind and gets addicted to chasing that high, must learn the hard truth that trying to force peacefulness is a real guarantee that peace will not visit. Since peace cannot be controlled, its visit will only happen at times of surrender.

I have slowly been learning that the best I can do is to open the door of my heart. I can only make a space for the Giver of Peace. If she wants to bless me with a sense of oneness with all that is, even for a moment, so be it. But chasing that experience is not a worthy goal. Inviting the presence of God is the real mission here.

As a child, I learned this Christian chorus: "Into my heart, into my heart, / Come into my heart, Lord Jesus; / Come in today, come in to stay; / Come into my heart, Lord Jesus."[2] Opening the door of the heart to the presence of Christ in this simple way is really what being a contemplative is all about. Like a child I say, "Come in today, come in to stay." Instead of grasping for peace, this practice of heart-welcome becomes far more satisfying. Peace then becomes a by-product of a more important relationship, and faking peacefulness can be replaced by actual communion.

I have already started delving into what a contemplative life brings: A day will come when I stand face-to-face with myself. In fact, many days will bring a mirror of self-reflection that I didn't ask to face. Cultivating inner stillness has such a nice ring to it, but what I find is that there is a very real reason why Americans avoid stillness at all costs. When I slow down, I come face-to-face with everything that is in me.

---

2. Taken from "Into My Heart" by Harry D. Clarke C 1924, Ren. 1952 Hope Publishing Company, Carol Stream, IL 60188. All rights reserved. Used by permission.

FAUX MONK

I recently fell into another layer of awareness that there was much more fakeness in me besides the pretense of peace. This new awareness was unsought and unwanted, and yet it came looking for me without an invitation. Openness has a way of bringing what we need, not just what we would prefer.

I went on an extended retreat at Saint Mary's Sewanee, an Episcopal haven in Sewanee, Tennessee, in January of 2012. Our group's purpose was to practice centering prayer all through our eight-day retreat. We entered into silence and maintained that quiet through most of the week. We ate together in silence, practiced yoga in silence, took walks in silence, and did all things in silence unless we needed to share a private session with a spiritual director. Of course, our hours of centering prayer were spent in silence.

A thick fog surrounded the mountain on the cold January day when we entered the grounds of the retreat center. Anna Maria and Maggie, two friends from our school, had also registered, and we traveled from New Orleans together. The fog in the air paralleled my inner fog for those first few days. I was practicing along with everyone else, struggling with the discomfort of long hours of sitting meditation, and trying to manage my false expectations to have meaningful experiences.

For the first five days, the retreat was pretty uneventful. Even in the fog and rain, the time to just *be* was proving to be enough for me. I knew not to try to force special experiences, but I secretly expected a good dose of feeling a sense of oneness with God. After all, such experiences are fairly common when I am sitting in my own home or with some of our groups. It made sense to privately expect to feel some of that spiritual connection while we were all practicing together through so much of the day.

Despite my expectations, for five days I wasn't feeling much spiritual connection. It was disappointing, but what could I do? I knew enough to know we can never control these things and that we can be sure nothing will happen when we try to force communion. I took a nap on the afternoon of day five, a luxury I rarely enjoy at home but treasured every day of the retreat.

When I awakened, the blustery day was blowing the tree branches around just outside my window. I sat up in bed watching the flapping of the fingertips of the trees for a minute when two words slammed into my mind. They came out of nowhere. The words were "faux monk."

I did not need an interpreter to receive the message. I did not question who had spoken the words (clearly this came from the Divine Voice). I did not want to hear the words, but there was a clear and simple truth in them. They named me for what I was and sometimes still am—a faux monk.

What this means is that there is a pretender in me, a poseur. There is that in me which wants to be seen as a monk without doing the requisite work of making that commitment to live that life. There is a desire in me to be seen as a super-spiritual guy. It is a flimsy defense against my own vulnerability and sense of inadequacy. It is an intrusion of an attitude of superiority to try to hide my sense of spiritual inferiority. It is an attitude of being a wannabe in the spiritual life I create.

The faux monk is a real part of my false identity. This fake monk is not as powerful or convincing as he would like to be, but he is still right here within me. Even as I write these stories, he is inside, sometimes beyond my awareness, helping me to choose which stories to share and which to conveniently forget. The faux monk will always be around, and despite what you might think while reading this, he is not the enemy. My work is not to try to expel him from my life or disintegrate him.

Defensive moves like trying to get rid of unwanted parts of ourselves are ineffective. They just do not work. Such moves only push parts of us down into the unconscious. Their seeming disappearance only gives the faux monk more power.

Since that first revelation of the faux monk on retreat, I have come to see him as a silly companion. I have watched his moves, learned to catch a glimpse of him sneaking around out of the corner of my eye, and laughed at him when he tries to steal the limelight.

I have also learned that my faux monk would like to be in charge of my life, to run the show and stay center-stage. He is like an endearing but irritating friend who nevertheless should not be belittled or put down. My faux monk just wants attention.

He might have been born out of my insecurity and uncertainty about how to be a monk in this world. He might have been born through a false belief that people would like me better if I looked holy or superhuman. The problem is that none of that is real. The faux monk persona actually distances me from other people, and so is counterproductive. Who wants to be around a spiritual know-it-all? Who wants to sit next to someone who believes they are better than the people beside them in the pews?

So what am I to do with this revelation that I have a faux monk in me? For one thing, I do not put him in charge of my life. When I can be self-aware, I do not ask him to make my decisions. Here is an example.

I spoke on contemplative living in a 2013 summer class on world religions at Tulane University. If the faux monk had taken charge, I might have walked in there looking like a Dalai-Lama-wannabe. I might have tried to seem ultra-peaceful, as though I stood above the fray of life. I might have remained silent for so long that the class would be made to feel uncomfortable, or spoken of the contemplative life in lofty terms as though it is superior to all other lifestyles, or pontificated as a supposed expert on contemplative living.

Here's the problem with all of that: There is no such thing as a contemplative expert! I once heard the real Dalai Lama, speaking at a Resilience Conference in New Orleans in May of 2013, say in honest humility that he is not a real monk, though he admires the genuine qualities of an older monk he knew. In a sense he was exposing his own faux monk, just putting him right out there in the open—and this coming from a man who spends five months a year in silent solitude. There is no doubt that he is a real monk.

His Holiness gave a good example of a way to address the faux monk in us. Bring him out into the light. Lovingly expose him for what he is, then point toward someone who is the real thing. When others try to project their image of our greatness onto us, deflect it firmly but playfully.

As I spoke with the students, I brought the faux monk out in the open to admit there is a contemplative poseur in me. I sought to speak the truth of my desire beneath the pretending: to simply experience union with God. That desire leads me to a commitment to practice the presence of God as best I can each day, by myself and in small contemplative communities. As I spoke with the class, I just left it at that and invited them to join us if they were interested.

I was not happy when the words faux monk came into my consciousness on that cold and rainy January afternoon. But because they are revealed truth, because the faux monk is part of me, I still need this awareness. And in such moments of graced self-awareness, I kind of like the little guy as he dances around seeking attention. I am glad to know he is there so I can give him that attention he needs and know when I am pretending. I help my own growth by remembering to not take my pretending too seriously.

You might not have a faux monk in you, but there just might be other pretenders and self-delusions hindering you on the contemplative path. Contemplative experience is likely to bring forth these pretenses, because truth comes forth sooner or later during the prayer of interior stillness. I call this process a dark side of contemplative practice because the difficult truths that emerge from this silence can be hard to take. Richard Rohr referred to such experiences as part of the dismantling of the false self when he spoke for our school in April of 2011. Such dismantling can lead to meaningful growth if we are willing to be lovingly gentle toward the parts of ourselves that usually prefer to hide in the shadows.

IMPERFECTION

Many of us who seek to live a spiritual life would like to imagine that we are making progress toward perfection. The United Methodist Church even asks a question that newly ordained clergy must answer yes to: "Do you believe that you will be made perfect in this life?" We can hope that a great deal of theological study and discussion on real-life experience takes place before the ordination candidate has to say a final "I do," but what is the deal with Christians and the obsession with trying to look perfect? When did the gatherings for followers of Christ stop being a refuge for struggling sinners and become a kind of suburban country club where we all say, "My, what a pretty dress you are wearing"?

Why is it so astonishing, and deeply refreshing, when a preacher actually acknowledges his or her own struggles as a human being and a spiritual follower? If spiritual leaders are hardly ever able to be honest about their own doubts, fears, questions, disbelief, hopelessness, and misplaced values, how likely is it that the regular people in the pews will step up to share their difficulties in walking the spiritual path?

I remember times in my youth when people would share testimony in church. Sometimes testimony would come from a person recovering from alcoholism or some other problem believed to be a sign of lapsed moral character. They would share their gratitude that Jesus had saved their soul from a life of sin with sincerity and sometimes tears. Regardless of the theology behind it, people were coming to church to admit how messy their lives had become and how happy they were that they were being set free.

I wonder why people don't come to church to say what a mess their lives are anymore. When they did speak such truths in the old days, the story was usually told after the fact, after God had done a miracle and made it all better. There aren't many stories at church about life being a wreck without a happy ending, but people in Alcoholics Anonymous (AA) do this all the time. When someone shares a story of radical imperfection in AA, people in the room clap and congratulate them for speaking honestly. I wish church people could speak out about our imperfections with that kind of honesty.

Since none of us will ever be perfect in this life, what makes it so hard for religious people to admit that? Or more to the point, how will we respond when we practice contemplative prayer and find that the inner stillness allows our imperfections to come welling up?

Here is a hard truth: Become inwardly still, and you will come to see yourself honestly. Who you truly are will arise: the good, the bad, and the ugly. Just as I could not escape the discovery of the faux monk part of my personality, I will also not be able to avoid seeing the whole mess of my inner life sooner or later in contemplation.

When I quit avoiding confronting these truths and settle into a simple practice of the presence of God, I also make my awareness vulnerable to the presence of all of me. It's myself *and* God who are in communion, and God seems to be pretty good at showing me to me. Here is yet another reason to avoid contemplation at all costs. If your goal is to avoid seeing yourself or your life as it is right now, then skip practicing contemplation. If achieving perfection is in your life plan, then I highly recommend you stop reading right now because that is not where we are heading. In fact, being in the Presence a little each day makes it clear to me that I will never reach perfection in this life—not even close!

If you decide to keep reading, or better yet, if you make it to the bonus round of the spiritual journey and establish a regular practice of the presence of God, you will also come to this realization: I am never going to be perfect, and that is completely okay. It's like admitting to ourselves: I'm not okay, you're not okay, and that's okay. Stay on this path and you might come face-to-face with grace.

One of the great gifts of practicing the Presence is receiving regular help with the Messiah complex, which is the secret belief that we have to be perfect *and* save the world from all of its imperfections. And being near the true One can also help us with our own God complex, by which we believe we have to run the world. Being in the Presence, even for a moment each day, really delivers a potent message that can be transformative: I am loved right in the middle of all my imperfection.

So here is how we begin to deal with the uncomfortable reality of our many imperfections, which always come bubbling up in the quiet times. We practice simple honesty in seeing ourselves as we are, and true humility in accepting ourselves as we are. No, this is not nearly as easy as it might sound. This is real work, inner work, the work of watching our messy lives emerge a bit at a time and asking for the grace to offer those imperfections right into the presence of the One who loves us so.

Rather than asking God to fix our mess and clean us up, contemplative prayer brings us into an intimate communion where we can be authentic with the One who already knows everything about us. Once there, we say a simple prayer, "Here is my messy life. Please help." As we fall into that wordless place with a little bit of trust, we turn it over to the Source of all help and comfort. Instead of hiding our imperfections from ourselves and everyone else, the contemplative path offers a wonderful freedom to speak our truth to God and to other people. What we come to find is that other imperfect contemplatives are relieved to know that we struggle too.

Regular contact with the Source of loving-kindness will help us embrace our foibles, even dark thoughts and impure motives. Daily rejuvenation of our sense of worth can help us take off the mask and risk saying, "I am the guy who gets overwhelmed by lust," or "I am the woman who can't seem to get past my old grief," or "I don't know if I even believe in God anymore, but I really wish I could." All this relief can be found through entering a contemplative learning community. We are not learning how to be more perfect. We are learning: My life's not okay, your life's not okay, and that's okay.

SNACK FOOD

Monasterians—people seeking to live in a monastery of the heart—will not be able to make it in this imperfect life without finding a way to sustain the practice of the inner sanctuary. For the presence of God is our food. Without it we quickly starve. We do not enter this path because we are good, or righteous, or spiritually superior in any way. We are just hungry. So much of what we have been offered in the American culture is nothing more than snack food, or worse than that—it's mostly junk food.

It's really no wonder that so many people, including religious people, are settling for substitutes for real spiritual food. Without the daily nourishment of soul food, what else can they do but seek any form of distraction from the discomfort of hungry bellies? It makes me sad to see so many of us trying to fill up on snack foods. How many chips and candy bars does it take to make the inner being feel full?

My most frequent snack food has been the hours dedicated to watching television. Maybe others try to slake their spiritual thirst with their favorite beer, while other people feed on the daily news. Others keep up with every single sneeze of every single one of their five hundred friends on Facebook. I am not decrying any of these things as bad in themselves, but it seems we can turn most anything into a form of overindulgence with snack foods that don't really satisfy. At times we all sense, somewhere in our awareness, that snack foods leave us spiritually hollow.

Monasterians, contemplatives, new monks, or whatever we call ourselves as spiritual seekers—we are all waking up to our dissatisfaction with our own forms of snack food. We want more, and even a nibble of the feast laid out in the sanctuary of the soul sends us on a quest for more.

But there is a rub in all of this: It is unpleasant to have to wake up and see that we have been subsisting on snack food. Once we are awake, it is embarrassing to see how often we still settle for those same inadequate foods as though they were ever enough. Something in us wants more, but something else in us is used to what we have been stuffing our souls with. Maybe this is one of the reasons so many of us overeat in our culture: We are trying to fill a soul-deep need. Perhaps this is why we also try almost any new spiritual technique, or trendy guru, or special spiritual site. Could we call it spiritual gluttony?

Contemplative experience is a balm to this pain of self-recognition. If we are awakened to the inadequacy of snack food in fulfilling the soul's hunger, then we can also be helped to find deeper satisfaction. For instance, moments of oneness with the Divine bring a sense of my own deeper wholeness. In those visits with the Presence, I know I am not alone. In the emergences of higher wisdom than my own, I am helped to find direction, guidance, and a sense of purpose. Such experiences fulfill me somewhere down beneath my habit of distracting myself with television shows that are more commercials than entertainment anyway.

Let's agree on the following truths: Snack foods never satisfy deeper hungers; I have an embedded pattern of settling for spiritual snack foods; and there is help for my addiction in practicing the presence of God, which will fulfill me as nothing else can.

ON CONTEMPLATIVE DISCOURAGEMENT

There have been plenty of discouragements in my long years of seeking to form contemplative communities. I have been disappointed in my own futile efforts to sustain daily contemplative practice through the early years. These days, I am frequently dissatisfied when I let myself get started with projects before I practice inner stillness. I know from experience that if I don't start the day in stillness, I rarely find time to stop later.

For many years I felt the longing to regularly visit in an inner sanctuary, but I could only live that life sporadically. I would wonder to myself, "If you love it so much, why can't you practice regularly?" That question gradually helped me learn that there is great resistance to spiritual growth in the human psyche. As much as we feel an innate impetus toward growth, we have an equally stubborn resistance to change. For the longest time my resistance won out over my desire to practice the presence of God on a daily basis.

Scolding myself never helped. Striving never helped. Reading books about practicing the Presence was inspiring, but books alone don't conquer resistance. Despite the common myth that says, "You can accomplish anything through willpower," I have learned two strategies that did gradually help me find a regular pattern of practicing the presence of God.

First, I ask for God's help, and second, I ask for other people's help. In my experience these approaches are both different from willpower. When I ask God in the simplest way to help me actually sit down and practice, she usually does. She does not seem to be filled with mountains of inner resistance like I am. In some ways this means I meet my resistance by giving up on willpower. When I can finally get myself to let go of trying to practice, and simply ask God to help me surrender, I am already moving into her Presence.

For many years I met the definition of insanity: trying the same thing over and over and expecting different results. I tried and tried with willpower alone, but it turns out that willpower is not as effective in spiritual matters. No wonder I was discouraged so often.

Trying to create a spiritual practice with willpower alone is about as effective as trying to paint the ceiling of the Sistine Chapel with a toothbrush. You mostly end up with a lot of frustration and discouragement because you are working with the wrong tool. What is the right tool? Surrender of our efforts into God's hands.

Years ago, my friend Lloyd taught us the simplest version of the first three steps from AA's twelve-step program in a meeting for family members and friends of alcoholics. Lloyd would often repeat these steps with a certain smug look that at first made me think he was showing off, for he quoted AA's Big Book so often that he earned the nickname of Big Book Lloyd. Later I decided he was just happy to have learned the formula for more successful living after decades of life as a drunk. I watched Lloyd, with his long white hair, as he summarized those steps of recovery in an ultra-simple prayer: "I can't. You can. I think I'll let you."

So there it is in all its simplicity, a secret of the spiritual universe. Lloyd's prayer was the first thing that actually worked to help me establish a more regular contemplative practice. The secret is a real and practical surrender of willpower—the opposite of what most of us try.

If you come to me now as a discouraged contemplative newbie, and you ask me to tell you the secret of practicing the presence of God on a regular, if messy and imperfect basis, I will not say, "You just have to keep trying harder." I will not offer you a how-to manual guaranteed to bring results. On a good day, if we get lucky and I remember the truth, I will tell you to stop trying, for surrender is the only solution. "I can't do this alone" is the starting point.

Unlike some coach on a playing field, I hope I will tell you to give up on doing it all alone and to try trusting a Power greater than yourself to help you. I hope I will remember Lloyd's prayer and encourage you to know that God can do what you can't. She can lead you into direct contact, into a relationship of simple Presence.

After I give up trying and say, "I can't," and after I cultivate a little trust that "you can," I take the full plunge of surrender: "I think I'll let you." Thank you, Big Book Lloyd, for teaching me a simple tool for overcoming my resistance to practicing the presence of God each day.

After some years of being annoyed with Lloyd's joyful attitude, which I interpreted as being a know-it-all because of my own sense of spiritual inadequacy, I now recognize he was serving us from his joy. Lloyd's life wasn't perfect, and he would regularly complain of the messed up relationships within his own family, but he grew a long way by learning the secret of giving up and turning it over.

The second approach that has eventually helped my own discouragement about practicing the presence of God regularly has been asking for help from other people. After too many decades of trying to be spiritual on my own and being too embarrassed to ask others for help, I finally gave up on my spiritual pride too. I had to—it was fake anyway.

Using Lloyd's prayer as a model, this second kind of asking for help might sound like this: "I can't. You can't. Maybe we can help each other." My rational mind says, "Wait a minute. How would two people who can't do something add up to helping anyone?" My rational mind makes a logical point, but it is missing the point.

When you and I get together in the sure knowledge that we can't do this thing alone, we ask God to help both of us. The request for her help is multiplied, and when a group of us get together to seek God's presence in this way, the divine math can add up to more than the sum of its parts. In a mystery beyond understanding, Jesus said, "When two or more are gathered in my name, there am I in the midst of them" (Matt 18:20). So the divine math goes something like: one person who can't plus another person who can't equals Presence!

I'm no good at math, but I know from experience that when I get together with others and we all give up trying and surrender to prayer, some version of "I can't. You can. I think I'll let you," then our discouragement often dissolves into a sense of Presence.

If I were a person of real faith, I'd say God's presence is always here. But I'm not. I know that theory, and in my best moments I do believe it. Doctrines don't do much for actual spiritual experience. What I am really seeking is not some stale, theological belief adopted in the Middle Ages called omnipresence. I want a Presence that I can count on now.

I'm not saying God has to give me warm and gushy feelings *all* the time. It's more like saying, "I could use a little help here." What I really want is to be in God's presence, even if there are no bells and whistles. For some people it is enough to have a firm set of beliefs all packaged in a tidy box, but beliefs just don't do it for me—I want experience.

I can believe that my wife exists all day long. I can establish firm doctrines about her and assent to all of these beliefs, but I am a contemplative, a seeker of direct experience! What I want is Carol's presence with me. For me, even a few moments of being with Carol is worth far more than any number of books or beliefs about her.

So what is a guy who wants to experience the presence of the Spirit to do? Besides asking her to come be with me, I also sit with others who want her Presence. We want together, and in some miracle outside our control, she often comes. Sometimes we can even sense her nearness, and that is a heavenly feeling.

Maybe this plan for dealing with discouragement is another window into what it means to form contemplative communities all around New Orleans. We are just regular people wanting God's presence together. I know that doesn't sound too flashy, and you might even ask why I think my mission to create contemplative communities means anything. I ask myself that all the time. Aren't we just little groups of people sitting around in silence?

In my better moments, I try to embrace the simple truth that I need to be with other people who want what I want, just as alcoholics seeking recovery need to be with other people who want to recover. Contemplatives need to be with other people who also want Presence, and that's all there is to it.

I birth and support contemplative communities because I need their help. It's a unique kind of selfishness. I do it for me. If someone else benefits, that's good too. I know it would sound a lot holier to say I do this to help all the people in our world who need God's presence. If it does help them I am glad, but in all truth I do this because I need to be with others who want God.

So there is my two-part formula for dealing with discouragement in practicing the presence of God. It goes like this: Stop trying and ask for help.

LOSS OF OUR CALLING

We who live in America often get addicted to being busy instead of honoring the need for stillness and inner listening. We are not trained as children to listen in stillness, except perhaps when we get on our parents nerves and are told to sit down and be quiet, which is not exactly training. As we develop through childhood and young adulthood, we learn that we will be assessed and measured by what we accomplish and produce. This is true for religious leaders as much as anyone. Nowhere are we trained to listen within for who we are or why we are here.

Even religious vocations so often get turned into a performance and an evaluation of the performance. A preacher listens for an evaluation like, "Great message, Pastor!" and hopes to avoid hearing parishioners say, "I didn't understand your point." Pastors are often evaluated based on an expectation for unending growth in church membership and donations. In some circles, this never-ending growth expectation is synonymous with effectiveness. American values, like the ones that say that bigger is always better, become dogma that infiltrates the church and its mission.

In the religious or secular world, it is all too rare to hear anything about the importance of slowing down, taking time for contemplation, or seeking wise guidance from the voice within. When we are so unfamiliar with such changes of pace, the very thought of stillness can trigger anxiety or guilt at not being productive and fear of what might come bubbling up. We don't have to question our purpose in this life if we just keep moving and looking busy.

Stillness might just bring us face to face with the awareness that we have yet to find a sense of purpose for our lives. Or if we ever did have a true calling, we might experience the painful loss of the mission we once had. Stillness might bring the immediacy of recovering our destiny, but we are afraid to even try a little stillness.

Once a good friend named David and I discussed the issue of purpose. After sharing our own understanding of why we walk this earth, we decided to bring the question to our men's group. Most of the men were in the latter years of their careers or retired. When we asked the question, not one man out of ten could form even a semblance of a response. Not one could articulate a sense of calling, purpose, or personal mission, which saddened me. It seemed clear that something about our American society and our religious culture is not working. I thought afterwards that it is no wonder that Americans avoid stillness at all costs, if the experience might bring up such an empty sense of having no purpose on this planet.

When we do begin to learn how to cultivate inner stillness through some retreat or workshop or spiritual group, we begin to get in touch with our own souls. The soul is the seat of creativity and imagination, so inner images arise as we take some first steps in contacting our own souls, and "a certain inner fire begins to burn. These images have to do with our deepest and perhaps most precious desires,"[3] according to the poet David Whyte.

---

3. Whyte, *Heart Aroused*, 230.

If excessive busyness leads to loss of mission, calling, and purpose, then inner stillness can bring us back in touch with our own soul. As David Whyte says, our souls want to help us connect with our deepest desires. Here begins the recovery of our inner calling, our possibilities for creative purpose, and our inner ear for a mission that matters. But we will never find that inner fire if we do not face the sad reality that we have been moving too fast to even know we have a soul. The contemplative practice of stillness leads us through the sadness of those lost years without purpose and into the inner fire. For this journey the soul always stands ready. It is never too late.

This is not a how-to book, but I do want to mention a way we can begin to renew the journey of establishing contact with the soul. We can begin by asking our family members and ourselves some questions about our childhood: What was I like? What did I love? What were my treasures and gifts? Who was I as a child? In this looking back we are seeking to see the original, one-and-only being who was born to a certain purpose before the world began to mold us into another image.

After locating some of those hints of our own early souls, we can ask similar questions for today. What experiences bring me joy? When and where and how does my soul seem most pleased? What do I long for more than anything, and what is the desire beneath that longing? When do I touch my own wholeness, and when do I feel my emptiness?

I believe the most profound modern author concerning the nature and care of the soul is Dr. Thomas Moore. If you want to recover your own sense of your soul, I can't think of a better place to start than to read his *Care of the Soul* and *Soul Mates*, books for helping us connect with the depth and beauty of our own souls.

FACING EMPTINESS

"Those with busy lives, but bereft of the inner images based on the soul's desires, have empty larders, and no fire in the hearth; they will starve if they are not fed something more nourishing."

—David Whyte[4]

The avoidance of our innate emptiness is probably one of the strongest motivators in our culture for keeping perpetually busy. Yet David Whyte

---

4. Ibid., 239.

calls our attention to how our addiction to staying busy feeds our own emptiness. In a disastrous, self-defeating cycle, our habit of saying "yes" to every call to action or service drains us of what the soul needs. Soul hungers are not fed by adding to our already jam-packed agendas.

No wonder establishing a discipline of contemplative practice can be so daunting. Some vague inner awareness senses that we are empty down in the soul, but paying attention to that discomfort is usually avoided at all costs. Nowhere are we trained in knowing the presence of our emptiness, facing it, or befriending it. So we run and run and never slow down, and the empty hunger of the soul keeps growing.

Training in contemplative practice involves learning to be with emptiness, inner stillness, inactivity, and simple being. This in no way implies that we are learning easy steps to get rid of emptiness. Let someone else write that book. We contemplatives are slowly learning to face our fear of emptiness so that we can learn the geography of our own souls. This means we will notice the emptiness within. We will practice not running away until we discover we can be with our emptiness and even come to rest in the wholeness beneath our brokenness.

There are times when the temptation to flee will be enormous. Here is an example: On my first silent retreat over a long weekend I, slow reader that I am, read five books on contemplation. I hope you will have a hearty laugh over that one. How ridiculous to go off on a silent retreat in the company of one hundred other men at the Manresa House of Retreats in Convent, Louisiana, and spend every waking moment reading about silence rather than actually experiencing it. Even in silence, I managed to fill up every inch of empty inner space with printed words rather than spoken. I was so effective that I hardly noticed how desperately I was avoiding my own emptiness.

Over that first weekend, there was a vague hint of inner awareness that all of this reading was unusual for me. I probably even had a tiny sense that something defensive was going on. But that intuition did not stop me from plunging headlong into information about the very silence I was there to experience.

I did the same kind of substituting when I first came across Thomas Merton's *Contemplative Prayer* in my late twenties. I was fascinated by his description of a landscape of the soul of which I had no knowledge. I would read a phrase and ponder over it for days. I would feel convinced of the truth in Merton's words intended for novice monks, for I too was a total novice. I felt like I was being invited on an adventure into a foreign country: The country was the inner world of my own soul and a deep relationship with God.

I remember feeling a sense of conviction in reading Merton's quote from an obscure monk, Isaac of Nineveh, who said, "Every man who delights in a multitude of words, even though he says admirable things, is empty within."[5] That phrase gripped me and would not let go. I wanted to believe it was about other people who liked to talk all the time, but the truth was calling me to look in a mirror: I am a man who delights in a multitude of words, and even though I might sometimes have said admirable things, I was empty within.

This truth also hints at why we humans might run from silence, stillness, slowing down, or turning away from the myriad distracting entertainments our culture offers us. Most of us do not want to encounter the truth that we are empty inside. No wonder I dove into reading all those books on that first silent retreat. I didn't know anything about my natural emptiness, and I sure didn't want to experience it.

Back then I did not know that we have emptiness built into our inner structure as human beings. I did not know that our very cells contain more empty space than substance. Check it out in some scientific journal. Google a picture of a human cell. Down to the core of our being we contain a lot of emptiness. This is not a problem unless we never have any training in how to be with empty space.

As I write this section, I am sitting alone beside large picture windows at my cousin's beautiful home in South Lake Tahoe, California. It's an incredible view. The green aspen leaves gently flutter in an occasional cool June breeze. The pine and fir trees of the forest stand erect, and their greenery reaches up to the bright sun and deep blue sky. They might be silently worshipping. The only sound is the wind rustling through their branches. Otherwise, everything is still and quiet, except for an occasional dog barking in the distance.

In this spaciousness I can feel my own emptiness. It rises each time I allow myself to open to this stillness. I do not need to tear through five books today. I no longer need to turn away from the empty inner space to read about contemplation. My emptiness is not an enemy. It will not devour me. My empty space is my own soul saying, "Here am I." This is

---

5. Merton, *Contemplative Prayer*, 5.

my being. This is my friend. This is the inner sanctuary of the soul where I am one with the Divine.

In this moment the awareness brings up quiet tears. I can still let myself get so busy that I get lost from my true home in God. Have I not learned the lesson by now? I pause between writing each sentence of this book to be present in this empty home. I pause again as the wind outside picks up enough to make the aspen leaves dance. I feel sorrow for all the moments I have missed, and at the same time, I know joy that I am home now.

So here is what I have begun to know in these decades of contemplative practice. There is an inner structure to being human, a geography of the soul. To begin this lesson, we must be willing to experience what words in books cannot teach us. We must practice being, which helps us begin to know our own being.

There are also layers of consciousness within this realm of the soul. The mind tends to dominate the topmost layer with its constant stream of thoughts. This world of thought includes memories from the past, immediate awareness of the present moment, and projections of what might be in future. Everyone knows they have thoughts. But not everyone has spent enough time observing the flow of thoughts to know that their thoughts are not who they are. The special realm of the mind is the producing and analyzing of thoughts.

Beneath these thoughts, and often attached to them, are our feelings. Emotions are at the second layer of consciousness, connected to the heart. Meditative practices sometimes include training in the observation of our feelings. This helps us know that we are not our feelings. No matter how intensely we might feel something, we are not our emotions.

I first learned this truth for myself during the eight-day mindfulness retreat I mentioned. We were immersed in long days of observing the flow of thoughts and feelings. Through such experiences, we learned that we could take the stance of silent witness observing the unending stream of thoughts and feelings.

Watching the way my thoughts and feelings keep changing from moment to moment helps me remember that I am neither my thoughts nor my feelings. They are simply passing through me. This knowledge can be a blessing to me when I am experiencing troubling thoughts or emotions, for it is a comfort to remember that they will pass. This understanding also helps me be a therapist who does not seek to help counseling clients rid themselves of troubling thoughts or feelings, but instead to come to peace with them. Discovering for myself that our thoughts and emotions are a never-ending stream offers great relief that we do not have to do anything about them.

Still, there is a lot more going on in our inner geography besides the flow of thoughts and feelings. Beneath the feelings there is empty space. I see this space as being within the territory of the soul. If we sit, or walk, or engage in any contemplative practice where we settle into the landscape of simple being, we will encounter this empty space.

I envision this emptiness as being like the inside of a large inner cavern. The thoughts are at the surface, above ground. The feelings are beneath, then there is the open space of the cavern itself. This I experience as the emptiness beneath thoughts and feelings. This cavern of emptiness can be explored just as spelunkers investigate caves beneath the ground. Long practice of inner stillness can afford us the opportunity to get comfortable with this cavern as it becomes familiar territory. With time, we can stop avoiding this empty place and come to face it with awareness, saying to ourselves, "Oh, there is my emptiness."

Sitting here in my own emptiness, with the snow-covered mountains in view out of one window to my left and the aspen leaves of June dancing in front of me, it is easy to go deeper in the layers of consciousness. I refer to this layer as the inner sanctuary of the soul. This is the floor of the cavern, a sanctuary that is the ground of being.

I think it might help to envision the whole geography of human consciousness. Beneath the stream of the mind's thoughts and the heart's feelings, and beneath the large cavern of emptiness within the soul, we find the soul's ground of being. I believe our deepest needs for oneness and longing for union with the Divine arise from this place. The contemplative practice of being in this oneness in the sanctuary of the soul is like the resolution of our emptiness.

The healing of our troubling thoughts, our memories of personal wounds, and our disturbing feelings can only come from being in touch with our fundamental wholeness beneath all of our brokenness. This wholeness is the ground of our being. I believe it arises from the sanctuary of the soul, the little altar where we experience oneness with the Presence. This inner sanctuary, the home of the living God, is at the center of our very existence. This is the Source of the wholeness beneath every form of brokenness. Dropping down into this place takes us through the emptiness and readies us for God to heal our many ills.

I have learned to trust this inner sanctuary of the soul as a source of healing when I am sitting with counseling clients. This knowledge comes from personal experience. It is not a theory to be debated. I have known the healing balm of my own inner sanctuary time and again. I have even been blessed to practice loving-kindness meditation to help me turn my attention down into that inner sanctuary and fill my heart with loving-kindness to dissolve the suffering. You too can rest assured that when you encounter your own emptiness beneath your thoughts and feelings, there is an amazing inner sanctuary beneath it just waiting for you.

LOSTNESS: WHEN DARKNESS FALLS

There are times of darkness on our contemplative way, entrances into the classical Way of Unknowing, which will be part of any contemplative path sooner or later. So what are we to do when the ground under our feet disappears, when we find ourselves falling into a downward spiral as our scaffolding gives way? How are we to respond when everything in our lives starts changing, when our sense of ourselves is rattled, shaken, or lost altogether?

Maybe you know what it is like when life has thrust you out into thin air like an acrobat suspended high above an invisible net—flying somewhere between the hand-hold of the former life you had to let go of, and the next hand-hold you have yet to grasp, the life that has not yet been revealed. This is a scary space that feels vulnerable, dangerous, naked, and susceptible to falling onto the concrete in a life-changing splat!

What are we to do about the times when the soul cries out with that strange, otherworldly sound that we can barely recognize as our own, when we are unsure of how to respond? What happens when the soul sound is not a clear message but just a wailing longing from the deepest place? Is there really a Spirit issuing groans too deep for words when we do not know how to give voice to our soul? Is there a Presence in our midst when we are frightened to the core by something we can't even explain?

This passage is one of the hardest parts of the dark side of contemplative practice. We are quite capable of completely losing our way on this spiritual journey. One of our school members is in the middle of this darkness. Andrea has been trying to leave behind the constricted religion in which she was raised, and she has been slowly embracing a more progressive form of Christianity that allows for and even treasures questions of faith. But the road has been rough on her soul.

Massive fears have arisen in Andrea asking: What am I doing? Where am I going? Who am I if not the person who followed all those religious rules for so long? Where is this path taking me? What if I end up losing my faith altogether? How can I cope with all these changes to the very core of my life?

Andrea has entered that time when darkness falls and the way ahead is not just foggy, it has gone black as night. At times it seems that no light can penetrate the darkness of her spiritual and religious vision. The temptation to try to go backwards is strong, but we can't ever really go backwards on a spiritual journey. Once we have seen through the false old ways of believing and behaving, we can't adopt those ways again. It would be like trying to convince our adult selves to believe in Santa Claus.

Along that lost path there is a sense that we are truly alone. We believe we have to find our own way, and this loneliness raises our anxieties sky-high. This path of seeking oneness with the One who we can't see or touch feels like wandering blind with hands outstretched and a yearning to grab hold of anything solid.

The contemplative path winds this way so that we must face our fear of falling and our fear of the dark. Lostness, or walking forward when we cannot see what is ahead of us, calls for a kind of faith we don't believe we have. This is not only Andrea's problem. This is my problem too. Maybe your struggle is the same. This is one reason why Andrea comes to see me as a spiritual director and why I go to see my own spiritual director. None of us want to walk in the dark alone.

The faith to keep walking when darkness falls cannot be forced. It is not our religious duty to try to create faith, despite the hundreds of sermons we may have heard telling us so. Hearing someone say, "You just gotta have faith," in no way produces faith, just the guilt of another false expectation. Let me say it clearly: Faith is not of our own creation.

Perhaps the confusion comes from people using the word "faith" as though it is synonymous with "belief." Faith is more like trust than belief. Faith leads me to take a step into the dark trusting that there will still be solid ground under the next step, even though my fear tells me there is nothing there. Faith is not the absence of fear. Yet it can be "the substance of things hoped for, the evidence of things not seen," as Paul, the apostle of Jesus, described it (Heb 11:1). Trust-faith happens when I take that fearful step into the unknown and my foot finds the ground. In that moment, I am able to receive a little faith.

Faith is actually a grace-gift, and sometimes it finds us individually. Sometimes our faith is enhanced by the sheer presence of friends who are experiencing their own faith. When Willie, one of my formerly homeless friends, told me about the possibility of receiving a housing voucher, he was expressing faith—trust that what had been promised would occur. In fact, each morning Willie stepped out of the Salvation Army's door to hit the streets of New Orleans, he stepped out in faith, trusting that his next meal would present itself. He was following an unseen hand's guidance, and Willie's faith strengthened mine.

This is not a vignette to take us back to the belief that "You gotta have faith," as though you could control it. This is a reminder that when the way grows dark, as it regularly does for people who live in reality, there is a way through. There is a very real Presence within, and there are companions who will support us when we are lost.

Perhaps you have not found a group of companions who accept you wherever you are on the spiritual journey. If so, now is the time to start looking around for a few spiritual followers who are seeking God's presence, who don't have all the answers, and who accept others with lovingkindness wherever they are on their spiritual path.

You do not have to have the same beliefs as these new friends because they are not the ones who have all those answers. You do not have to look or sound like these new friends because they are not into conformity. You do not have to act like you are not lost because they have been lost too.

Start by seeking out people who practice centering prayer or other contemplative practices as part of their spiritual disciplines. You can find the nearest centering prayer group through the Contemplative Outreach website listed in the "Resources" section at the end of the book. You might also contact the nearest retreat center to see which groups come through for contemplative retreats. These contemplatives have already started the path of practicing the presence of God. They too have been lost, and this path has brought them to encounter the Being who guides us through times when darkness falls.

Finally, rather than offering a pat answer on easy steps to conquer your sense of lostness, I suggest you seek out a personal spiritual director who is willing to serve as a guide and spiritual companion. You can locate the nearest spiritual director through Spiritual Directors International, which is listed in the "Resources" section. This new friend will walk along with you through your lostness, for spiritual friendship is an immense help when darkness falls. It is not a shortcut on the spiritual journey that we need, but a community of people to help us remember we are not alone.

NOWHERE TO HIDE: FEELING PAINFUL FEELINGS

Another of the difficulties of this contemplative lifestyle became clear as I was launching a new class on "Ten Ways to Meditate." Nineteen people registered to meet in our apartment in the heart of New Orleans. On the first day of class we were exploring the foundational practice of mindfulness meditation when I asked the group to imagine where, when, and how they would like to try their new practice of mindfulness.

One of the participants decided to bare her soul for a minute to say she was finding it hard to imagine practicing at home, since she is never alone by choice. She said she feels loneliness all the time and isn't too sure she wants to sit still all by herself. We listened to her describe a loneliness we all feel sooner or later.

Another group member agreed, "Yeah, because we are the culture addicted to distraction. It sounds like a book title that would sell a million copies." We laughed and then grew quiet. Those students had hit on one of our greatest human resistances to practicing inner stillness. When we grow still, we tend to truly feel our feelings. If we have emotions we would prefer to avoid, like loneliness, we have a strong motivation to avoid stillness.

If you have ever tried to practice meditation or contemplation, you know what we were talking about in class. Most of us are willing to try most any distraction, and even some addictions, if they promise escape. We need immense courage to start and sustain a meditation practice. We can't avoid feeling our emotions in the stillness, but we can acknowledge them and learn to work wisely with them.

Learning I needed a tooth implant was a good example. That is not nearly as serious as people facing cancer, death, divorce, abuse, or the many other traumas in the world of terrible feelings, but it offers a hint of how things work when we learn there is nowhere to hide on the contemplative way.

I had been having dental work in hopes of curing a toothache that had been bothering me for several months. I went in for a crown, but things did not go as planned. I left the office with half of the tooth broken off, an exposed root, and in need of an extraction and a tooth implant.

The visit with the oral surgeon did not comfort my soul. Hearing the surgeon detail the removal of a tooth with roots anchored into my jawbone sounded gruesome. The idea of drilling a screw down into that same bone sounded dangerous. Reading the list of all that could go wrong on the medical release raised my anxiety even higher. Do they always have to list death as a possibility in any surgery?

That evening as I was joining one of the centering prayer groups I found it unusually hard to concentrate on the presence of God. In fact, I could think of hardly anything but what might happen to me the next day and worry about where the money for the surgery might come from.

Although the practice of centering usually involves the gentle release of all thoughts and feelings as they arise, there was no release for me that evening. There was no protection from the fears either. The contemplative way never offers magical help. It is not a quick-fix path. There simply is nowhere to hide in the practice of opening our hearts to the presence of God. This is true of the hardest feelings that assault us, and it is true of smaller fears like my anxiety over my tooth implant procedure.

Even when we have the hope of finding the presence of a living God within ourselves, we still also have that fear of stillness and of our own feelings. So what are we to do? I suggest we make use of two small steps to help us walk the contemplative path despite our fears. I find we need to first set our intention, and second, to practice in groups.

When I say we set our intention I do not mean we have to harness the power of positive thinking and make ourselves do something whether we want to or not. This is not a manipulation of willpower, which just strengthens our resistance. What I do mean is that we can look beyond the wish to avoid our painful feelings to discover a deeper place within ourselves where we long to find our true home.

Admitting that we will be imperfect in our efforts, we do what my twelve-step friends do in the third step of their recovery program: "Make a decision to turn our will and our lives over to the care of God." This is one form of setting our intention.

We give voice to our deeper longing aloud or within by saying, "I want to practice the presence of God." This is our intention, and stating it simply and clearly might help keep us in touch with the longings beneath our fear of feelings. Find your own way right now and practice saying your intention to yourself: "Deep in my heart I long for . . . and I intend to . . ."

We also help ourselves address our fear of painful feelings when we practice setting our intention in groups. Some of us have been through terrifying trauma, and the nightmares, memories, or even flashbacks don't just go away because we are seeking God. We have good reason to want to avoid such dark places in our psyches, and perhaps we have even fallen prey to addictions to try to numb things that we just can't face alone.

We do not need to face these things alone. There are serious dangers in going into some places in the psyche without the help and support of wise guides like therapists and spiritual companions. Even the small normal agonies of human experience still deserve the supportive care of nonjudgmental companions.

So let us commit to expressing our desire for spiritual communion in groups where we will find loving help. In the company of others, we might set our intention out loud by saying, "I want to practice the presence of God as best I can," or "I want to let love rule in my life," or some other personal expression. We practice in groups to strengthen our resolve, which will always waver and falter when we try it alone. When we hear the commitment of others, it helps to consecrate our own intention.

I have also learned that there is something about the intention of others during group practice that helps me sense God's presence. I believe there is a place beneath thoughts and feelings and emptiness where together we can land in the inner sanctuary of the soul, where we are all connected by an invisible web of divinity. Shared contemplative practice seems to strengthen our awareness of our interconnectedness. We regularly feel a sense of oneness with each other as well as with the Divine. In fact, group practice sometimes feeds a sense of our interconnectedness with all beings and the entire world. I can offer no explanation, only my own direct experience and that of fellow group members.

When we are ready to face our own feelings as best we can by setting our intention and practicing this intention in groups, we can set a course for contemplative practice in a thousand ways. Once we know we want to practice the presence of God in our lives, we get to choose approaches to practice that work best for us. It is time to experiment, and many of us find we can actually have fun if we take a light-hearted approach to spiritual practice. Here our AA friends can help in admitting as they do that we are "seeking spiritual progress, not perfection." So when you are ready, dive into the next section and find your own way to practice the presence of God.

5

Practicing the Presence

TEN WAYS TO MEDITATE

THERE ARE THOUSANDS OF ways to practice God's presence. The best ways are whichever ways work for each of us. In our classes at the School for Contemplative Living, we have found the practices listed in this first section to be some of our favorites, but they are only a sampling of the myriad ways to practice the Presence. So I am beginning this chapter with ten of our most recent practices.

Sitting meditation is the most common form of meditation among people who are intentional about their practice. If you have not tried this form yet, you might have an image in mind of some yogi on the floor in a lotus posture. That is one way to sit, but limber legs are not a prerequisite to practicing sitting meditation.

In fact, physical posture is not the main thing. Intentional consciousness, or mindfulness, and heartfulness are the main things. Still, it does help to sit upright in a posture of wakefulness for sitting meditation. Drop your shoulders, relax your hands in your lap, and raise your head as though a light string is gently lifting you towards the sky. It helps to have good back support if you intend to sit for more than a few minutes.

Sitting meditation, like most forms of meditation, is mostly about cultivating a particular state of consciousness. While there are many ways to sit and meditate, all share a common intention. Once you have taken your seat, it is good to set that intention. The mind rambles around like a stray cat, changing directions with every whim, darting to and fro without any form of guidance. Feelings arise and distract our attention. Streams of thought with no apparent connection sweep us along so that within a minute we can forget why we began to meditate in the first place.

This is why we begin meditation by setting our intention. Rather than letting the mind wander aimlessly in all directions, we set an intention to be attentive. We might pay attention to the stream of thoughts themselves, observing the emergence of our feelings, attitudes, interests, and impulses as they come and go. This is an aspect of mindfulness practice.

But we can also set our intention toward a specific focus like cultivating relaxation, or peace, or loving-kindness, or prayers for a loved one or friend, or simple attention to the presence of God. Setting intention does not mean blocking thoughts out. It just means cultivating awareness in a particular direction.

Even now as I pen these words, I am intent on keeping my focus of attention on this writing. My thoughts still come and go, but my intention is to communicate with you about something that matters to me. So I release the other thoughts and keep bringing my attention back to this writing.

In sitting meditation, we notice these passing thoughts with the simple intention of paying little attention to them. We keep turning our attention back to our focus, whatever that may be. I first learned about this letting go during my eight-day immersion experience in mindfulness with Jon Kabat-Zinn and Saki Santorelli in 1998. Through their guidance, we learned to pay attention to the place within us called the silent witness. This is the observing aspect of consciousness. Instead of getting lost in the stream of thoughts and emotions all day long, sitting meditation teaches us to stay in touch with the witness, the aspect of ourselves that notices our thoughts, feelings, and impulses as they come and go.

At that 1998 retreat, I was amazed by how constantly my own mind kept shifting from one thought and feeling to the next. As we practiced that attentive consciousness from six a.m. to six p.m. each day, I found it comforting to notice that no matter how powerful an emotion or how persistent a thought or attitude, they all kept changing. The lesson went a bit like this: Whatever comes up, just stick around long enough and it will go away to be replaced by the next.

Discovering the impermanence of every thought and feeling this way was life-changing. Before trying meditation, I tended to feel at the mercy of each passing emotion. Perhaps you have too. What a relief to discover that sitting meditation can offer a deeper and more pervasive part of ourselves where we can sit in a state of equanimity to watch our passing thoughts and emotions. This is one of the gifts of sitting meditation, one that can also be cultivated through other forms of meditation.

If meditation is coming to our middle, or our center, then the various forms of meditation are simply alternative ways of coming to center. The form is not the point. The experience of centering is our purpose here. I will list several other forms of meditative practice briefly before returning to the real story, which we will discover when we shift from attending to the stream of thoughts and emotions to sustaining our consciousness in the presence of the Sacred.

Mindfulness meditation is the act and art of being awake to the present moment. Mindfulness can be practiced in any setting, with any object. You can be mindful of the curious mind itself, or the curious tiny curves of a single raisin rolling around the mouth. You can be mindful of your own body sitting in the chair as you read these words, or mindful of how busy your thoughts are in this moment.

Mindfulness is a particular state of consciousness in which we pay attention to anything in the present moment without judgment. This nonjudgmental mindfulness is also helped by attitudes of non-doing, by which we simply pay attention without trying to accomplish anything, and non-striving, by which we do not strive to bend reality in any preferred direction. Non-judging, non-doing, and non-striving can help us enter a state of pure awareness in which we become the one who observes. Mindfulness meditation can be practiced in conjunction with sitting, walking, moving, eating, or any other form of practice.

Walking meditation is another meditative form. In this case, the body is moving but the intention is still set on staying aware of the present moment and on keeping the focus wherever we set it. I recommend walking slowly for walking meditation. The purpose is not to go anywhere, but instead to arrive at an inner peace, so why hurry? The intent of walking meditation is to find our center, so taking time to breathe as we walk can slow us down to a pace that allows awareness with every step.

We can also use a mantra or prayer word to guide our attention as we walk. This combines the slow stepping and attentive breathing of walking meditation with a focus that helps us stay attentive to the present moment. You may select any word, phrase, or prayer that works for you, so choose a word and stick with it as you walk. A prayer word can facilitate a sense of carrying the presence of God with us as we walk.

Once I was practicing walking meditation by quietly pacing our living room on a cold winter morning. Our son Ted, then eleven years old, woke up and saw what I was doing as he came down the stairs. Without saying a word, he began following me around the room. We walked along in silence for some time. Once we finished, Ted asked me, "What were we doing?" I was impressed that he could take part without any explanation, so I simply answered, "Walking meditation is a calm and peaceful way to be present in this moment." Ted just said, "Oh," and we carried on with our morning routine.

Walking meditation can also be done in nature to allow the living world to become our focus of attention. I practiced this form in the Rocky Mountain National Park recently. One cold afternoon, I parked the car and strolled out across a snowy field. I meandered along the Colorado River, where the only sounds were water tumbling over rocks and the occasional breeze through the evergreens beside me.

Each step I took was slow and mindful, following in the tracks of the elk that had walked there before me. I wandered into the forest in slow motion, eyes and ears attentive as I experienced moments of emptiness and aloneness that later passed. I felt I was in a wilderness where only God and her creatures abide. My body tired after about four miles, and as snowflakes gently landed on my face, I returned to my starting point.

Walking meditation can also be done around a labyrinth. Wandering along the circular path that leads to the labyrinth's center can help our wandering minds learn to find their way back to the center of our beings. Labyrinths also teach us that we do not have to know the way ahead. We can learn to trust that the path will take us to the center even when we do not know which way it will turn. This following along in trust is an apt metaphor for the spiritual life.

Moving meditation takes many forms. In addition to walking meditation, you might have experienced yoga, tai chi, or a related form of meditation meant to bring us to our center as the body moves through various poses. I personally enjoy practicing and teaching an ultra-simple form of sacred yoga. I also love to watch friends engage in the flowing and meditative movements of tai chi. Several friends have also led us in meditative dance forms while the group chants or moves wordlessly to the music. My friend Amina refers to her practice as "Dances of Universal Peace," and our groups have enjoyed sharing them.

In the sacred yoga practice I teach, we set our intention toward our devotion to God. We use a variety of postures known as hatha yoga for gentle stretching and relaxation. Our focus of attention is not primarily on either our breath or the postures, though we use both. Instead, our main attention is on opening ourselves to the presence of God within us.

We conclude the series of postures with four bows. We bow in reverence, with our hands folded beneath our chins in a prayer pose, either standing or kneeling, and hearts full of reverence for the Divine. We bow in surrender, with our bodies prostrated on the floor, arms stretched forward, foreheads resting on the ground, and an inner attitude of surrendering our lives into God's care. We bow in openness from a seated posture with our hands resting on our knees and our palms open toward the ceiling or sky. Our attitude is one of opening ourselves to the presence of the Holy in whatever way she might want to be in us and work through us this day. Finally, we begin a bow of simple being in which we continue sitting with our hands resting in our laps with one hand resting in the other and the tips of our thumbs touching. Our circled hands express our wholeness beneath all our brokenness. In this last bow, we adopt the attitude of simply being, just as we are. Here we sit, resting in the stillness for as long as we choose.

Lectio divina, or sacred reading, is another form of meditation. In this form, we use a period of reading to practice the presence of God. The reading does not need to be long, since we are not reading for information. We are reading for inner formation. We choose a favorite Scripture, poem, or other form of inspirational reading and read the words until a particular phrase speaks to us. When the words shimmer or shine for us as if they are trying to get our attention, we pause there and stay with the phrase.

In the classical practice of *lectio divina*, brought to us especially by the Benedictine monks around A.D. 500, there are several phases to this form of meditation. When a phrase draws our attention as we read, we pause to meditate with it. From *lectio* (reading) we move into *meditatio* (meditation). We reflect on the meaning of the words that catch our attention and wonder why the phrase is speaking to us. We consider how the words apply to our lives or to our current situation.

After this period of reflection, we move into *oratio* (praying or speaking). In this phase, we let our heart speak. How do we desire to pray this phrase? What do the words want to express in our hearts? How would we express the words or their meanings toward God?

Finally, *lectio* becomes *contemplatio* (contemplation). This is an experience of letting ourselves move beyond the words, thoughts, and images toward a state of simple being. We let the movement of our hearts bring us into God's presence. This movement is always a gift, and although it is never under our control, we can set our intention to be open. Then we just let the Presence come as it comes, even if only for a moment.

Scriptio divina, or sacred writing, is another form of meditation. In this practice, we use the process of writing as our way into the center. We might start by writing something we would want to say to God or something we believe God might be saying to us. We might write in response to something we have read, or write out our feelings, our sense of what is happening in our lives, or whatever else seems to be bubbling up from our souls.

Next, we shift our focus from our writing to what those words might be saying to us. We meditate on them. We might let the words pray through us—that is, to find expression through us without our conscious control. Eventually we might let what we have written help us shift into a wordless state of open presence for God. Again, we let our thoughts or feelings about what we have written dissolve and bring our consciousness into the heart, where the living God dwells.

Tilden Edwards has a wonderful phrase for this process. He calls it "bringing the mind into the heart."[1] The intention of *lectio divina*, *scriptio divina*, and similar forms of meditation is to facilitate this shift into contemplation and invite union with the Divine. Here we are no longer reflecting on words or their meanings. We are no longer consciously praying the words. We are *being* the words in our hearts, at least for a fleeting moment.

I practiced *scriptio divina* with a group of African-American women at the Mercy Endeavors Senior Center here in New Orleans. The women and I were writing about our lives as part of a lesson on spiritual journaling. We were seeking to practice the presence of God through sacred writing in community.

My instructions were simple: "Listen within and write from the place where God lives inside of you. There is only one rule: Keep this writing

---

1. Edwards offers a thorough explanation of this process in *Embracing the Call to Spiritual Depth*. Edwards' text includes exercises and practical guidance on ways to deepen the contemplative dimension of life from a wise and seasoned contemplative friend.

private so you can write honestly and freely without worrying about what others might think. Set your intention to let your life speak to you."

We opened with five minutes spent in silence together. We sought to get in touch with the place where we are one with God. As I sounded the chime to close the silence, we began to write from that oneness. Using music for inspiration is optional, but sometimes music helps the flow of writing. Sometimes it is a distraction, so I gave the ladies the option of writing to the tune of Andrea Boccelli singing Italian love songs, and they chose to write with the inspiration of musical beauty.

Ten minutes into the writing, I noticed several of the senior women were not writing. One woman sat gazing out the window in her red sweater. She looked as though she had gone somewhere else in her mind. Another lady with a sky blue hat and matching blouse held her journal close to her face, the better to see the page as she wrote intently.

One woman dressed in black looked over what she had written and lapsed into thought for a moment. She usually led the women in Bible study at that hour on Tuesdays. I wondered if she was bored, or maybe a little agitated that she was not getting to lead her Bible study, though perhaps she was just enjoying listening to Boccelli's soaring voice.

Next I noticed several other ladies looking over their writing. One was hanging over her table as though she was going to sleep, with her wrinkled hands cradling her head. Who knows, maybe she was praying.

Vicky, the activity director for the program, wore a white dress. Her hair was cropped close and dyed blonde. She seemed intent on her writing, as if her life was speaking to her. Soon I discovered that Vicky was reviewing her words to see what she might share.

Many of us in American culture have little or no experience with spiritual autobiography or *scriptio divina*, and letting the Spirit speak to us through our own writing is rarely taught. We are not usually trained to listen within, to value our inner lives, or to trust that the Inner Voice has secrets to tell and wise guidance to offer, so I had offered the whole exercise with some fear and trembling that most of the women might not get the significance of the practice

I was beginning to think the little adventure in sacred writing was not making much of an impact on this group of senior women. I wondered if at least one of the ladies would begin to hear and value her own voice. My prayer was that they would at least have a slight hint that a Spirit Voice resides within us and wants to befriend us, when we are ready to listen. I hoped that even one among them might discover what it is like for words to flow from the heart into the hands and out onto the page.

Then Vicky spoke up. She asked if she could share a little of what she had written. Vicky's contribution triggered another woman's sharing. Then came another and another. Not only had many of the women found their spiritual flow in the writing, they also wanted to bring their experience into community. They read passages about learning how to love all people, even during a time when people of color were treated like second-class citizens in America. I wish we could say those days are over. The women shared church experiences, private spiritual epiphanies, family memories, and individual revelations.

These ladies didn't want to keep all of their thoughts to themselves. They wanted to commune, to let sacred writing turn into sacred sharing. By the time we closed for lunch, I was glowing inside. I was also embarrassed at myself, for it seemed that "O ye of little faith" meant me (Matt 8:26). Just when I feared the exercise had not touched anyone at all, they proved me wrong.

Audio divina, or divine listening, is a similar practice with music. During this sacred listening we seek to let go of the rational mind and its tendency to analyze experience. We don't assess the quality of the music, but instead ask to be escorted into the presence of God through the medium of music.

Once I was enjoying a piece of music by Ashana,[2] listening as her Tibetan singing bowls sounded various notes in the same key. Her voice began to soar through the music without words. Soon I was singing in harmony with her. I was being drawn into an experience of Presence by both the sounds and by my own singing.

The most dramatic experience of *audio divina* I ever had happened quite unexpectedly during a breath-work training with our men's group. After an extended period of deep, rapid breathing to the rhythm of powerfully evocative drumming and music, a new piece of music went down into my soul. I later learned it was Ennio Morricone's orchestral piece entitled "The Mission" that moved me so. By the time the chorus began to sing with angelic sounds I was not only crying, but sobbing. The music was loud and I didn't care what others might think. Something within me came bubbling up and without consciously intending to, I began singing along.

---

2. Ashana, *Jewels of Silence: Meditations on the Chakras for Voice and Crystal Singing Bowls*, with Thomas Barquee, recorded September 15, 2008, Angelic Tones B001IDJ2BG, compact disc, http://progressivechristianity.org/resources/jewels-of-silence-ashana/.

It was like my soul was singing its own harmony to the music's melody. The syllables that flowed forth from my mouth became "Al-le-lu-jah." I sang the word repeatedly, slowly. I sobbed. I laughed. I felt like I had entered another realm, a heavenly dimension at the center of all of existence. There was no time or place, just the music and voices and all of us in union with the All. Nothing like that had ever happened to me, and it was a glorious taste of heaven.

Those moments of *audio divina* became a mystical experience. For me, it was like crossing dimensions into a realm where nothing else mattered but singing praise. All of the suffering I had been through during Carol's cancer journey came pouring out in the tears and the laughter. I laughed as hard as I ever had right in the middle of the sobbing, all while singing as loudly as my strained voice would allow.

An experience of ecstasy like this is rare. You can't orchestrate mysticism or spiritual experience. Trying to achieve it is like trying to control the birth of a star. You can only be in the moment and stand, sit, or lie down in awe and wonder. Everyday mystics are the ones who open themselves and surrender to the presence of God wherever, whenever, and however she comes into our awareness. Presence is really our ultimate home. No wonder we seek it in as many ways as we can.

A word of warning here: Seeking to be in God's presence is a way of saying yes to a reality that is already here. We do not strive for some special mystical or ecstatic experience. We do not try to force feelings of closeness with God. If ecstasy is given to us, as it was in my experience with *audio divina*, we can be extremely grateful for the gift, treasure the experience, and let go of all efforts to have the experience again. Otherwise we are attempting to manipulate ourselves and God, which never works.

Visio divina, or divine visioning, is similar to the other practices except that we use visual images such as icons, art, or nature. In each of these art forms, the movement is the same: From initially looking and seeing what is before us, we move into reflecting on what we are seeing, praying with what we are seeing, and finally releasing the images altogether into simple union with the Creator.

Twice we have invited icon painters to be our teachers of this sacred seeing at the School for Contemplative Living. Each teacher explained the sacred act of participating in the art as a form of prayer. Their devotion was clear. Both described a sense of being led as they painted. For these teachers, the creation of each icon was a communion with the

Divine. And for us, looking at their creation with eyes of wonder became a form of divine communion.

We have also invited artists to display their work and to share their experience of the connection between art and spirituality. Their artistic creation was one form of spiritual expression, and our viewing of their art was another form of communion with the Spirit of all creativity. These workshops in sacred seeing are only one example of the many ways we can practice seeing the Holy. The challenge is not to try to control our experience, but to open the eyes of the heart and allow the Sacred to appear to us as it will.

Conversatio divina, or sacred conversation, is a little trickier. In this practice, our meditation starts with a simple conversation. Although we may have been taught good listening skills, we are not usually taught to stop listening carefully to the words in a conversation so that we can attend to the heart. If I were practicing with you, as I do with people in spiritual direction all the time, I would gradually turn my attention away from what you are saying. Instead I would begin to focus on your being as a child of God.

I don't mean that I would stop listening to your words altogether, but I would shift my consciousness toward your inner life, your heart, your needs, and your being. In effect, I would seek to see you through the eyes of God. Sometimes this shift is helped by how easily a conversation can turn sacred on its own. Sometimes the nature of sharing between us moves into the heart without our even trying.

Those sacred moments of communing set the stage for *conversatio divina*, where what passes between us is spiritual union rather than mere information. In such moments of sacred conversation between us, I might directly experience a sense of union with God as I am helped to be in God's heart for you. The moment becomes holy as it will, not through our efforts to make it so.

Sacred conversations can also take place in groups. When we share stories from the heart and our listeners offer their nonjudgmental and receptive hearts as containers for our stories, the moment can become holy. Without intending to make the conversation spiritual, and without necessarily even using religious words, this kind of heart-talk can be the place where the Spirit enters and unites us.

Such moments can also happen in those silent pauses when the group is so moved by someone's sharing as to fall silent. Right in that gap between words, the very presence of a living God can enter and draw participants into communion. If sacraments are means of grace, then I have experienced many times when group sharing from the heart became a sacrament.

Loving-kindness meditation can be experienced while sitting, standing, walking, or moving through postures that express what is in our hearts. The real focus of this form of meditation is on centering ourselves in a state of loving-kindness. We begin by cultivating a state of loving-kindness for ourselves. In this sense, we are filling our own inner reservoir full of compassion first.

We start by picturing ourselves as the human beings we are, just as we are. We cultivate a nonjudgmental attitude toward ourselves. We might use a phrase like this: "In stillness I fill my heart with loving-kindness to dissolve the suffering in me." We could keep it even simpler: "I fill my heart with loving-kindness." We stay in that state of grace, reciting the phrase in our hearts for as long as we need to.

After sufficient time, we begin to shift our attention to another person, perhaps someone we already love. We direct loving-kindness toward that person. We send them love in the belief that we are all connected with an invisible web of divinity. Our compassion is directed along that web from our heart into theirs, from our life into theirs. We can send loving-kindness with inner words, saying, "I fill my heart with loving-kindness to dissolve the suffering in you." Or we could keep it even simpler: "I send you loving-kindness." Again, we practice for as long as we need to feel communion.

Next, we might move our focus to direct compassion toward others. We sometimes gather up the courage to set our intention on our enemy's need for compassion. Amazingly, sending love toward our enemy can help to dissolve some of our own animosity toward that person or group. Sometimes cultivating loving-kindness toward these people helps us to remember that they are beings who suffer just like us. You might also try seeing the other as a child, or as the wounded human that they are. If this seems impossible, ask for help from the Great Love. This part of the practice is in keeping with the call of Christ to love our enemies (Matt 5:44).

Finally, we can direct our loving-kindness toward any group of people, or toward the natural world, or to the whole globe. Then we finish by returning our focus once again to holding ourselves in our own hearts and directing loving-kindness into ourselves for a closing moment.

The following is an expression of a loving-kindness meditation that can be recited one phrase at a time:

For myself:
I fill up with loving-kindness for this being I am, just as I am.
I allow my needs, hurts, feelings, and even emptiness to come bubbling up.
I direct loving-kindness to gently touch any hurts or needs in me.
I become a center of loving-kindness radiating throughout my being.
I release problems, stresses, needs, and let them be cleansed from me.
I dwell here in the place of loving-kindness.
I slowly say, "In stillness, I fill my heart with loving-kindness to dissolve the suffering in me."

For others:
I begin to imagine those who need my love.
I see them as little children. I visualize their essential beings.
I direct loving-kindness toward them—enveloping, surrounding, pouring through them and their needs.
I say, "In stillness, I fill my heart with loving-kindness, to dissolve the suffering in _____."

Going further:
I can now direct loving-kindness toward anyone, even those who have caused me harm, if I so choose.
I say, "In stillness, I fill my heart with loving-kindness to dissolve the suffering in _____."
I radiate loving-kindness within and without, sensing my connection with all living beings.
I rest in the sanctuary of loving-kindness.
When I am ready to, I pause this practice, knowing I can return whenever I wish.

These ten ways to meditate are simply examples of practices we use and teach in our School for Contemplative Living. There are really thousands of ways. You might meditate while gardening, bathing, lighting candles, imagining, floating in a river or pool, hearing a voice guiding you, and on and on. Ultimately, our practitioners in the School for Contemplative Living seek oneness with the Divine through our practice.

This seeking is part of what defines a contemplative: a seeker of the presence of God. The seeking can also be quite the adventure, because finding the sacred comes when it comes. Chapter 6 offers my poetry expressing some of the twists and turns along this journey. Sometimes the poems express the ecstasy, and sometimes the agony that can be part of the journey we call contemplative living.

BEGINNING STILLNESS: AN EXERCISE

In case you are ready even as you read, here again is the simplest of outlines for a way to find the peace of knowing the Divine: Be, be still, let go, relax, let your concerns fall away, and cease your striving. Take a moment right now to experience the psalmist's words for yourself: "Be still and know that I am God" (46:10). Pause from your reading, breathe, and just *be* for a few moments. This is the prayer of *rapha*, the Hebrew word for "be still, relax, let go, cease striving," or "let it fall."

STEPPING THROUGH THE DOOR: AN EXERCISE

In the example of Saint Augustine from chapter 2, less is more when it comes to seeking God. We come now to seek God where God may be found, in the inner sanctuary. We do not try too hard. We do not look outwardly. We turn our attention within. This is the real meaning of solitude.

Try using the image of the inner door. Close your eyes. Picture a door as you wish it to be. See its color, size, handle, and any other details you need to bring it to your mind's eye. Begin to sense that there is Someone on the other side who also wants to greet you, who is just waiting for you to open the door. Feel your own desire to meet, to be together, and to stand face-to-face. If being so close to God causes uncomfortable feelings, fears, or other reluctances and resistances, take the time to be aware of each passing feeling. Do not rush. Note the discomfort. Be aware that there is no handle on God's side of the door, so God will not open it for you. God will wait as long as it takes for you to be ready.

Comfort yourself by tuning in to your heart's desire to know this One. Feel the depth and breadth of your longing. Remember how long you have wanted to open that door. Pay attention to the part of your heart that just wants to be loved, seen, and accepted as you are right now. Notice the gentle patience of the One who is waiting to offer the love you have been seeking.

Gather your courage. Reach for the door handle. Touch it, grasp it. Realize that you alone can open this inner door. Slowly turn the handle. As the door cracks open, what do you see? Perhaps light will be streaming through, or mist, or the beautiful sounds of a symphony or birdsong. Perhaps there will be simple silence. Let your desire and your own imagination lead you as you open the door further.

Who do you see? In what form is your Guest appearing? Is God more like a mother or father, a brother or sister, or like a friend? Does God appear to you as light, or cloud-like with no particular form at all beyond the invisible Presence you feel? See God in a form or formless way that brings you comfort. Take your time, your own careful time. Be leisurely. Stroll around in your imagination, or just stand or sit, as you wish. Be as near or far from God's actual presence as you wish. Trust that God only seeks your wellbeing. Spend as much time as you wish in the presence of God, inside your own inner sanctuary. Let the time unfold at your own pace.

When you need to part for a while, close out your time together as you choose. Let your heart lead you. Approach the door again. Do you wish to close it for a bit? Would you rather leave it cracked open, so that you can stay in touch with the Great Love within your soul any time you want? It is your door—yours to open and yours to close by your own choosing. Just remember that the door to your inner sanctuary is there. You do not ever have to search abroad again. You can come to the One who is at home inside you whenever you choose. Do not be a stranger in your own home!

PRELUDE TO THE INNER SANCTUARY: A RELAXATION EXERCISE

Begin by focusing the mind on one simple thing. Perhaps the sound of a bird calling outside your window, beautiful music, a breeze coming through a window, a calming word or prayer requiring no thought, the ticking of a clock, a comforting image that eases your mind, the feel of the breath flowing in and out of your lungs, or whatever focus you choose. Let the mind rest on that one simple thing.

When other thoughts come along, and they will, gently release them. Let them float on like a cloud. Do not fight them off. Do not try to clear the mind of all thoughts. Do not pay much attention to them at all.

Just notice that the mind is thinking a thought, or conjuring some mental picture, or analyzing your current experience, and let that go. Keep letting these intrusive thoughts go as they come, one by one. Return your attention to your one simple focus. Let the relaxation response come as it comes. Do not try to make yourself relax. Do not try to make anything happen at all. Just focus.

If you are a social person or are new to the practice, joining others to practice can be an encouragement to keep practicing. Sometimes others' intention to practice can strengthen your own commitment, but you can also practice in the presence of others who do not know you are relaxing inwardly as you sit near them. Even when others are conversing, you can focus your attention on your word, or breath, or whatever you choose, and let other thoughts go. Others may think you are daydreaming, but you will be doing the opposite. Instead of getting lost in thought, you are simply focusing your attention on one thing in a kind of gentle wakefulness. Practice wherever you find yourself.

If you are a spiritual person, this relaxing practice may serve as a prelude to spiritual experience. Open the heart to God as you focus. Be present to the Presence. Know that the Giver of Life is as near as your breath. Keep practicing.

ENTERING THE INNER SANCTUARY: THREE WAYS IN

Spiritual experience can be entered into through many avenues. This is not a one-size-fits-all endeavor. A practice that helps one person find peace may be disturbing to the next person. As you consider nurturing your own spiritual practice, I highly recommend Robert J. Wicks' practical guide to spiritual growth, *Everyday Simplicity*. Wicks offers practical suggestions and helpful examples for creating your own rule of life.

The following spiritual exercises are offered to help you enter your own inner sanctuary. I invite you to experiment with them or create your own. Let your intuition lead you to the practices that work best for you.

Whatever practice you choose, remember to approach the whole experience with a gentle touch. Do not believe that we need only wish for spiritual experiences to find the right formula. We are not in control of spiritual experiences. You might remember the words of Anthony de Mello, a Jesuit priest who lived in India and served as a contemplative retreat leader and author:

"Is there anything I can do to make myself Enlightened?"
"As little as you can do to make the sun rise in the morning."
"Then of what use are the spiritual exercises you prescribe?"
"To make sure you are not asleep when the sun begins to rise."[3]

These words capture the essential attitude of wakefulness that is the prerequisite for so many practices. The practices described in these pages are additional tools for cultivating our readiness. These exercises are intended to prepare the soil of the heart, for our attitudes are as important as the practices themselves. So as you become ready, settle into your humility, openness, and willingness. After that, the rest is up to the Spirit.

Physical Experience

Many of us come into spiritual experience best through some form of visceral physical experience. One example is found in the potter who relishes the touch and feel of clay. Another example is seen in the dancer entranced in the rhythm of movement. We can also look to the naturalist who loves the feel of the ocean's spray. Some find sexual passion and union to be quite spiritual. The mindfulness meditation tradition encourages several physical practices such as yoga, walking meditation, and eating meditation. These and many other physical experiences can help us nurture our spirituality and can actually enhance our sense of the presence of God. Awareness of the physical sensation of the breath can be one such experience.

Attention to the breath as a form of meditation is almost universal. The breath is used as a tool for prayer and meditation in all the world's major religions. After all, breathing is free, comes naturally without effort, and requires no training. For me, breathing is a visceral experience. I can sometimes enter into deep states of relaxation, prayer, and meditation through the simple act of feeling the flow of air in and out of my body. I hope the following exercise will help you find a visceral way into your own inner sanctuary.

A Breath Exercise

Sit quietly with a sense of dignity, keeping your back upright but not rigid. Rest your hands in your lap comfortably, and let your shoulders

---

3. de Mello, *One Minute Wisdom*, 11.

fall, releasing any tension. Let your eyes close or open as you wish, but do not look intently at anything. If you choose to keep your eyes open, maintain an unfocused gaze. Focus your attention instead on the simple experience of breathing in and out, and keep your awareness there for a while. As other thoughts enter your consciousness, gently let them go and return your focus to the breath.

Do not fight these passing thoughts or try to clear your mind. That's too much effort. Just keep returning your awareness to how it feels to breathe, moment by moment. Settle into the simple act of breathing in and out. Let time pass. Resist the urges that come to get up and go do something. Commit enough time to the practice so that you can relax into the process. Let yourself begin to know that you *belong* in this place of simple breathing and being.

As you continue to just sit and breathe, let your heart open to God's presence. Do not try to think about God or speak to God. Just let your open heart become a quiet place where you and God can comfortably be together. Stay there, resting in the inner sanctuary as you can. As other thoughts come, let them go. Even if a sense of communication from God comes to you, just notice it and leave it alone. Now is not the time for conversation. You will remember the words later, if they are needed.

Open yourself to the One who loves you so intensely. Sense the love within you, for wherever we find love, we find God. If no such awareness arises, do not be concerned. We do not dictate our own spiritual experience. We just accept what comes. We rest in the simple knowledge that we *are* loved, whether we feel it or not. Let your breath be the incoming flow of divine compassion into your deepest being. Stay as long as you like. This is your sanctuary, your home, your place of belonging.

Some of us find our way into spiritual experience best with our eyes. Once when taking a boat ride many miles out from San Diego Bay, we saw a pair of migrating whales surface. Their blowholes would release a tremendous breath before they dove back below the surface of the Pacific Ocean, using their breathing to return to the inner sanctuary of the water. We passengers watched in silent amazement as the whales offered up a visual demonstration of spiritual practice: breathing into the deep. Can you picture it?

A Visual Exercise

Try letting your deepest longings come to surface. Silently wait for them to bubble up in some thought or image that might capture your imagination. Prepare yourself to let your inner longings become a vision that can take you down below your surface. Do not try to force it to come. Do not try to control your experience. Get out of your own way and simply watch for its appearance. There is a part of your soul that already knows how to breathe into the deep, and how to take you there.

Imagine your own inner sanctuary, a place down in your own depths. What might that look like for you? Pause here long enough to let some image form. How do you see yourself in your inner sanctuary in your mind's eye? What do you notice around you? In what form or image does your soul express itself? Are you ready to enter your sanctuary?

Take time right now to let a scene unfold in your mind. Your soul wants to take you down into the inner sanctuary where you can feed, find nourishment, and fill up. This is the place where your deepest longings can be satisfied. What image is coming? Will you let this image carry you away down into the inner sanctuary?

Is your God there? If so, how are you seeing your God? Is God speaking or silent? If speaking, what do you hear? If silent, what is happening in the silence? Is God being active in some way, or just still? As you draw near to what Thomas Kelly calls the "Divine Center,"[4] what is this like for you? Will you let a scene come to mind that brings you into this Presence? If so, stay there as long as you like. See if you can stay long enough to feel a sense of belonging. Know that you are now entering into the holy of holies, the place where the soul and the Maker are one.

The imagination is amazing! The image we need can arise from the depths in a synchronicity beyond our control. Over the years of my work with spirituality groups in the psychiatric hospital, I came to know several counseling clients who were open to trying this visualization exercise. One was a deeply depressed woman we will call Betty, who had been especially troubled by persistent thoughts of suicide despite her best efforts.

Betty said she just needed some magic dust to free her of this painful disease. I decided not to dismiss her wish. My intuition said that her soul's imagination was providing an image. Such spontaneous images often prove helpful if we can trust them to lead the way. I asked Betty to close her eyes and, at her own pace, to let an image of magic dust come

---

4. Kelly, *Testament of Devotion*, 3.

into her consciousness. I suggested she invite the scene to happen in her mind, take the time to let the scene unfold, and tell me when she was done.

Soon Betty was reporting that she had begun to see shimmering magic dust falling from the sky. As it fell around her, the dust began to form a kind of protective cocoon. She could not see through the walls of the cocoon, but she felt safe in there. She felt warmth, and love. Betty somehow knew she could stay as long as she wanted and leave as she wished. She also realized it was *her* magic dust cocoon, so she could return anytime she needed to. In fact, Betty committed to return there as a form of spiritual practice to help her through her depression. She decided to remain open in case the image of magic dust changed in some way that would further her healing.

To many people, Betty's experience might sound contrived, artificial, or insubstantial. Many people do not trust the psyche at all, but over decades of helping counseling clients through terrible traumas, I have come to trust that the psyche-soul is much wiser than we are. There is an inner wisdom that can show us the way to healing. In Betty's case, the tool of seeing her magic dust cocoon became a way to ease her depression, release suicidal thoughts, and find the courage to face the sources of her depression.

Tatiana, another woman in those years, was struggling with the high anxiety that came with her bipolar illness. She felt she was near a manic phase and that there was little she could do about it. She had been in a psychiatric hospital before and hated the thought of having to return. Tatiana described her experience as being "like a dam that has a crack in it. The walls are bulging and ready to burst open. A leak has already begun." Instead of trying to rid the mind of this disturbing image (which rarely works anyway), we decided to use it to help her through her fear.

The exercise took immense courage on Tatiana's part, but she agreed to close her eyes and let the scene unfold in a way that would bring her back into her innate wholeness. She did not try to force anything to happen. Despite the desperation of her feelings, Tatiana was able to surrender control to her own soul. She let the following images come on their own.

Tatiana began to see herself floating on her back on the surface of a lake. Soon God's hands were underneath her, holding her up. Her cares melted away in the beauty of being able to look up into the sky. She felt the sun's warmth. She relaxed and let the bulging hole in the dam's wall be smoothed by God until there was no more leak. Holding back the floodgates was no longer her responsibility. A solution had presented itself, and Tatiana did not have to handle her anxiety by herself.

Tatiana's experience was a healing rediscovery of her wholeness. In her imagination, she was assisted by God to find just what was needed. A most remarkable aspect of the experience was that her high anxiety disappeared in the process. Some people find sudden healing, while others experience transformation over time. If we could have monitored Tatiana's internal body chemistry in that moment, I believe we would have seen a transformation from the rush of adrenalin that comes with the fight-or-flight response to the flood of endorphins that characterizes the relaxation response, as described by Dr. Herbert Benson in his "Spirituality and Healing in Medicine V" conference.[5]

Tatiana's experience also reminds me of the power of being attentive to what the mind is up to. There are times when we need to redirect the mind away from disturbing images and toward more helpful images. Examples of guiding the mind into visualizations that can facilitate healing are found in the mountain, the lake, and the loving-kindness meditations Dr. Jon Kabat-Zinn describes in his book titled *Wherever You Go, There You Are*.[6]

Another example of a visual entrance into the inner sanctuary came to me in one of my favorite experiences while on a silent retreat. I wrote a poem expressing my own direct experience, and although it is not necessarily intended as a model for your experience, I hope it will be an example of how profoundly we can be moved by silent watching. Even imagined scenes can bring us into the heart of the inner sanctuary. In the case of this poem, I was recording what it was like to allow actual sights to move me into the arena of the soul. You can find my experience rendered in poetry in chapter 6, under the title, "Tasting Light: Breakfast of Tears and Mist."

Many people find their best way into spiritual and healing experience through hearing. Sounds of nature and music can soothe us like nothing else. I once wrote about this feeling on a silent retreat. Even though we were practicing silence, we had been using many forms of music to bring us closer to the soul and into God's presence. Some people prefer nature sounds when they want to relax and center themselves. Others prefer

---

5. I heard Dr. Benson discuss these chemical changes in his role as a moderator at the "Spirituality and Healing in Medicine V" Conference, Harvard Medical School, Houston, TX, March 22–24, 1998.

6. Kabat-Zinn, *Wherever You Go*, 57, 64, 78.

music. Each person has specific musical tastes that resonate with his or her own soul and can bring a sense of calming and introspection.

One example of the healing gift of music is seen in the way a song can come back to our minds at just the right time. Since I grew up in the church, I was raised on hymns. There are times when I awaken to a hymn in my mind that I haven't sung for years. Other times, songs emerge from my memory with a specific message that seems to fit my current situation. This synchronicity is like being given a message from God—a phrase that fits the moment or a melody that soothes the mind or heart. Has this happened to you? Maybe you too can find your way into your own inner sanctuary through the gift of listening.

A Hearing Exercise

Try playing a piece of music you find soothing and beautiful, or turning your attention to the sound of water falling, or listening carefully to a bird's song. Whatever sound you choose, *truly listen* for a little while. Let yourself be carried away by the sound. Allow yourself to enter into the beauty. Stay there as moments pass. Hear with your soul. Let your body relax, and allow other thoughts to pass by as they come. Do not pay them any mind. Your one aim is to hear with all your being.

As you listen, allow the music or sounds to move you to your depths. Slowly drift down into the place we call our soul. Let the Creator of music and sound be with you there. Hear the silent voice of God in rhythm with the sound, or hear the speaking Voice Thomas Kelly referred to in the notes or words of the song.

Let the One who cherishes you as you are come to you through the music or sound. Feel the heartbeat of the Great Love of your soul beating through the symphony of sounds. Know that here you are loved, wanted, and never to be forsaken. Know that you are also a song being written as you listen, breath by breath. This is your place of belonging, your home and destination. Do not leave too soon! Let your ears become your passageway down into your soul. Stay until you are fulfilled.

Your way into the inner sanctuary may come through the breath or some other physical experience. Your way may come through visual experience, or through the music of your favorite sounds. However you find your way, go there.

Go there alone. Go there with others. Go there as often as you can. Find your best times and places and ways to practice each day. Become familiar with the amazing inner sanctuary of your soul. Set aside formal times to practice, and continue to practice informally during the day as you work or play. If you forget, just begin again, as you are.

Devote yourself to the practice. Believe that you deserve the time to be rejuvenated each day, even if you have to give up some other valuable use of your time. Your body, mind, and soul will thank you. I believe your awareness of God's presence will grow. Resistances and hindrances will arise, and the way will not be easy. The important things in life never are, but if you commit to keep practicing, you too can come to live in the inner sanctuary. Your true home is God's great gift to you. You belong there. *Be.*

RETREATS

Going down into my inner sanctuary—my true home—so that I can practice being without interruption is what draws me to embark on contemplative retreats. There is no adventure like the inner adventure of stalking the Wild Divinity. There is no other gift quite like the joy of dropping down below my usual consciousness into the country of oneness. One of the most important practices for cultivating the experience of God's presence is to go away on contemplative retreats.

I have heard the word "retreat" used to refer to concentrated times of work. Such work retreats tend to mean a group of coworkers getting away from their usual environment in hopes of becoming even more productive than usual. Contemplative retreats, on the other hand, are about dropping all efforts to be productive, except perhaps in inviting God to work within us. The centering prayer practice is specifically aimed at consenting to God's presence and action within. So yes, there is some work going on—God's work—but it is nothing like taking on the work of accomplishing some task all by myself.

My contemplative retreats have become a kind of work over the past twenty years, for they have given me the opportunity to work on myself. Yet this work is not under my control. My work does not take the usual form of productivity in that no product is created. This work is about my willingness to let the presence of God be active in me. This often means being willing to see things about me that I need to see, whether I want to recognize them or not. This work is part of a transformation process guided by God to help me grow. Sometimes it means the scaffolding I have carefully constructed to hold up a certain image of myself has to come crashing down. But even that revelation is not really my job. That is God's work. My work is to show up, practice inner stillness, surrender myself to God, and let the guidance of God's Spirit reveal whatever I need to see or experience.

These contemplative retreats have involved a pulling away from my usual responsibilities for a while, but the goal is not to retreat from myself. I have traveled to a Jesuit house on Labor Day for four-day silent retreats for the past eight years. I have served on the staff of four-day silent retreats through the Academy for Spiritual Leaders in Louisiana for ten years. I have attended five-day and eight-day centering prayer retreats in Tennessee and Louisiana, and I attended an eight-day mindfulness-based stress reduction retreat in New York, dedicating most of this time to silence. In every case, I showed up and so did God.

Teachers from Contemplative Outreach recommend that once we have established a daily practice of centering prayer, we should participate in an annual centering prayer retreat, preferably for five to ten days in length. The purpose of these retreats is to deepen our contemplative practice. Such retreats usually involve centering in community for three or four hours each day and dedicating the rest of the day to eating, walking, reading, and resting in silence.

Contemplative Outreach teachers also suggest participants dedicate one day each month for a Sabbath, a quiet day spent alone with God. I have never adopted this practice for myself. Perhaps I still have some growing to do. None of these suggestions are intended to create unrealistic expectations of becoming spiritual superheroes. Instead, these invitations are a call to a lifestyle of being in God's presence so we can be transformed into full union with the God who is love.

Whether you are just beginning to attempt a daily contemplative practice or have been practicing on your own for many years, you too could benefit from retreating to a place where you can open yourself to God's presence for an extended period each day in the company of other seekers of God. Trying to transform ourselves all alone rarely lasts with any depth; seeking transformation in contemplative community offers a powerful process tested by thousands of people over several thousand years. To locate a retreat center near you, enter the words "retreat center" into your search engine or consult the "Resources" section at the end of this book to contact Contemplative Outreach for the nearest centering prayer retreats.

SACRED CIRCLE: SHOULDER RUBBING PRACTICE

Contemplatives who practice contemplative service with a small group may discover a secret: Giving and receiving love belong together. This is one of my favorite group experiences to share a sense of oneness with each other and with the Great Love.

To practice, group members form a circle and stand close together facing the center in a tight circle. Each person's shoulders touch the shoulders of the person to their right and to their left. Then everyone turns to face to right. Everyone should be close enough to easily reach the shoulders of the person who is now in front of them. If the group members are too far apart, everyone should simply take a step in towards the center of the circle.

Now open the heart to the Source of all loving-kindness as your hands rest on the shoulders in front of you. Know that this person before you is a sacred being, a fellow child of God. Let your own heart fill with the Great Love who is God, and allow love to flow from your heart through your arms and hands into the shoulders of the one in front of you. Let love flow. Rub that love into the shoulders of the person in front of you. Receive the love being rubbed into your own shoulders. Be in the flow of love. As you let your hands rest on the shoulders of the person before you, whisper a silent prayer: "May you be filled with wellbeing."

Next, everyone should pause and turn back to the left to repeat the practice in the other direction. Give to the one who was giving to you, and vice versa. Let love flow until you all simply *must* stop or be overwhelmed. Notice how your shoulders can remember the feel of the love that was rubbed into them. This practice invites us to experience the presence of God as a gift that we simultaneously give and receive. This exercise is a physical expression of a spiritual truth and demonstrates contemplative service at its best.

CENTERING PRAYER

Centering prayer is by far the most frequently used practice in our School for Contemplative Living. Thomas Keating, Cynthia Bourgeault, and others have written much about this form to share their teachings on centering prayer.[7] Our initial centering groups around New Orleans were

---

7. See Thomas Keating's *Open Mind, Open Heart* and Cynthia Bourgeault's *Centering Prayer and Inner Awakening* as examples.

founded and trained in centering prayer by Contemplative Outreach facilitators like Vivien Michals and Anna Maria Signorelli. They used their long experience in centering to draw the rest of us into a practice and a path that has now spread throughout the region.

From our original centering group that met once a month in New Orleans, we have grown to support eleven weekly groups and three monthly groups (although a few groups were birthed in hospitals, nonprofits, and churches that no longer meet regularly). You can find one group or another settling into our inner sanctuary as a contemplative community most days of the week. Enriched by those times of sourcing, we head back out into the wild world to serve. If you want to know more about this central practice as a means of opening yourself for contemplative prayer, visit the Contemplative Outreach website detailed in the "Resources" section.

6

Poems of Practicing the Presence

THE POEMS INCLUDED HERE have been inspired by my contemplative experiences over the past twenty years. I recommend that you read them slowly and reflectively as a form of meditation. I suggest that you read one at a time and give each poem time to speak to you. If you come across a word or phrase that shimmers or otherwise catches your attention, pause there and stay with that phrase. Take the time to see what arises within you. Resist the impulse to hurry on to the end. My prayer is that sharing these poems will offer some avenue into your own sense of the inner sanctuary.

THERE IS A STILLNESS

There is a stillness
that waits
beneath every thought.

There is a calm,
unperturbed rest
waiting still
below every action.

The stillness is waiting for you,
waiting, for *you*.

Quiet spring,
Source of your personal giftedness,
deep well,
river source flowing.

Do not act too soon,
do not think too much
before you go deep
where the waters flow free.

Drink deeply.
Drink long.
Drink to satisfy longing.
Let the inner drought end.

Best actions still always spring
from that stillness.

This is the wise one's way:

From the bone-chill winter
to the dry-drought summer,
best actions still always spring
from the stillness.

REGARDEZ ET ECOUTEZ

The spiritual life happens like this:
You watch and you listen.
That is all.
But in so doing, you
come into the presence of the Holy.

Watch for the Holy,
whose appearing may come at any moment
out of hiding and into your life,
but only noticed and felt
if you are watching,
if you have eyes to see.
Cultivate eyes to see!

Listen when this Voice comes
like your life depends on it.
For it most assuredly does.
And your days will not be the same
if you miss the whisper
that changes everything.
Cultivate ears to ear!

Don't you see?
It's just this watching,
this listening,
that changes everything, changes *you*,
and brings the Holy to your heart's door knocking.
Answer every moment!

HOLDING NEAR THE DEEP PRESENCE

Sacred moments
come to be held.
Come to be held . . .
Treasure in the eyes,
longing to be shared,
longing to be kept secret.

Let us whisper
and say barely a word
of the sacred things
we hold dear.

Let us draw near,
let us come to the deep Center
and stay a while
and whisper sacred things
into the quiet holding.

Come to be held
as the slow-motion fall
into the dark
appears,
as the low-horizon yellow moon
and the penetrating stars call out,
telling the return
of the deep blue night.

Lights out now
and all is well,
midnight stands forth
and all is well.

Rest now,
curtain falls,
rest deep,
hold near the deep Presence.
Come to be held.

Come to stand still
and do not be afraid
for long
as the coming One comes
as the holding draws near.

MOUNTAIN IN RAIN

Being mountain in rain.

Rain gently falling
on my surface,
pooling,
rolling down in trickles and streams,
seeping in
down into fertile, dark earth.
Being mountain in rain.

This is simple being,
no other tool but being.
Being comes first.
All else follows.

Much being
readies one
to share being
by being.

Today I *am* mountain in rain.

TASTING LIGHT: BREAKFAST OF TEARS AND MIST

Tears have dried on my face,
  those tears I was just crying;
    their residue clings to my skin,
      their emotion hovers over my soul.

Just outside my window—
  dawn is streaming across treetops
   over and through the mist
    illuminating droplets of haze
     moving across the lake's surface
      drifting,
       rising,
        ethereal light—substantial reality—temporary visitor.

Nearer still,
  droplets of morning glisten on winter leaves
   and evergreen pine,
    early light falls across the field,
     shadows stretch across wet earth,
      tiny lavender flowers push up and out,
       seeking a drink,
        seeking morning's light.

Frost, there across the lake,
  so thick it looks like snow
   protected by shade
    from sun's first heat.

Fountains springing up,
  cadences of silent motion,
   perpetual rising and falling
    glistening liquid light beams
     resonating off bird-wing,
      these very morning birds I mean,
       silhouetted, flitting, preening.

All these silent sights,
   breakfast more filling than food,
      as though morning mist
         could be tasted, devoured,
           tasting light,
              breakfast of tears and mist.

WHEN THERE ARE NO WORDS: SPIRIT!

Down in the country of the soul
where there are no words,
no fitting theories, or right explanations,
for how this life breaks us open
and spoils our plans for the perfect day.
Spirit is drinking what it needs
through centuries, or eons,
of silent nourishment
in the unseen world below.
Embracing the call to spiritual depth,
we must leave the country of assurances,
ambitions, all the dreams of the high-flyer,
and let Spirit make love with the soul
in the place where only the moon and stars
offer their dim light.
For we have spent entirely too long
chasing the upward call
of the American dream of enough,
which never was present, as promised,
in the country of rising ever higher.
It is *another country* we need now,
where wildness, utter surprise,
and glimpses of eternity
prove to live in the inner world,
underworld,
alongside unsought sorrows,
and the loss of all direction—
as we traverse the splendid ocean of the soul
in the dark of night.

So sooner or later,
this soul life, your life and mine,
calls us to the unwanted descent,
bringing the mountain height of Spirit
through the crucible of transformation
into that inverted region of dark soul.
This deepening Source of Life

wants our surrender
to the rudderless voyage
of sailing downward together.
And we might say God wants this too.

TODAY I TAKE MY SEAT

Today I take my seat
right here
in the country of the overwhelmed,
in the middle of these latest storms,
tree limbs slapping our windows,
rain drops hurled at us with greatest force,
electricity lost for days now,
and oh, by the way,
cancer trying to run/ruin/defeat our life,
illnesses compounding the uncertainties
landing us in the hospital again
on the verge of moving away
from our safe haven on the bayou
and then I lose my voice.

Today I take my seat
right here
in this place.

My good friend
has just reminded me
I sit with everyone who ever suffered,
one great congregation,
a cloud of witnesses
spread in all directions.
Together we all sit
right here
in this place,
for we are not alone as we seem.

There is a silent witness within,
the One who knows,
and our shared witness around us,
the ones who know,
all sitting with little lamps of the soul
in our laps,
belonging here in this community
with this lamplight,
in this darkness
and this vast sea of compassion.

IF I MISS SEEING

If I miss seeing
the first opening
of the pink lotus blossom
in the early dawn
of its very first morning,

on my way to see
my first hospital patient
of the day,

then
I'll probably miss seeing
the expression on his face
as he waits to place his heart
in a surgeon's hands too.

And if I miss seeing
the way the moon at dawn
still catches light
in its three-quarter radius
just above our cypress swamp,

on my way to see
my first hospital patient
of the day,

then
I'll probably miss
hearing the way his throat catches
as he tells me he can't pray too well
'cause his tears always take over
after the second word
until he can't speak at all.

Don't you see?
If I'm not here in every moment
of utter stillness in the bayou,
of morning dew pooling on the red caladiums,
of dawn light falling across the grass,

I won't be there
when a moment that means everything
comes from the mouth
or rises in the face
of the ones I will love today.
If I'm not here right now
with all my being,
I won't be there either!

THE MANY DIFFERENT FEET

Tonight the many different feet
are walking the same path
together
on a blue and beige labyrinth
in a monastery
out in the Louisiana woods.

The feet of these ecumenical monks
are male and female together:
naked and sock-covered feet,
white and milk chocolate feet,
gay and straight feet,
old and young feet,
healthy and ill feet.

And every single one of us
are very broken people
in our own ways
and yet, O so very whole tonight . . .
Walking to live music
created by the Great Artist
through the fingers and hands
of my good friends.

And don't I just love
seeing those feet
stepping gracefully
right through the inner doorways of their lives
walking away from what was—
stepping into what will be—
across sacred thresholds and liminal spaces
on a blue and beige labyrinth
in a monastery
out in the Louisiana woods.

And some people are crying,
the lucky ones,
and some are wishing they could,
and everyone who wants to
"gets saved" in a way tonight—right here
in a monastery
out in the Louisiana woods.

And some people are just watching,
reluctant to take the leap themselves,
maybe scared
of the Something
or the Nothing
they might find
on the "magic carpet ride"
of a blue and beige labyrinth
in a monastery
out in the Louisiana woods.

And that's where the story bends,
'cause it's my turn now
to put my feet
on a blue and beige labyrinth
in a monastery
out in the Louisiana woods.

ON THE EVE OF A NEW YEAR

Mary Oliver, you spoke part of the truth
when you wrote in your latest poems
that the stillness
is a sanctuary.

Why, just this morning,
on the last day of the year,
I felt your Truth.

But wasn't the rest sacred too
when I did things
like take my family to the beach
to see the shorebirds
and take care of some business
that had to be handled
and bring them home again?

And won't it be sacred
on the last evening of the year
if I gather the will
to go back out into the cold
and walk on the labyrinth
spread out on that church floor,
which won't be very still at all?

Maybe I best read
the rest of your poems, Mary,
so I can laugh at myself
when I remember
you saw the sacredness
of any act done with heartfulness.

Maybe I best remember
it was always the inner stillness
you were talking about,
and maybe I will follow you there
right now.

ON THE EVE OF THANKSGIVING

On the eve of Thanksgiving
the western sky is coruscating pink bands
across the deepening blue
and reflecting itself
across Bayou Saint John's stillness
and our mid-city New Orleans home.

Coruscating—
giving off or reflecting light
in bright beams or flashes,
which some people also do.

And now she is just showing off up there,
but quietly,
so that only the mindful notice,
and I am quietly grateful.
Something told me to look
over my right shoulder in time.

For I was busied
drowning a little
in self-pity
as Life's necessary suffering
had pushed me past my own resources
and held me under for a while.

Then my friends come to mind
who are suffering too
and we exchange messages,
which draw us near each other,

and my gay neighbors
are playing the grieving music up loud
with no welcoming family on this holiday,

and then I start wondering
if I can even think of anyone
who isn't at least knee-deep
in this thick stuff,

and my heart spreads wide open
to each of you
one by one.

A little love
enough
coruscates
toward all my brothers and sisters
without effort.

This is what oneness is
on the eve of Thanksgiving.

ON THE VIRTUES OF BEING BLIND AND DEAF

Sometimes eyes and ears
grow weary.
Noisy opinions flood the space
and crowd out the Presence
'til I long for deafness.
O Lord, make it so.

And sights of the human ant pile—
one crawling over the other—
the over and under of whose way is right
and who deserves the most stuff,
"To the victor go the spoils."
Tragic sight
carried in the faces and the flesh
until the Way
becomes invisible altogether.
So I long for blindness
blind eyes to see the Invisible.
O Lord, make it so.

Let my eyes and ears shut for a while
and go internal
and wait
and rest

'til the Quiet Voice
without words
has spoken—
blessed sound—

and the imageless One
appears before me,

the only sight and sound
there is.

Blessed blindness,
virtuous deafness
come.

THERE IS THIS OTHER KNOWING

There is this other *knowing*
whose center is not in the head,
whose thoughts are not facts,
but are oh so real:
known by another knowing.

There is this freshness in the chest
in the Other Center
knowledge untouched by dispute:
the *imago dei* united in the *imago humanitas*,
such gorgeous creatures are we.

And when our moments are graced,
we see *imago dei* through *imago humanitas*.
It looks like we're waiting for the music to start at Tipitina's,
but we're really watching for an appearance of the Sacred.
We're standing outside the doors
of the arts district gallery openings.
But the art we seek
is the holy in the human images.
We thought we joined the choir
to make beautiful music,
but it's really the beauty of human fellowship we're after.

Poor Jesus.
You tried so hard to tell us
that the kingdom we all seek is already so very near.
But we couldn't believe you,
so focused were we
on all the ways the world got broken.

But you saw through *imago humanitas*.
You already knew the secret in your youth
that what we came for, *imago dei*,
is still right here!

Your knowing was not like the facts
from some class you took,
not a set of opinions
tied together with a string.
You knew in your inner being
Ultimate Reality.

And this is why we loved you so,
and hated you too.
You kept trying to wake us up
to see the *imago dei*
in the woman caught in the act.
We weren't ready to see it then.
And you saw it in little Zacchaeus, the tax collector.
But we only saw his wrong,
his *imago humanitas*.
And you saw it in all those stinky, stupid fishermen.

No wonder you told them, and us,
"Come follow me,
and I'll show you how
to fish for people."
You got it so early in life
that we are already the beloved community.
And you were here
to help us find *that* salvation,
to see how we must turn from our blindness
and be given new eyes
to know in our souls right now
God alone.

Born, every one of us,
to *be* the kingdom of God
in how we see and live now
(not someday),
and to gather our brothers and sisters,
the enemy and the outcast,
to be one with us too.
(How much they need to know, as we do,
that they are already your beloved.)

And so we take up the call now
to wake up again
to how you are in us now,
and to simply, clearly
invite every neighbor
on every corner
to come be
the kingdom of God, with us,
the beloved community,
together
in this place.

And so we begin . . .
Amen

Desperation
An Epilogue

Through thirty years of illnesses threatening my wife's life, I searched for an inner sanctuary each day out of desperate need, not some superspiritual holiness. Desperation is a great motivator, though it can sometimes move us toward addictive escapism rather than toward finding our true home. By grace, desperation has helped me find my true home again and again.

In the beginning, we faced Carol's diagnosis of kidney disease, which left her one kidney functioning at just 20 percent for ten years. The terrible news came with the premature birth of our son when we were in our late twenties. We were told Carol's kidney failure would come any day for a decade.

Then came the first transplant with a kidney donated by Carol's sister Jan, while her sister Gayle and her parents wished they could offer the same gift. From the first week following Carol's transplant, her surgeon warned us that the new kidney could fail on any day, without warning. There was no promise of anything more than one day at a time.

That organ lasted for fifteen years before the transplanted kidney began to fail as a result of the very medications Carol's doctors prescribed to prevent its rejection. In those desperate times, we learned that I too was a match. The second surgery went well, and we named the life-saving organ T. J., a nickname for Truly Joyful, as he seemed to thrive in his new home. Then, less than three years later, my dear wife was diagnosed with an aggressive stage-three breast cancer.

The daily stress of the ever-pressing possibility of the latest threat taking my wife created a kind of quiet desperation. Sometimes the threat was intense. Sometimes it retreated to the back of my mind. But every day for thirty years, we have known that today is all we have. Through this long journey with daily desperation, I have needed two gifts: First, an inner sanctuary for practicing the presence of God, and second, a community for practicing the presence of God.

One of the miracles of birthing the contemplative communities we collectively call the School for Contemplative Living is that it was born during the pangs of our second kidney transplant and our shared journey with breast cancer. As of this writing, Carol has completed her first year of breast cancer treatment and is in her second year of preventative treatment. And so far, the little kidney we call T. J. is still holding his own inside Carol.

I have shared how the birthing of our school's communities happened in the wake of the Hurricane Katrina. More recently, we all survived the effects of Hurricane Isaac in 2012. That storm destroyed the pier I had built by hand from our backyard out into the Doubloon Bayou behind our home. The storm also threatened the sale of our home, which was under contract when the storm hit. Even worse, Isaac brought a virus in the storm's winds that partially paralyzed my vocal chords and took my voice for most of a year. All of that happened as my wife was just beginning treatment for breast cancer. Did I mention desperation?

There is good reason for connecting the experience of desperation in life's circumstances with the need for an inner sanctuary and a community for practicing the presence of God. In a way, our personal journey in South Louisiana tells the story of the human community. When life brings desperate circumstances, as it always seems to do, don't we all need some form of inner sanctuary and a community for mutual support?

Each day we all awaken with some form of need, sometimes desperate need. The question is not whether we have the need, but whether we acknowledge it. If we are blessed with enough self-awareness to awaken to our need, it can lead us to search for shelter. So where do we find shelter during these storms of need? One of my own greatest discoveries, in addition to finding an inner sanctuary and a practicing spiritual community, has been finding shelter in my love for my wife. Perhaps this next vignette will offer instruction for your own discovery of sheltering relationships in times of need.

WE SHELTER EACH OTHER

She awakened from ten hours of sleep still exhausted. Two long days of travel from New Orleans to Denver, Colorado, and across the state had pushed my wife past the limits of her energy. Having passed over to the wrong side of that threshold, exhaustion manifested in Carol as a sense of overwhelmed emptiness. She was depleted, and there was only one place she belonged: in the shelter of my arms.

After some tears expressing her feelings and need, and after some hot chocolate and cookies, we went back to bed on that snowy October morning. Carol rested her head on my shoulder. She leaned against me and snuggled into her cocoon-space, her shelter in my love.

Carol's only job in that moment was to be her vulnerable, human, real self by expressing her need. My job was to simply open my heart to her need and radiate loving-kindness. The baby cried. The milk was released. The snowflakes drifted gently down. She slept several hours.

This is how the world is meant to be. The baby of our need cries out. The milk of loving-kindness is released from the breast of our open heart. We shelter each other. Time passes as gently as snowflakes falling. Life is rejuvenated. This is how the world is meant to be.

Draw near when your own need is crying out. Do not turn away. Seek shelter in each other. Let the milk of loving-kindness flow. Watch the drift of the snowflakes of time. Trust life to rejuvenate itself.

The rest of the story is this. My wife had become exhausted in her effort to shelter my need. Let me explain. I wanted to interview with a group of spiritual leaders at an interfaith chapel on the far side of Colorado. The meeting felt like an important opportunity, even though we were on vacation. My life was asking me to say yes, but I did not want to take the adventure alone.

We had just spent the previous day making the long trek from New Orleans, which is below sea level, to Denver, the mile-high city. The early awakening, trip to the airport, first flight, layover, second flight, and drive into the mountains from Denver had already been exhausting. Asking Carol to leave with me early the next morning for eight hours of driving was asking a lot.

Still, I wanted my wife at my side. I needed her support and love. I needed her to help me stay grounded in my own vulnerable being. I needed her to shelter my dream of a new potential birth. I needed her to help me by talking things through before and after the meeting. I could have "manned-up" and made the trip alone, but I felt my need for support and expressed it to her.

The baby of my need cried out. The milk of her loving-kindness answered. She spent the day sheltering me in her arms.

We shelter each other. I say again: This is the way the world is meant to be.

I take this little vignette from two days in our personal life as a model for what the human community needs across the globe. We are vulnerable beings. Every day we awaken to our own needs and to those of the human family around us. Every day we need the shelter of one another. So how important is it that we learn to express our vulnerable needs and to radiate loving-kindness to each other? Immensely important!

This importance leads me to issue a call to the whole human family. We need each other so much more than we know. The time is now to tip the scales toward a worldwide community of people cultivating heartfulness, people who live from a *leb shalem*, or whole heart. Our little adventure of creating contemplative communities across the storm-tossed city of New Orleans is not just an interesting story. I believe it is a model for a desperate global community. I believe the swing of people polarizing against each other has gone far enough. I believe this world needs people practicing the presence of God together across the globe, no matter their differences in political or religious ideologies.

So take this book of stories about birthing a School for Contemplative Living as a desperate call to a desperate world, an encouragement to join us in forming communities who radiate loving-kindness as our first priority. How can we get there? Loving-kindness arises most naturally when we are practicing the presence of God. Our practice is an entry into the Source of loving-kindness. This means it is critical that we create contemplative communities where people practice the presence of God together. We shelter each other best, as a global community, by cultivating heartfulness, practicing the presence of God together, and bringing loving-kindness into the world around us.

The hour is late. The time is now.

Resources

THE CENTER FOR ACTION and *Contemplation* was created by Father Richard Rohr in the early 1990s as a resource for people seeking to unite contemplative practice and service. This ministry, based in Albuquerque, New Mexico, became the home-base for Father Rohr's international speaking and writing. More recently, the Rohr Institute's Living School for Action and Contemplation was created to expand the work of teaching this lifestyle of contemplative action.

We were blessed to have Richard Rohr spend four days with us in 2011. He also led us in a local workshop from his books, *The Naked Now* and *Falling Upward*. You can order books, DVDs, training programs, and other educational resources online at https://cac.org or find more information on this lifestyle by phone at 505-242-9588 or by email info@cac.org. You may also contact the organization PO Box 12464, Albuquerque, NM, 87195.

Contemplative Outreach was formed by Father Thomas Keating and several other monks in the early 1980s to help spread the practice of centering prayer around the world. Over time, the international organization began to teach the contemplative practice of *lectio divina* (sacred reading) and the Welcoming Prayer (a prayerful process for accepting whatever reality brings into our lives).

Father Keating and others have written numerous books and created many DVDs on the contemplative life available through the Contemplative Outreach website at www.contemplativeoutreach.org. Find your local chapter online or by contacting the organization by phone at 973-838-3384 or by email at office@coutreach.org. You may also contact Contemplative Outreach at 10 Park Place, 2nd Floor, Suite B, Butler, NJ, 07405.

The New Orleans chapter of Contemplative Outreach helped create the first centering prayer groups in our region. We continue to host centering prayer groups birthed by these friends.

The School for Contemplative Living serves people in the New Orleans region with centering prayer groups, classes, workshops, and retreats on contemplative living and service. For more information, you can visit our website at www.thescl.net, contact us by phone at 504-899-3431, or visit us at 1130 Nashville Avenue, New Orleans, LA, 70115. The School for Contemplative Living gladly accepts tax-deductible charitable donations in support of our mission online or by mail.

The Shalem Institute for Spiritual Formation was created by the Reverend Dr. Tilden Edwards, an Episcopal priest, author, and retreat leader, in the early 1970s. This international organization has trained thousands of people in contemplative living.

In early 2013 we were blessed to have Tilden Edwards lead us in a local workshop from his book: *Embracing the Call to Spiritual Depth*. You can learn about current programs and offerings of the Shalem Institute through their website at www.shaleminstitute.org, by phone at 301-897-7334, by email at info@shalem.org, or in person at 3025 NE 4th Street, Suite 22, Washington, DC, 20017. I also recommend any of the books by the Reverend Dr. Tilden Edwards or his founding faculty members, Dr. Gerald May and Sister Rosemary Dougherty.

Spiritual Directors International is a great place to locate a spiritual director near you. Spiritual directors can be invaluable in supporting your spiritual journey and your desire to integrate contemplative practices into your life and service in the world. To locate potential spiritual directors near you, I recommend you search online at www.sdiworld.org or by contacting Spiritual Directors International by phone at 01-425-455-1565 or by email at office@sdiworld.org. You may also contact the organization at PO Box 3584, Bellevue, WA, 98009. If you want to learn more about contemplative living through personal direction, I recommend asking potential directors about their own experience and interest in the contemplative dimension of the Christian life.

Bibliography

Benedict, Saint, Abbot of Monte Cassino. *The Rule of Benedict*. Edited and translated by Carolinne White. London: Penguin, 2008.

Benson, Herbert, and Marg Stark. *Timeless Healing: The Power and Biology of Belief*. New York: Scribner, 1996.

Bondi, Roberta C. *To Love as God Loves: Conversations with the Early Church*. Philadelphia: Fortress, 1987.

Bourgeault, Cynthia. *Centering Prayer and Inner Awakening*. Cambridge, MA: Cowley, 2004.

———. *The Wisdom Way of Knowing: Reclaiming an Ancient Tradition to Awaken the Heart*. San Francisco: Jossey-Bass, 2003.

Cameron, Julia. *The Artist's Way: A Spiritual Path to Higher Creativity*. 10th anniv. ed. New York: Putnam, 2002.

Chittister, Joan. *The Monastery of the Heart: An Invitation to a Meaningful Life*. Katonah, NY: Bluebridge, 2011.

Chödrön, Pema. *The Places That Scare You: A Guide to Fearlessness in Difficult Times*. Boston: Shambhala, 2001.

Claiborne, Shane. *Irresistible Revolution: Living as an Ordinary Radical*. Grand Rapids: Zondervan, 2006.

de Caussade, Jean Pierre. *Abandonment to Divine Providence*. Mineola, NY: Dover, 2008.

de Mello, Anthony. *One Minute Wisdom*. Garden City, NY: Doubleday, 1986.

Dillard, Annie. *Teaching a Stone to Talk: Expeditions and Encounters*. New York: Perennial, 1988.

Eckhart, Meister. *Meister Eckhart: The Essential Writings*. Translated by Raymond B. Blakney. New York: HarperCollins, 2009.

Edwards, Tilden. *Embracing the Call to Spiritual Depth: Gifts for Contemplative Living*. Mahwah, NJ: Paulist, 2010.

Einstein, Albert. "The World as I See It." In *Living Philosophies*, edited by Albert Einstein, 3–7. New York: Simon and Schuster, 1931.

Fitzpatrick-Hopler, Gail, et al. *Contemplative Service: The Contemplative Life Program 40-Day Practice*. Contemplative Life Program Year 2: "Dispositions." Butler, NJ: Contemplative Outreach, 2006.

Foley, Leonard, and Pat McCloskey, eds. "August 28: Augustine, Bishop and Doctor." In *Saint of the Day: Lives, Lessons and Feast*, 257–58. 6th rev. ed. Cincinnati: Saint Anthony Messenger, 2009.

Griffin, Emilie. *The Reflective Executive: A Spirituality of Business and Enterprise*. Eugene, OR: Wipf and Stock, 1993.

Heath, Elaine. *The Mystic Way of Evangelism: A Contemplative Vision for Christian Outreach*. Grand Rapids: Baker Academic, 2008.

Heath, Elaine, and Scott Kisker. *Longing for Spring: A New Vision for Wesleyan Community*. Eugene, OR: Cascade, 2010.

Johnston, William, ed. *The Cloud of Unknowing and the Book of Privy Counseling*. New York: Image, 1996.

Judy, Dwight H. *A Quiet Pentecost: Inviting the Spirit into Congregational Life*. Nashville: Upper Room, 2013.

Kabat-Zinn, Jon. *Full Catastrophe Living: Using the Wisdom of Our Body and Mind to Face Stress, Pain, and Illness*. New York: Delacorte, 1990.

———. *Wherever You Go, There You Are: Mindfulness Meditation in Everyday Life*. New York: Hyperion, 1994.

Keating, Thomas. *The Mystery of Christ: The Liturgy as Spiritual Experience*. New York: Continuum, 1994.

———. *Open Mind, Open Heart: The Contemplative Dimension of the Gospel*. 20th anniv. ed. New York: Bloomsbury Academic, 2006.

———. "The Rewards of 'Divine Therapy.'" Interview by Rich Heffern. *National Catholic Reporter*, July 22, 2011.

———. "The Theological Foundations of Contemplative Outreach." *Contemplative Outreach News* 15 (2001) 1–5.

Kelly, Thomas R. *A Testament of Devotion*. New York: Harper, 1941.

Lamott, Anne. *Bird by Bird: Some Instructions on Writing and Life*. New York: Anchor, 1995.

Lawrence, Brother, of the Resurrection. *The Practice of the Presence of God*. Grand Rapids: Baker, 1967.

May, Gerald G. *Simply Sane: The Spirituality of Mental Health*. New York: Crossroad, 1993.

———. *Will and Spirit: A Contemplative Psychology*. San Francisco: Harper and Row, 1987.

May, Rollo. *Man's Search for Himself*. New York: Norton, 1953.

Merton, Thomas. *Contemplative Prayer*. Garden City, NY: Doubleday, 1969.

———. *New Seeds of Contemplation*. New York: New Directions, 1974.

Moore, Thomas. *Care of the Soul: A Guide for Cultivating Depth and Sacredness in Everyday Life*. New York: Perennial, 1994.

———. *Meditations: On the Monk Who Dwells in Daily Life*. New York: HarperCollins, 1994.

Muller, Wayne. *Sabbath: Restoring the Sacred Rhythm of Rest*. New York: Bantam, 1999.

Norris, Kathleen. *Dakota: A Spiritual Geography*. New York: Houghton Mifflin, 1993.

Nouwen, Henri J. M. *Making All Things New: An Invitation to the Spiritual Life*. San Francisco: Harper and Row, 1981.

Oates, Wayne E. *The Presence of God in Pastoral Counseling*. Waco, TX: Word, 1986.

O'Donohue, John. *To Bless the Space between Us: A Book of Blessings*. New York: Doubleday, 2008.

Pennington, Basil M. *Daily We Touch Him: Practical Religious Experiences.* Kansas City: Sheed and Ward, 1997.

Reininger, Gustave, ed. *Centering Prayer in Daily Life and Ministry.* New York: Continuum, 1998.

Rohr, Richard. *Everything Belongs: The Gift of Contemplative Prayer.* New York: Crossroad, 1999.

———. *Falling Upward: A Spirituality for the Two Halves of Life.* San Francisco: Jossey-Bass, 2011.

———. *The Naked Now: Learning to See as the Mystics See.* New York: Crossroad, 2009.

Rumi, Jalal ad-Din Muhammad. *The Essential Rumi.* Translated by Coleman Barks with John Moyne, et al. Edison, NJ: Castle, 1997.

Rutba House, eds. *School(s) for Conversion: 12 Marks of a New Monasticism.* Eugene, OR: Cascade, 2005.

Safransky, Sy, ed. *Sunbeams: A Book of Quotations.* Rev. ed. Chapel Hill, NC: Sun, 2012.

Teasdale, Wayne. *A Monk in the World: Cultivating a Spiritual Life.* Novato, CA: New World Library, 2003.

Teresa, Mother, of Calcutta. *Jesus, the Word to Be Spoken: Prayers and Meditations for Every Day of the Year.* Edited by Angelo Devananda Scolozzi. Ann Arbor, MI: Servant, 1999.

———. *A Simple Path.* Edited by Lucinda Vardey. New York: Ballantine, 1995.

Teresa, Saint, of Avila. *The Interior Castle.* Translated and edited by Ellison Peers. Garden City, NY: Image, 1961.

Tvedten, Benet. *How to Be a Monastic and Not Leave Your Day Job: An Invitation to Oblate Life.* Brewster, MA: Paraclete, 2006.

Whyte, David. *The Heart Aroused: Poetry and the Preservation of the Soul in Corporate America.* New York: Crown, 1996.

Wicks, Robert J. *Everyday Simplicity: A Practical Guide to Spiritual Growth.* Notre Dame, IN: Sorin, 2000.

Winner, Lauren F. *Mudhouse Sabbath.* Brewster, MA: Paraclete, 2003.

www.ingramcontent.com/pod-product-compliance
Lightning Source LLC
Chambersburg PA
CBHW060602230426
43670CB00011B/1936